Frommer's®

Provence & the Riviera
day BY day®

2nd Edition

by Anna Brooke

WILEY

Wiley Publishing, Inc.

Contents

Published by:

Wiley Publishing, Inc.

111 River St.
Hoboken, NJ 07030-5774

ISBN 978-0-470-87482-0 (paper); ISBN 978-0-470-94393-9 (ebk); ISBN 978-0-470-94394-6 (ebk); ISBN 978-0-470-94588-9 (ebk)

Editor: Jennifer Polland
Production Editor: Katie Robinson
Photo Editor: Richard Fox
Cartographer: Andrew Murphy
Production by Wiley Indianapolis Composition Services

For information on our other products and services or to obtain technical support, please contact our Customer Care Department within the U.S. at 877/762-2974, outside the U.S. at 317/572-3993 or fax 317/572-4002.

Wiley also publishes its books in a variety of electronic formats. Some content that appears in print may not be available in electronic formats.

Manufactured in China

5   4   3   2   1

A Note from the Editorial Director

Organizing your time. That's what this guide is all about.

Other guides give you long lists of things to see and do and then expect you to fit the pieces together. The Day by Day guides are different. These guides tell you the best of everything, and then they show you how to see it *in the smartest, most time-efficient way*. Our authors have designed detailed itineraries organized by time, neighborhood, or special interest. And each tour comes with a bulleted map that takes you from stop to stop.

Hoping for a fresh picnic lunch amid lavender fields or a meander through a medieval perched village with staggering views of the provençal landscape? How about swimming along the Côte d'Azur and then drying off in the sun in a cove between the white cliffs of the Calanques? Or rolling the dice, elbow to elbow with billionaires, in the Monte Carlo casino? Whatever your interest or schedule, the Day by Days give you the smartest routes to follow. Not only do we take you to the top attractions, hotels, and restaurants, but we also help you access those special moments that locals get to experience—those "finds" that turn tourists into travelers.

The Day by Days are also your top choice if you're looking for one complete guide for all your travel needs. The best hotels and restaurants for every budget, the greatest shopping values, the wildest nightlife—it's all here.

Why should you trust our judgment? Because our authors personally visit each place they write about. They're an independent lot who say what they think and would never include places they wouldn't recommend to their best friends. They're also open to suggestions from readers. If you'd like to contact them, please send your comments our way at feedback@frommers.com, and we'll pass them on.

Enjoy your Day by Day guide—the most helpful travel companion you can buy. And have the trip of a lifetime.

Warm regards,

Kelly Regan Editorial Director
Frommer's Travel Guides

About the Author

British born **Anna Brooke** has spent the last 10 years of her life in France juggling between travel writing (*MTV France, Paris Day by Day, Paris Free & Dirt Cheap, Paris & Disneyland with Your Kids, France Day by Day, Time Out, Sunday Times Travel, Financial Times* magazine); acting in cabarets, shorts, ads, and the occasional French feature; and singing electro pop music for her band MONKEY ANNA (www.myspace.com/musicmonkeyanna). She is currently writing the first album. Contact Anna at annaebrooke@yahoo.fr.

Acknowledgments

Un grand merci to Jen Polland and Maureen Clarke for their excellent editing and undying patience. Thanks too to my family, and all my friends—you know who you are. And an extra special thanks to mon chéri Pascal Chind *que j'aime*.

Dedication

To Aunty Dawn

An Additional Note

Please be advised that travel information is subject to change at any time—and this is especially true of prices. We therefore suggest that you write or call ahead for confirmation when making your travel plans. The authors, editors, and publisher cannot be held responsible for the experiences of readers while traveling. Your safety is important to us, however, so we encourage you to stay alert and be aware of your surroundings.

Star Ratings, Icons & Abbreviations

Every hotel, restaurant, and attraction listing in this guide has been ranked for quality, value, service, amenities, and special features using a **star-rating system.** Hotels, restaurants, attractions, shopping, and nightlife are rated on a scale of zero stars (recommended) to three stars (exceptional). In addition to the star-rating system, we also use a **kids** icon to point out the best bets for families. Within each tour, we recommend cafes, bars, or restaurants where you can take a break. Each of these stops appears in a shaded box marked with a coffee-cup-shaped bullet ☕.

The following **abbreviations** are used for credit cards:

AE	American Express	DISC	Discover	V	Visa
DC	Diners Club	MC	MasterCard		

Travel Resources at Frommers.com

Frommer's travel resources don't end with this guide. Frommer's website, **www.frommers.com**, has travel information on more than 4,000 destinations. We update features regularly, giving you access to the most current trip-planning information and the best airfare, lodging, and car-rental bargains. You can also listen to podcasts, connect with other Frommers.com members through our active-reader forums, share your travel photos, read blogs from guidebook editors and fellow travelers, and much more.

A Note on Prices

In the "Take a Break" and "Best Bets" sections of this book, we have used a system of dollar signs to show a range of costs for 1 night in a hotel (the price of a double-occupancy room) or the cost of an entree at a restaurant. Use the following table to decipher the dollar signs:

Cost	Hotels	Restaurants
$	under $100	under $10
$$	$100–$200	$10–$20
$$$	$200–$300	$20–$30
$$$$	$300–$400	$30–$40
$$$$$	over $400	over $40

How to Contact Us

In researching this book, we discovered many wonderful places—hotels, restaurants, shops, and more. We're sure you'll find others. Please tell us about them, so we can share the information with your fellow travelers in upcoming editions. If you were disappointed with a recommendation, we'd love to know that, too. Please write to:

Frommer's Provence & the Riviera Day by Day, 2nd Edition
Wiley Publishing, Inc. • 111 River St. • Hoboken, NJ 07030-5774
frommersfeedback@wiley.com

20 Favorite **Moments**

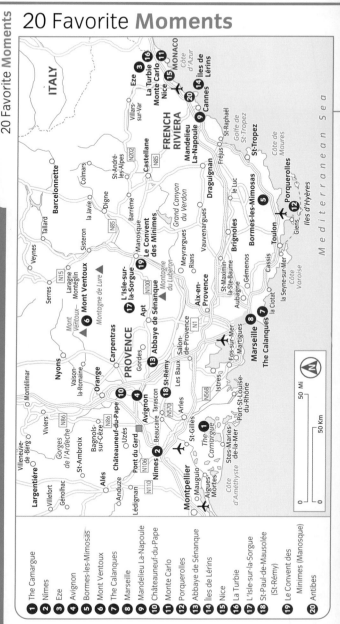

Previous page: Sunflowers and lavender abound in Provence.

From Provence's plush fields of lavender, Roman ruins, sun-drenched olive groves, sloping vineyards, and medieval villages to the glamorous resorts, glitterati-clad beaches, gastronomic restaurants, and clear seas of the Côte d'Azur, this region has inspired generations of artists and continues to compel *visitors* from all over the world today. Here are 20 of my own favorite experiences in the South of France.

① **Riding the white horses of the Camargue like a cowboy.** The desolate marshy flatlands of the Rhône Delta are home to pink flamingos, bulls, and white horses ridden by salty French cowboys, called *gardians*. Saddle up with La Bergerie de Maguelonne (see p 77) or Mas de Peint (see p 108), where you'll discover a world of rare birds, salt lagoons, and sweeping panoramas unreachable by car.

② **Visiting the Roman Arena in Nîmes,** a marvel of ancient civil engineering. Even if you've seen Roman Arles, you'll be bowled over by the grand fortitude of Nîmes' 1st-century amphitheater, built to stage bloodthirsty gladiatorial battles and chariot racing. *See p 175.*

③ **Indulging in a gastronomic meal at a provençal table d'hôte.** When you're dining at Michelin-starred Château de la Chèvre d'Or, in the chocolate-box village of Eze,

perched 429m (467 yds.) above the Mediterranean, life doesn't get much better. *See p 34.*

④ **Ambling through the animated streets of Avignon at night.** Pretty by day but even more striking by night, the former papal city comes into its own on a summer evening. Artsy cafe patrons flood the streets, and the air rings with lively conversation, lending even medieval alleyways a contemporary sophistication. *See p 128.*

⑤ **Following the Mimosa Trail.** Between January and March, the Côte d'Azur comes alive with sweet-scented balls of yellow mimosa flowers. Follow the Mimosa Trail, a fabulous 130km (80 mile) path along the hilly back-lands between Bormes-les-Mimosas and Grasse, the capital of perfume, and watch the landscape bloom with the fragrant buds. *See p 62.*

French cowboys (gardians) *of the seaside Camargue region.*

La Route du Mimosas.

creeks and beaches snuggled between the jagged, white cliffs between Marseille and Cassis. En-Vau, the prettiest calanque, is known for its sandy beach and needle-like rock formations. *See p 111.*

8 **Eating bouillabaisse in Marseille's Miramar.** As the light shimmers off the old port, grab a table on Miramar's sunny terrace, order a crisp white wine, and wait for the bouillabaisse to arrive. This rich, ancient traditional recipe—made from many kinds of impeccably fresh fish, saffron, and orange zest—is reason alone to visit Marseille. *See p 157.*

9 **Stealing kisses at Château de la Napoule.** There is something hopelessly romantic about Mandelieu's mock-gothic Château de la Napoule. Stroll through the topiary-filled gardens and marvel at the fantastical sculptures, designed by American artists Marie and Henry Clews, who purchased the castle in 1918. Then steal a kiss on the turreted terraces overlooking the sea. *See p 141.*

6 **Posing for a photograph at the summit of Mont Ventoux.** Whether you attempt the steep 5-hour hike, struggle up on a bike, or (sensibly) drive 1,912m´(2,084 yds.) to the top, the nor'easter that gusts over this dazzling white limestone cap will give you the ultimate windswept look. *See p 88.*

7 **Bathing in the Calanques.** Explore the hidden splendor of

10 **Tasting Châteauneuf-du-Pape wine.** In the green vineyard-studded

Abbaye de Sénanque in summer, engulfed by lavender.

Nice's pre-Lenten carnival.

hills around Châteauneuf-du-Pape grow France's most famous product. When you're driving around the Vaucluse, don't hesitate to pop into one of the many châteaus whose Côte du Rhône wines are among the best in the country. See p 84.

⓫ **Raising the stakes at the casino in Monte Carlo.** You may not even mind *losing* money at this beautiful palace on the Riviera. Play blackjack in the opulent Salons Privés, roulette in the Belle Epoque Salons Européens, or sip champagne beneath the risqué frescos on the ceiling of the Rose Bar. See p 158.

⓬ **Eating a picnic lunch on Porquerolles,** the most paradisiacal of the Hyères islands, is a must for nature lovers, who will adore the expanses of pine forests, olive groves, vineyards, and glorious beaches. See p 56.

⓭ **Visiting the Abbaye de Sénanque in bloom** is possibly the most clichéd summer activity in Provence. But that doesn't make the seas of lavender surrounding the 12th-century Cistercian monastery any less breathtaking, especially when approached from Gordes. See p 48.

⓮ **Sunbathing on the St-Honorat Beaches.** When bawdy mobs and jet-set frivolities get to be too much, take a boat from Cannes to the Îles de Lérins, a scenic islet owned by Cistercian monks, whose peaceful outcrops and beaches are a perfect antidote to crowd fever. See p 140.

⓯ **Attending Nice's annual carnival**—the most colorful festival in the South of France. What began in the Middle Ages as a masked pre-Lenten street party has turned into an explosive weeklong extravaganza, with giant puppets, oversized head-masks, flowers, and bright costumes. After the parades, heavy partying ensues (late Feb–Mar). See p 167.

⓰ **Basking in the glory of Rome** in the bougainvillea-scented village of La Turbie. The gigantic *trophée des Alpes* was erected to celebrate Emperor Augustus's victory against the Ligurians in 13 b.c. It used to

Antiques shopping in L'Isle-sur-la-Sorgue.

series of illustrated panels shows his works on the sites where he painted them. For fans, it is a moving experience. *See p 109.*

⑲ Recharging body and mind at le Couvent des Minimes. As the sun sets over the Haute-Provence hills, let the Couvent des Minimes knead away your tensions in the spa (the only one in France to use Provençal Occitane products). Later, dine on fine Mediterranean cuisine in the hotel restaurant. You may never want to leave! *See p 97.*

⑳ Filling up at Antibes' Provençal market. Colorful, bustling, and bursting at the seams with delicious produce, charcuterie, and cheeses, Antibes' covered market makes a plum spot to stock a picnic basket. *See p 101.* ●

Local olives for sale at Antibe's covered market.

mark the frontier between Italy and Gaul, and it still affords triumphant views over Cap Ferrat and Eze. *See p 104.*

⑰ Sifting through antiques in L'Isle-sur-la-Sorgue. Whether you covet an original Louis XIV chair, or seek a 1920s reproduction of an 18th-century bed, or just fancy perusing other people's junk in search of hidden treasure, pretty L'Isle-sur-la-Sorgue, with its crystal-line river and old waterwheels, is a paradise for antiques lovers of every stripe. *See p 86.*

⑱ Experiencing the haunting tranquillity of the St-Paul de Mausole monastery, where Vincent van Gogh committed himself after lopping off his ear in Arles. The tormented artist whiled away many an hour, silently painting the medieval cloisters and monastery gardens. A

1 Strategies for Seeing the Region

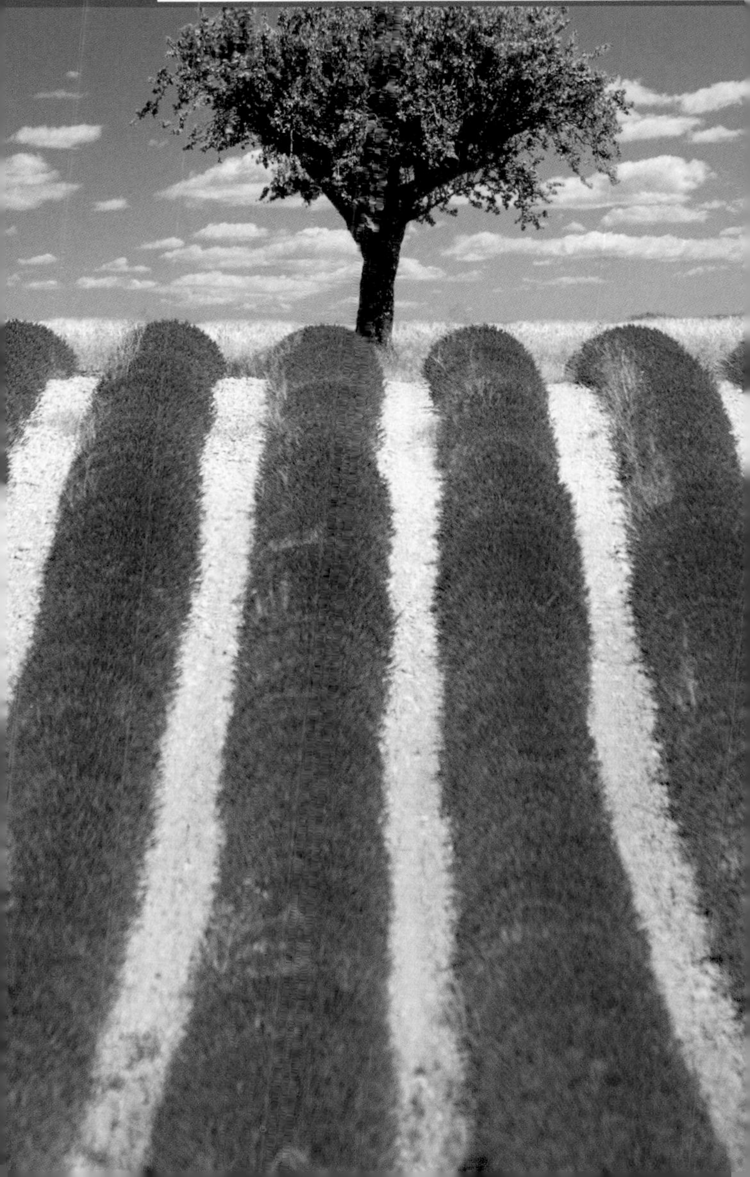

Strategies for Seeing the Region

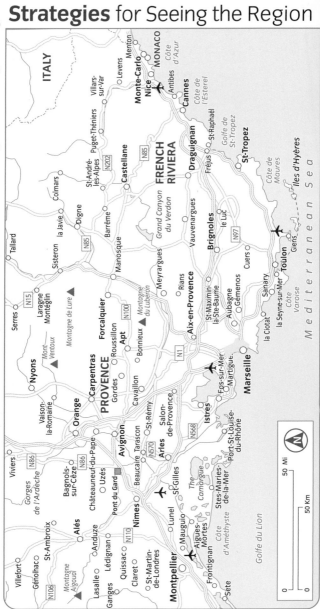

Previous page: Lavender field in summer.

Provence and the Riviera are regions to experience rather than "see"; life moves more slowly in the South of France, and hasty sightseeing cuts against the grain of daily life. With so many compelling small towns, villages, and rural landscapes, you'll be tempted to visit them all; but, if you rush, you'll miss the essence of the place. Here are strategies to help you enrich your time and travels.

Rule #1: Allow for down time

Don't cram your days full of activities. Build in plenty of time to unwind; to stop and smell the lavender; to eat long, hearty lunches; to slowly savor the wine and admire the views. These humble experiences could well become the pinnacle of your trip. To make the most of your time, decide what you want to do most that day, and then plan your other activities in the same area.

Rule #2: Take distances into account

Provence and the Riviera are as easy to traverse as a small U.S. state or a U.K. county. Under normal conditions, you can drive between many of the region's most popular stops in less than an hour. In traffic, however, certain destinations—particularly those away from the *auto-route* (highway)—can take much longer to reach during peak periods. If you're visiting in summer, around school vacations, or on public holidays, tack at least 30 minutes onto estimated drive times (even longer on the Côte d'Azur). As a general rule, roads are well maintained and sign-posted, but carry a detailed road map. See p 202 for crucial driving tips in France.

Rule #3: Time your visit right

If it's your life-long dream to see lavender fields, don't visit in spring; lavender blooms in July and August. Skip summer, however, if you want to experience the region at its most authentic—minus hoards of tourists. Opt for March and April or

September and October instead, when the weather is warm, but tourists are back at work. February can also be lovely on the Riviera, when Menton's Lemon festival, Mandelieu's mimosa festival, and Nice's carnival brighten the streets. See p 197 for a calendar of events.

Rule #4: Decide whether to hotel-hop or stay in one place

Many of the region's most popular stops are near one another. By choosing a base for several days (or even for the entirety of your trip) and exploring the surrounding area on day trips, you'll save time checking in and out of rooms, packing and unpacking. Avignon, St-Rémy, Les Baux, Nîmes, and Arles are so close

A quayside coffee break in Marseille.

you'd do best to bed down in just one town. On the Côte d'Azur, Nice is a fine station from which to explore Monaco, Menton, and the coastal villages around Cagnes, St-Paul-de-Vence, and Biot. A good way to stay put in one place is to rent a self-catering *gite* (a French cottage or farmhouse), from which you can visit the region at your own pace and cook at home. See "Hiring a *Gite*," on p 204.

Rule #5: Plan trips around lunch

If you're driving from town to town, it's best to arrive before lunch. Most restaurants serve from noon to 2 or 2:30pm sharp, and many shops close at noon for the midday meal. If you don't want to follow such a strict schedule, pack your own food and follow your heart's desire to a picnic spot under the provençal sun.

Rule #6: Plot your point of entry and means of transport there

Provence has small airports in Marseille, Nîmes, and Nice. Although there are some international flights that arrive in Nice (there are direct flights from New York City to Nice), most visitors to the region take off from Paris at either the Charles de Gaulle or Orly airports. Planes are a time-effective means of transport for Nice and the Riviera: Nice's airport is practically in the town center and receives daily flights from Paris and other European cities. The quickest and most cost-effective way to access Provence from Paris, however, is on France's legendary high-speed TGV trains. Avignon takes just 2 hours, Aix-en-Provence 2½, and Marseille a little under 3. You can rent cars at all the region's airports and train stations (see p 202 for a list of agencies). If you drive from Paris, the main *autoroutes* into the region are the A6, A7, and A8. From Paris, you should allow at least 6 hours to reach Avignon, 8 for Marseille, and up to 10 for Nice. ●

A cyclist near the village of Suzette.

2 The Best Full-Day Tours

Provence in **Three Days**

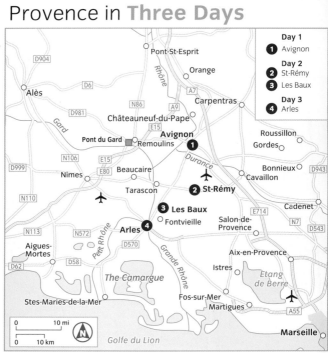

Day 1
1 Avignon

Day 2
2 St-Rémy
3 Les Baux

Day 3
4 Arles

Pont-St-Esprit
Orange
D904
D6
Alès
N86
A7
Carpentras
D981
A9
Châteauneuf-du-Pape
E15
Roussillon
Gard
Avignon
Gordes
Pont du Gard
Remoulins **1**
N106
E15
Durance
N999
E80
Beaucaire
Bonnieux
D943
Nimes
Cavaillon
Tarascon
2 St-Rémy
N110
Cadenet
E714
3 Les Baux
Salon-de-
N7
Fontvieille
Provence
D543
N113
N572
Arles 4
Aigues-
D570
Mortes
Grande Rhône
Aix-en-Provence
D62
D58
Istres
Etang
The Camargue
de Berre
Fos-sur-Mer
Stes-Maries-de-la-Mer
Martigues
A55
0   10 mi
Marseille
0   10 km
Golfe du Lion

rom the seaside salt flats of the Camargue to the *village
perchés* spilling down the rocky plateaus of the Lubéron,
Provence's landscapes are so varied, you don't have to travel far for
a dramatic change of scenery and atmosphere. The region's varied
yet compact scale is a blessing if you have just 3 days to explore it.
This tour covers four requisite stops: Avignon, Provence's elegant
cultural capital; the chocolate-box town of St-Remy and the nearby
cloisters where Vincent van Gogh convalesced during his final years;
the gravity-defying Les Baux; and Arles, with its Roman vestiges,
bullfights, and other strong provençal traditions with a Spanish twist.
START: Avignon. Trip length 41km/26 miles (82km/51-mile loop).

Travel Tip

For hotels, restaurants, and detailed
information on sights in these towns,
see chapter 6: Avignon p 128; St-
Rémy p 180; Arles p 122.

Previous page: The port of Cassis.

1 Avignon. Contained within
medieval ramparts, beautiful,
UNESCO-protected Avignon is easy
to explore on foot. Most sites surround the **Place de l'Horloge,**
named after the 15th-century clock
that dominates the square. From
there, it's easy to reach the

Dining alfresco at night in Avignon.

fortresslike **Palais des Papes (The Pope's Palace).** This Gothic castle was built as the headquarters of Christendom when the papacy fled to Avignon—officially from 1309 until 1376, followed by the reign of two antipopes that lasted until 1417. Equally emblematic is Avignon's half-fallen 12th-century **Pont St-Bénézet** (Pont d'Avignon), just outside the city walls. Art enthusiasts should flock to the nearby 12th-century **Musée du Petit Palais,** with its fine medieval paintings and Roman and Gothic sculpture; the **Musée Calvet** (a beautifully restored fine arts museum); or to the **Musée Angladon,** with an eclectic collection of furniture and fauvist canvases. The **Musée Lapidaire** is an archaeological museum in a stunning 17th-century Jesuit church. And the **Collection Lambert** holds an extensive avant-garde and Conceptual art collection.

If culture is not your prime concern, consider some retail therapy on **rue des Teinturiers, rue de la République, rue des Marchands,** and **rue St-Agricol.** Or head for the glorious **Les Halles** covered market on Place Pie (no phone; Tues–Sun 6am–1:30pm). On most Saturdays, at 11am, foodies flock

here to watch the region's top chefs perform cooking demonstrations.

The whole city becomes a stage in July, during the world-famous **Festival d'Avignon.** Unless you want to see theater, however, it's best to avoid the crowds at this time.

After a meal and a wondrous night of roaming through Avignon's floodlit streets, bed down and then head out early to St-Rémy. 🕐 *1 day. Avignon tourist board, 41 cours Jean Jaures.* ☎ *04-32-74-32-74. www.ot-avignon.fr. For more on Avignon, see p 128 in chapter 6.*

From Avignon, take the N570 (av. de Tarascon), and then continue on the D570n. Cross the Pont de Rognonas bridge and, at the next island, turn left onto the D571 to St-Rémy (via Châteaurenard and Eyragues). Distance: 21km (13 miles).

❷ **St-Rémy.** Arrive in this affluent, quintessentially Provençal town as early as possible on your second day to check into your hotel (unless you decide to stay in Avignon or Arles for 2 nights or have hired a *gite* nearby). If you arrive early on Wednesday or Saturday, stroll around the buzzing street markets. In the morning, you can visit the 14th-century **Collégiale**

St-Martin (St-Martin collegiate church), walk past **Nostradamus's birthplace** on rue Hoche, wander around the stunning 18th-century **Hôtel Estrine,** with its van Gogh–themed displays, marvel at the 16th-century galleried courtyard of the **Musée des Alpilles,** or opt for the fragrant displays at the **Musée des Arômes et des Parfums.**

After lunch, either continue exploring St-Rémy or detour to the nearby Gallo-Roman ruins at **Glanum** (just outside the town center on the D5) or the **St-Paul-de-Mausolée** monastery, where van Gogh convalesced and painted during the final year of his life (north of Glanum on the D5). In any case, head off to Les Baux by midafternoon. ⏱ *½ day. St-Remy tourist board, pl. Jean Jaurès.* ☎ *04-90-92-05-22. www.saint remy-de-provence.com. For more on St-Remy, see p 180 in chapter 6.*

From St-Rémy, take the D5 for 6km (4 miles), and then turn right onto the D27 to Les Baux. Distance: 10km (6 miles).

③ Les Baux. Wander in awe through the center of this medieval engineering marvel, teetering on a steep, bare-bauxite ridge. Les Baux is small, so even if you arrive in the late afternoon, you'll have time to see the former **Hôtel de Ville** (city hall

and 16th-century chapel); the 12th-century **Église Saint-Vincent** (church), with stained glass windows by Max Ingrand; the former 16th-century **Temple Protestant;** the present city hall in the **Hôtel de Manville;** and **Place St-Vincent,** which affords panoramas over the Fontaine valley, the Alpilles, and the Val d'Enfer (Hell's Valley). If you can bear the crowds and have the time, don't miss sunset here.

At the end of **rue du Trencat,** which is carved from bedrock, lies the **Musée d'Histoire des Baux,** which affords access to Baux's ruined citadel, chapel, and towers. This is a hauntingly beautiful and interesting sight, especially when actors in period costume assail the citadel with medieval catapults (this happens four times a day; check times when you arrive). Before you leave, don't miss the ancient quarries at the foot of town, which come alive with light and music shows in the **Cathédrale d'Images** (rte. Val d'Enfer D27; open daily 10am–5pm, except Jan and Feb). Then head for Arles. ⏱ *½ day. Les Baux tourist office, rue Porte Mage.* ☎ *04-90-54-34-39. www.lesbauxdeprovence.com. For detailed information on Les Baux, see p 35, chapter 3, and p 109, chapter 5.*

The ruins of Les Baux.

Arles' annual feria.

Tip

On your second day, you could skip Glanum or the St-Paul-de-Mausolée monastery in the afternoon, and head straight to Les Baux for a slower-paced visit.

From Les Baux, take the D27 then the D78f. After 3km (2 miles), take the D17 (via Fontvieille). At the island, take the D570n to Arles Distance: 10km (6 miles).

4 Arles. Either you arrived in Arles the night before or you're checking into your hotel. Either way, prepare for a jam-packed day. Before you visit Arles' Roman vestiges, the **Musée d'Arles Antique** is the best way to grasp how Arles would have looked in ancient times. From here, make sure you tour the 1st-century *arènes* (Roman arenas), once the site of bloody gladiatorial battles, and now the region's leading bullfight venue. Other requisite ancient stops include the **Thermes de Constantin** (Roman baths), the **Théâtre Antique** (Roman theater), and **les Alycamps** (graveyard), and the two columns on **Place du Forum.** Whether you stay in the **Hôtel d'Arlantan** or not, pop into the lobby to see Roman ruins exposed under a glass floor.

Art fans must visit the **Espace van Gogh,** one of the former Provençal hospitals that sheltered the artist and became the subject of his paintings, the **Fondation van Gogh** tribute museum, and the **Musée Réattu.**

As you wander through the streets, make a detour to the lovely Romanesque **Eglise St-Trophime** (church) and cloisters, and the **Hôtel de Ville** (city hall).

Arlesians have a strong sense of identity—Provençal with a Catalan twist. The **Musée d'Arlatan** is a folklore museum devoted to Arles' costumes and traditions as well as the Provençal language.

The Easter *feria* is a particularly fun time to visit, when revelers descend on Arles (often in traditional dress), restaurants stir up enormous pans of paella, bulls fight in the Roman arena, and a spirit of bacchanalia prevails. ⏲ *1 day. Arles tourist office, esp. Charles de Gaulle/ bd. Craponne.* ☎ *04-90-18-41-20. www.tourisme.ville-arles.fr. For detailed information on Arles, see p 122 in chapter 6.*

To return to Avignon after this whirlwind tour, take the D570n from Arles. After 28km (17 miles), take the N570 to Avignon.

Provence & the Riviera
in **One Week**

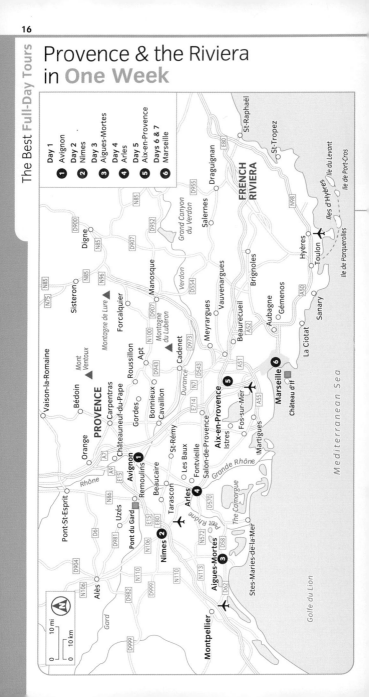

Day 1 Avignon ➊

Day 2 Nîmes ➋

Day 3 Aigues-Mortes ➌

Day 4 Arles ➍

Day 5 Aix-en-Provence ➎

Days 6 & 7 Marseille ➏

With a full 7 days, you can dip down to the Mediterranean coast and still have time to explore the diverse inland regions of Provence. This trip begins in Avignon and takes you into the Roman heart of Nîmes, with its ancient amphitheater; Aigues-Mortes, ensconced by ramparts and salt marshes; Arles, known for its Roman vestiges and bullfights, chi-chi Aix-en-Provence, birthplace of Paul Cézanne and former capital of the region; and gritty, exotic Marseille, where you will spend 2 days exploring the city and its surrounding coastal attractions, with a chance to wind down over a glass of wine and some fine seafood. For a more leisurely rhythm, you could take 10 days to cover this route. START: **Avignon. Trip length 253km/157 miles (350km/217-mile loop).**

Travel Tip

For hotels, restaurants, and detailed information on sights in these towns, see chapter 6: Avignon p 128; Nîmes p 174; Arles p 122; Aix-en-Provence p 114; Marseille p 144.

① **Avignon.** At one time, Avignon was the capital of both Provence and Christendom. Today it is one of France's most important cultural centers with a world-renowned theater festival. It is also celebrated for its sumptuous town houses, medieval streets, and the centuries-old children's song (Sur le Pont d'Avignon), inspired by its tumble-down medieval bridge. Try to arrive the night before, or in the early morning to make the most of your day, before wining and dining in one of the city's great restaurants. After a night in a hotel, head for Nîmes first thing the following morning. ⏲ *1 day. For a 1-day itinerary, see bullet ①, "Provence in Three Days," above. For detailed information on Avignon, see p 128, in chapter 6.*

Travel Tip

Unless your hotel has a private car park, it's nearly impossible to find space inside Avignon's ramparts. Park in one of the paid lots around the perimeter or ask your concierge where to park.

The 2,000 year-old Pont du Gardé, near Nîmes.

Exit Avignon via la Porte de l'Oulle and join the N100. After 20km (12 miles), join the A9 and follow signs to Nîmes, exiting the highway at junction 24. Distance: 45km (28 miles).

2 Nîmes. Although it's technically outside Provence, in the Languedoc region, Nîmes is essentially Provençal. Feed your belly on food specialties such as *brandade de morue* (see below), almond biscuits called *croquants,* and marinated olives; and feed your mind on its numerous attractions. Check into a hotel, and then prepare yourself for one busy day during which you can see such highlights as the **Ampitheatre Roman**—a two-storied vestige, more complete than the Colosseum in Rome; the miraculously conserved **Maison Carré** (Roman temple); the **Carré de l'Art,** a modern architectural take on the Maison Carré that houses the contemporary art museum; the stunning **Jardin de la Fontaine** gardens, lined with trees and more Roman and pre-Roman ruins; and the **Castellum,** a Roman water tower.

Aigues-Mortes.

If you'd rather spend time in museums, head for the **Musée des Beaux Arts,** which showcases 17th- to 20th-century painting and sculpture; the **Musée des Cultures Taurines,** devoted to *tauromachy* (bullfighting); and the **Musée du Vieux Nîmes,** which recounts the city's history. *1 day. Nîmes tourist office, 6 rue Auguste.* ☎ *04-66-58-38-00. www.ot-nimes.fr. For detailed information on Nîmes, see p 174, in chapter 6.*

A Regional Specialty

Don't leave town without sampling *brandade de morue*—a cod and potato purée that is one of the region's best dishes when it's prepared correctly. You'll find it on restaurant menus and in supermarkets, where authentic *brandade* comes in a tin to take home.

Leave Nîmes early for Aigues-Mortes, and follow signs for the A9 toward Montpellier. Leave the A9 at junction 26, and follow signs to Aigues-Mortes (via N313, D6313, and D979). Distance: 42km (26 miles).

3 Aigues-Mortes. This medieval, grid-patterned settlement is spellbinding in the way its ancient battlements and defense towers rise sharply from the melancholy, salty flatlands of the Camargue. Aigues-Mortes is tiny and easy to cover on foot. Much of its charm comes from narrow streets teeming with art galleries, cafes, and crafts shops. Once you check into your hotel, however, you may want to take the good 1½-hour tour run by the tourist office (Place St-Louis; ☎ **04-66-53-73-00**). It will give you an overview of what to see and do.

As you wander around, look out for the beautiful baroque **Chapelle**

A Romantic Vineyard

Picture this: Waking up inside a little house on a working, organic vineyard with nothing but Syrah, Cabernet Sauvignon, and Grenache grapes ripening on the vine-trestled hills around you. Sound tempting? If you're a couple looking to unwind, stay at the romantic Villa Minna Vineyard, which lies between Aix-en-Provence and Arles (near Saint-Cannat) in the shadow of the Sainte Victoire mountain, which was immortalized by Cézanne. There are oodles of walking, picnicking, and cycling opportunities on site, plus wine tasting, with reds and whites lovingly produced by the friendly owners. **Villa Minna Vineyard.** Just off D17, Roque-Pessade, 13760 Saint-Cannat. ☎ **04-42-57-23-19.** www.villaminnavineyard.fr.

des Pénitents Blancs, the 17th-century **Chapelle des Pénitents Gris,** and the **Église Notre-Dame-des-Sablons**—a Gothic church once used as a salt warehouse. The ramparts encircle the entire town, but they're accessible from Place Anatole France **(Porte de la Gardette).** You can enter the **Tour de Constance**—a humongous, circular keep, once used as a prison. Also look out for the grisly **Tour des Bourguignons,** a 15th-century tower used to house the salted bodies of dead Bourguignon soldiers during the Hundred Years War.

If you have time in the afternoon, jump into the car and head 3km (2 miles) southwest along the Route du Grau-du-Roi to the **Salins du Midi** (☎ **04-66-73-40-02**). Much more than a simple working salt farm, the Salins du Midi also has marshes that harbor endangered flora and 200 species of birds, including elegant pink flamingoes. You could also opt for a relaxing **boat tour** along Le Grau-du-Roi canal. ⏲ *1 day. Aigues Mortes tourist office, pl. St-Louis.* ☎ *04-66-53-73-00. www. ot-aiguesmortes.fr. For detailed*

information on Aigues-Mortes, see bullet ❸, p 108.

From Aigues-Mortes, take the D979; after Aimargues, join the D6572, and then follow signposts to Arles (on the D572N, N572, and N113). Distance: 55km (34 miles).

❹ **Arles.** Day 4 takes you to Arles. For detailed suggestions on how to make the most of Arles in 1 day, see p 15 in "The Best of Provence in Three Days," above. ⏲ *1 day. For detailed information on Arles, see p 122, in chapter 6.*

Leaving Arles, follow the N113 for 19km (12 miles). Near St-Martin-de-Crau, join the A54 and follow signs to Aix. They will take you onto the A7 and the A8 (exit jct. 30A Les Milles). Distance: 77km (48 miles).

❺ **Aix-en-Provence.** This chic spa town encompasses the best of Provence: gorgeous 17th- and 18th-century town houses, medieval streets, bustling markets, fine food, thronging cafes, Roman baths, and former artist residents (Cézanne and Zola) whose legacies have helped to

Baths in Aix-en-Provence.

former bourgeoisie. ⏲ *1 day. Aix-en-Provence tourist office, 2 pl. Gén de Gaulle. ☎ 04-42-16-11-61. www.aixenprovencetourism.com. For detailed information on Aix-en-Provence, see p 114, in chapter 6.*

From Aix, join the A8 highway, and then follow signs to Marseille (via A51 and A7). Distance: 35km (22 miles).

❻ **Marseille.** We recommend spending at least 2 days in France's fascinating oldest town and the European Capital of Culture 2013—an honor designated by the E.U., which allows the city to showcase its cultural life for 1 year. Granted, it has all the undesirable trappings of any big city—crowds, commerce, crime, and car fumes—but showcases its monuments, restaurants, bars, cafes, and markets. Marseille's nerve center is its ancient port, crackling with energy and change. Fishing and pleasure boats are crammed in rows like pretty sardines, and characters come and go from all over the world, chiefly Europe and Africa. Stroll through the traditional **Panier** district to visit the intriguing **Vieille Charité,** which houses several excellent museums. For far-reaching vistas

shape France today. Once you've checked into your hotel, you can easily spend the day wandering through the streets. The **cours Mirabeau** is the main drag, dotted with fountains; **rue Gaston-de-Saporta** is littered with shops; and the **Mazarin** quarter is the peaceful, grid-patterned district of Aix's

Vallon des Auffes, a tiny fishing port tucked behind a bridge in Marseille.

across the town and coastline, climb up to Marseille's emblematic **Notre-Dame de la Garde basilica.** Other noteworthy religious buildings are the **Cathédrale de la Major** and the **Abbaye St-Victor.** The **Vieux port,** protected by two old forts (**St-Jean,** with its Mediterranean civilization museum, and **Fort St-Nicolas**), is the hub of town and the setting of a wonderful morning fish market. Art lovers could visit the **Musée Cantini** (post-War art and fauvism), the **Musée Grobet-Labadie** (rare paintings and furniture), and the **Musée de la Faïence** (ceramics). Shoppers can get their kicks on the **cours Julien, rue St-Ferréol, rue Sainte,** and **rue de la Tour.** To learn about Marseille's history, head for the **Musée d'Histoire de Marseille,** the **Musée des Docks Romains,** and the **Maison Diamantée.** To see Marseille's splendid Belle Epoque architecture stroll up the **Canebière** towards the richly decorated **Palais Longchamp.** For a dose of modernity head out of the center to Le Corbusier's **Cité Radieuse** or to **MAC,** the award-winning contemporary art museum.

On day 2, we recommend exploring Marseille's coastline. If you don't mind sharing sand with droves of sunbathers, the **Prado beaches** foot the bill nicely. Boats frequently leave the Vieux Port for excursions to the **Château d'If** island fortress and Marseille's wild

Fresh lunch on a beach in the Calanques.

Frioul islands. **Les Calanques,** the stretch of picturesque rocky creeks between Marseille and Cassis, are truly hypnotic. North of town, **l'Estaque** is the fishing port prized by many Impressionist and Fauvist painters. ⏱ *2 days. Marseille tourist office, 4 La Canebière.* ☎ *04-91-13-89-00. www.marseille-tourisme.com. For detailed information on Marseille, see p 144, in chapter 6.*

To return to Avignon, take the A7 (toward Aix), and exit at junction 24 to join the N7.

Provence & the Riviera
in **Two Weeks**

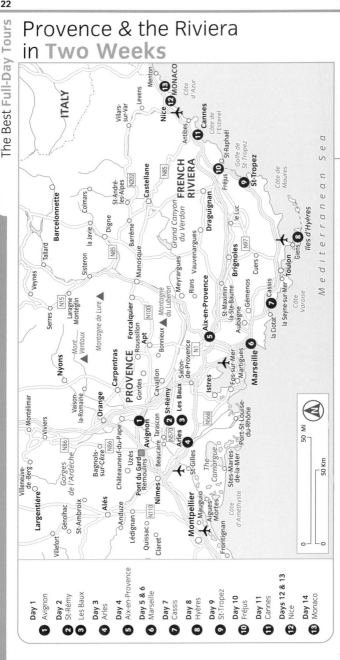

Day 1
1 Avignon

Day 2
2 St-Rémy

3 Les Baux

Day 3
4 Arles

Day 4
5 Aix-en-Provence

Days 5 & 6
6 Marseille

Day 7
7 Cassis

Day 8
8 Hyères

Day 9
9 St-Tropez

Day 10
10 Fréjus

Day 11
11 Cannes

Days 12 & 13
12 Nice

Day 14
13 Monaco

This tour combines destinations covered in both the 3-day and weeklong tours. You'll spend your first week in Provence, before continuing along France's sunshine coast through the pretty port of Cassis, Hyères and its offshore islands, glamorous St-Tropez, quaint Fréjus, star-studded Cannes, and buzzing Nice, to the principality of Monaco. If you wish to return to Avignon, tack an extra day onto your tour to allow ample driving time and give yourself the chance to visit any places you might have missed. **START: Avignon. Trip length: 428km (266 miles) (plus 270km/168 miles back from Monaco to Avignon).**

Travel Tip

For hotels, restaurants, and detailed information on sights in these towns, see chapter 6: Avignon, p 128; St-Rémy, p 180; Arles, p 122; Aix-en-Provence, p 114; Marseille, p 144; Cannes, p 136; Nice, p 164; Monte Carlo, p 158.

1 Avignon. Celebrated for its quality theater, architecture, and history, Avignon is your first port of call. Arrive the night before, or early in the morning, to make the most of your day. For a 1-day itinerary, see bullet **1** of the 3-day tour. ⏲ *1 day. For detailed information on Avignon, see p 128, in chapter 6.*

From Avignon, take the N570 (av de Tarascon), and then continue on the D570n. Cross the Pont de Rognonas bridge and, at the next island, turn left onto the D571 to St-Rémy (via Châteaurenard and Eyragues). Distance: 21km (13 miles).

2 St-Rémy. Get to St-Rémy as early as possible, so you can squeeze in a maximum number of sights in the morning, before heading off to the village of Les Baux in the afternoon. If you would rather concentrate on just one town, spend the day and night in St-Rémy, and make time to visit the Roman vestiges in nearby **Glanum;** or see the beautiful **St-Paul-de-Mausolée** asylum, where Vincent van Gogh convalesced after lopping off his ear. For a ½-day itinerary, see bullet **2** of "Provence in Three Days." ⏲ *½ day. For detailed information on St-Remy, see p 180, in chapter 6.*

From St-Rémy, take the D5. After 5km (4 miles), turn right onto the D27 to Les Baux. Distance: 10km (6 miles).

3 Les Baux. Famous for its wines, olive oil, ruins, and panoramic views, Les Baux makes for a memorable visit. If you want to treat yourself to some luxury, try the

The streets of St-Rémy.

A day's work in Cassis.

L'Oustau de Baumanière (see p 35) hotel and restaurant; it costs a pretty packet, but boy does it impress. For a ½-day itinerary, see bullet ❸ in "The Best of Provence in Three Days." ⏱ *½ day. For detailed information on Les Baux, see bullet* ❻*, p 109.*

From Les Baux, take the D27 and then the D78f. After 3km (2 miles), take the D17 (via Fontvieille), then the D570n to Arles. Distance: 18km (11 miles).

❹ **Arles.** If you arrive early in the morning, you can easily cover both Roman and medieval Arles in 1 jampacked day, plus photograph several sites that inspired van Gogh. For a 1-day itinerary, see bullet ❹ in "Provence in Three Days." ⏱ *1 day. For detailed information on Arles, see p 122, in chapter 6.*

Leaving Arles follow the N113 for 19km (12 miles). Near St-Martin-de-Crau, join the A54 and follow signs to Aix. They will take you onto the A7 and the A8 (exit jct. 30). Distance: 77km (48 miles).

❺ **Aix-en-Provence.** Refined and beautiful Aix competes with Marseille as the unofficial capital of Provence. Make up your own mind by getting here early enough to soak up as much of it as possible. For a 1-day itinerary, see bullet ❺ in "Provence & the Riviera in One Week." ⏱ *1 day. For detailed information on Aix-en-Provence, see p 114, in chapter 6.*

From Aix, join the A7 highway, and then follow signs to Marseille (via N296 and A51). Distance: 35km (21 miles).

❻ **Marseille.** Because there is so much to see and do here, schedule at least a 2-night stopover. Your first day could be spent exploring the city itself, leaving the second day free to visit Marseille's wild and somewhat romantic off-shore island of **If** (with its François I military stronghold), and the **Frioul isles**—havens for birdlife and flora. For a 2-day itinerary, see bullet ❻ of the "Provence & the Riviera in One Week" itinerary. ⏱ *2 days. For detailed information on Marseille, see p 144, in chapter 6.*

From Marseille, join the A50 and follow signs for La Valentine. Leave the highway at junction 8 and continue on the D559a to Cassis. Distance: 31km (19 miles).

7 Cassis. This small and attractive fishing resort lies in a bay dominated by the massive **Cap Canaille** cliff, famous for the way in which its rocky facade changes color throughout the day, according to the weather and sunlight. This is a place in which to relax. Sit in one of the cafes on the **port** and watch the world go by. Meander in and out of the narrow streets lined with boutiques, or work on your tan on one of four beaches. If you can't sit still, the tourist office can organize guided walks over the surrounding **Calanques** cliffs, or you could opt to see them by boat. Just before sunset, one of the most memorable things you can do is drive up the nearby **Route des Crêtes** (21km/13 miles long) for sweeping panoramas over the coastline, when the orange and purple light reflects off the tranquil sea. Spend the night in Cassis and leave for Hyères in the morning. 🕐 *1 day. Cassis tourist office, quai des Moulins.* ☎ *08-92-25-98-92. www.ot-cassis.com. For detailed information on Cassis, see bullet* **11**, *p 111.*

Exit Cassis on the D559 and take the A50 (dir. Toulon-Centre). Once in Toulon, follow signs to Hyères on the A57, which eventually becomes the A570. Distance: 63km (39 miles).

8 Hyères. Famous for its palm trees and mild climate, this winter resort has been popular since the 19th century. The main town is split into medieval Hyères and 19th-century Hyères, and you can cover it in 3 to 4 hours. Early in the morning, head for the old town. You'll need to be fit to walk around: Streets are uneven, narrow, and often steep. **Place Massillon** has a daily market, near the **Tour St-Blaise** (a 12th-c. tower linked to the Knights Templar), and **Place St-Paul,** by the **Collégiale St-Paul** (12th- and

17th-century) affords some fine views. On one of the highest points, you'll find the **Villa Noailles,** famous for extravagant parties thrown by artists such as Picasso and Dali in the 1920s; now it's a cutting-edge art exhibition space (closed lunchtime and on Tues). Back in the new town, don't miss the faded but beautiful **Godillot District,** with its Belle Epoque hotels and villas—testimony to Hyères' popularity among aristocrats.

After lunch, leave the center along the D97 to the tip of Hyères at la **Tour Fondue,** where boats embark for the **Île de Porquerolles**—a magnificent island with 54km (33miles) of cycle paths, pine and eucalyptus forests, and vineyards (see chapter 3, for detailed information). After your excursion, enjoy dinner back in the main town and get a good night's rest. 🕐 *1 day. Hyères tourist office, av. Ambroise Thomas.* ☎ *04-94-01-84-50. www.hyeres-tourisme.com. For detailed information on Hyères, see p 92, in chapter 5.*

The cliffs of Hyères.

The docks of St-Tropez.

From Hyères, join the N98 (past Bormes-les-Mimosas); at Port Grimaud, turn right onto the D98A to St-Tropez. Distance: 50km (31 miles).

9 St-Tropez. St-Tropez's glamour is infamous, but this sexy image betrays the port town's humble alter ego as a fishing village. Spend the morning wandering around the center, through the **port,** its tiny **fish market,** and around the former fishermen's quarters, the **Ponche district.** Don't miss the **Château Suffran** (remains of the former St-Tropez Seigneurs' castle) on Place de l'Hôtel de Ville, or the views along the coastline from the **Môle Jean Reveille** jetty, or from the lofty heights of the **Citadelle** ramparts. One of the best spots for coffee or a meal is **Place des Lices**—a tree-shaded square prized by *boules* players and marketgoers alike. If you have a sweet tooth, this is a fine spot for a nibble on St-Tropez's specialty cake, *la tarte Tropézienne,* sold by a bakery of the same name on the square.

Two wonderful museums are worth exploring: the **Musée de l'Annonciade,** with its fantastic modern art collection, and the **Maison des Papillons**—an old-world Provençal house entirely given over to butterflies. If the weather's fine, don't forget your bathing suit. St-Tropez has several beaches for all tastes. Spend the night here, and then get up bright and early for Fréjus. ⏲ *1 day. St-Tropez tourist office, quai Jean Jaurès.* ☎ *08-92-68-48-28. www.ot-saint-tropez.com. For detailed information on St-Tropez, see p 186, in chapter 6, and p 93, in chapter 5.*

From St-Tropez, take the D98A to Port Grimaud. Pick up the N98 past Sainte-Maxime, then join the D1098 (on the left) to Fréjus. Distance: 36km (22 miles).

10 Fréjus. Although it's renowned as a beach town, the shore is not Fréjus's main attraction, even if it does reel in bathers by the dozen. Once you've checked into your hotel, spend a leisurely day wandering the old town, crammed with charming cafes and boutiques. Fréjus is also known for its **Roman amphitheatre** and **aqueduct,** on the outskirts of town. Another fine historical site is the **Groupe Episcopal** with its **baptistery, cathedral,** and **cloisters.** If you're traveling with kids, you could spend the afternoon at Fréjus's **Parc Zoölogique** (zoo) or at **Aqualand** waterpark. Sleep here and head off the next morning to Cannes. ⏲ *1 day. Fréjus tourist office, 325 rue Jean Jaurès.* ☎ *04-94-51-83-83. www.frejus.fr. For detailed information on Fréjus, see chapters 3 and 5.*

Leave Fréjus on the D37, and then join the A8 to Cannes, exiting at junction 40. Distance: 38km (24 miles).

11 Cannes. Thanks to its world-famous film festival, Cannes attracts the rich and famous like bees to honey. There are three parts to the city: **La Croisette** is where you'll find flashy shops, restaurants, beaches, and hotels, as well as the **Palais des Festivals,** with its famous red carpet and surrounding **Allée des Stars.** The old town of **Le Suquet** is where you'll see authentic Cannes, with its Forville market and Musée de la Castre (ethnic and 19th-c. art museum)—complete with a 12th-century watch tower and adjacent 17th-century church (Notre-Dame de l'Esperence). **Les Îles des Lérins** are Cannes' peaceful offshore islands, one of which is cared for by Cistercian monks. Get here early, and then choose the Cannes you'd prefer to see. After a night on the tiles, drive to Nice. 🕐 *1 day. Cannes tourist office, Bureau Palais des Festivals La Croisette.* ☎ *04-92-99-84-22. www. palaisdesfestivals.com. For detailed information on Cannes, see p 136, in chapter 6, and p 68, in chapter 4.*

The Musée d'Archéologie in Nice.

La Croisette in Cannes.

Leave Cannes along the D6285 past Le Cannet, and head for the A8 toward Nice. Exit at junction 54. Distance: 41km (25 miles).

12 Nice. We recommend spending 2 days in Nice. On the first day, use your morning to visit **Vieux Nice.** Here you'll breathe the scents of Nice's street food and see the vibrant *Cours Saleya* market, the baroque *Chapelle de la Miséricorde,* the *Chapelle de l'Annonciation* dedicated to Ste-Rita, the eerie **Palais Lascaris,** and the **Cathédrale de Sainte Réparte.** After lunch and a scroll along the **Promenade des Anglais,** jump on the **Grand Tour** bus, which will give you an excellent commentated overview of the whole city, allowing you to decide which areas to revisit the next day. One ideal destination for Day 2 is **Cimiez,** where you can see Roman remains in the **Musée d'Archéologie** and marvel at the **Matisse** museum. Other fantastic museums include: **Musée National Message Biblique Marc Chagall,** the **Musée d'Art Contemporain** (modern art),

Monte Carlo's Jardin Exotique, overlooking the Côte d'Azur.

Musée des Arts Asiatiques (Asian arts), the **Musée des Beaux-Arts** (fine arts), and **Musée International d'Art Naïf Anatole-Jakovsky** (Naïve Art). Sleep here, and then head for Monaco. ⏲ *2 days. Nice tourist office, 5 pr. des Anglais.* ☎ *08-92-70-74-07. www.nicetourisme.com. For detailed information on Nice, see p 136, in chapter 6; p 103, in chapter 5; and p 32, in chapter 3.*

From Nice, rejoin the A8, and follow signs to Monaco. Distance: 21km (13 miles).

⑬ **Monaco.** The principality of Monaco impresses visitors with its cleanliness and friendliness. Check into your hotel, and then head straight for the **royal palace** and its museums, on "the Rock." At 11:55am, make sure you are outside to witness the changing of the guard. From here, the fabulous aquarium in the **Musée Océanographique** or the sea views from the **Jardin Exotique** make for a good visit, followed by a commentated tour around town on the **Azur Express Tourist train.** Once you have gawked at the stylish bodies thronging the beaches along **avenue Princesse Grace,** head for a flutter in the world-famous **casino** in Monte Carlo. ⏲ *1 day. Monaco tourist office, 2 a bd. Moulins.* ☎ *92-16-6116. www.visit monaco.com. For detailed information on Monaco, see p 158, in chapter 6, and p 104, in chapter 5.* ●

3 The Best Special-Interest Tours

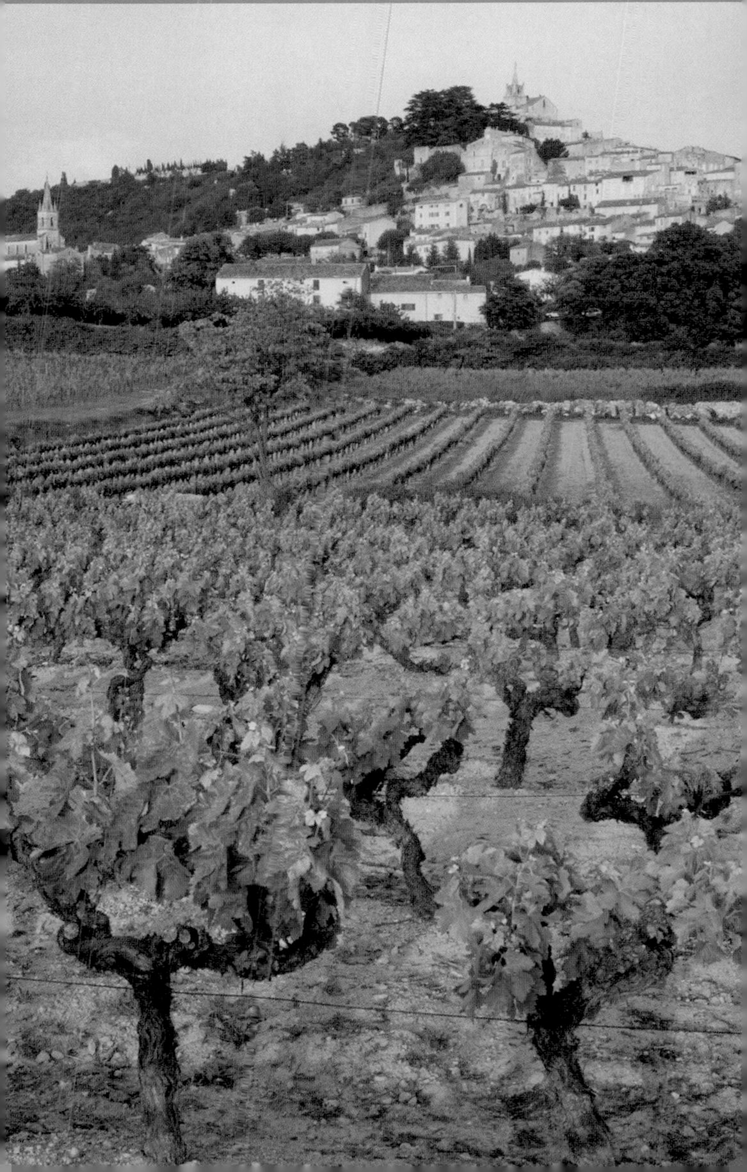

Provence for **Gourmands**

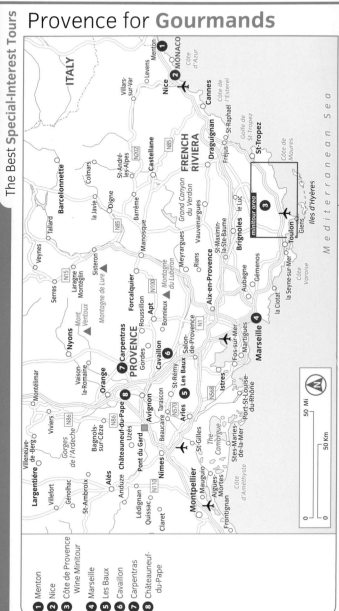

1 Menton
2 Nice
3 Côte de Provence Wine Minitour
4 Marseille
5 Les Baux
6 Cavaillon
7 Carpentras
8 Châteauneuf-du-Pape

Previous page: A vineyard near the village of Châteauneuf-du-Pape.

Fertile soil baked in sunshine, sprinkled with just the right amount of rain along a lengthy coast, Provence's climate has all the right ingredients for glorious harvests of wine grapes, olives, tomatoes, eggplants, zucchinis, peppers, garlic, fresh herbs, truffles, melons, lemons, and more. And locals know what to do with the goods. Centuries-old culinary traditions influence every *Provençal* kitchen, where age-old specialties and contemporary creations are based on some of the world's finest olive oils and produce picked that very morning. You're never more than an hour from the Mediterranean in this region, so fresh seafood takes pride of place on most tables. To top it off, fine local wine—Côtes du Rhônes, including Châteauneuf-du-Pape, and crisp Côte de Provence rosés—fuels lively chatter and makes dining here an indelibly memorable experience. **STAR: Menton (30km/19 miles East of Nice). Trip length: 7 days.**

Travel Tip

For recommended hotels, see chapter 6: Nice, p 171, and Marseille, p 156.

1 ★★ **Menton.** Wedged between the sea and an amphitheater of mountains, between Monaco and Italy, Menton is blessed with the mildest weather on the Riviera. Its microclimate has made it a center for citrus-fruit cultivation since the 1500s. During the annual **Fête du Citron** (Lemon Festival), from mid-February to early March, the town becomes a roiling mass of vivid yellow, as locals decorate floats, windows, streets, and themselves with lemons. *Tarte au citron,* France's delicious, biscuit-based tart with lemon cream, is a Menton specialty; ★★ **La Cigale's** heavenly versions, at 27 av. Carnot (☎ 04-93-35-74-66), are the best in town. In August, foodies flock to **La Fête des Les Bazaïs,** on the quai Henry Bennett, for a giant cauldron of bean, meat, and vegetable soup. The festival dates from the Middle Ages, when Menton's plague-ravaged villagers cooked an immense stew to show barbaric invaders that they had enough resources to withstand a siege. Another sweet specialty is the *Fougasse Mentonnaise,* a doughy cake, flavored with orange flower and coated with sugar and aniseed. For something savory, look

Menton during its annual Lemon Festival.

out for *stockfish*—dried fish cooked in garlic, onion, parsley, potatoes, and white wine, and then flambéed in cognac. *Menton tourist office, 8 av Boyer 06500.* ☎ *04-92-41-76-76. www.menton.fr.*

From Menton, drive west onto the A8. Turn off at junction 55 and follow signs to Nice.

❷ ★★★ **Nice.** Nice thrived as an Italian protectorate until 1814, and the boot's imprint on Niçoise cooking remains distinct. As in Italy, many traditional dishes begin with superb olive oil. **Socca** is a thin-crusted, piz-zalike bread, made from chickpea flour and olive oil; a delicious variant is **pissaladière**—*socca* topped with anchovies and caramelized onions. Both are sold at **Chez Thérèsa** (in the boutique and on the market stall in the Cours Saleya; see p 169) and **Chez René Socca**, 2 rue Miralheti (☎ 04-93-92-05-73), which doubles as a wine bar.

The restaurant-shop **Oliviera** (see Nice, p 173) sells what may be the Mediterranean's best oils. Passionate owner Nadim can tell the story of every oil he sells and readily conducts blind taste tests.

Other Niçoise specialties include the giant sandwich called **pan-bag-nat**—bread dipped in olive oil and filled with tuna, eggs, and salad—once the prized meal of fishermen. **Salade Niçoise** is Nice's most exported dish. The traditional version is a toss, however, rather than an arrangement, of salad leaves, tuna, eggs, anchovies, tomatoes, cucumber, onion, black olives, and

The owner of Chez Thérèsa with fresh-baked socca, a Niçoise specialty.

garlic. **Omelette de poutine** is a delicious local omelet made with parsley, olive oil, fresh lemon juice, and **poutines**—baby sardines caught over a 30-day period in February and March. Another local delicacy is **beignets de fleurs de courgette**—batter-coated zucchini flowers, deep-fried and served in a tomato sauce. **Soupe au pistou** is a hearty bean, tomato, and zucchini broth, flavored to taste with garlic, olive oil, and basil pesto.

As you wander the old town, look out for bakeries selling **tourte aux blettes**—a sugar-coated pie made with cabbage *(blette)*, raisins, and pine nuts. A savory variant swaps the sweet ingredients for rice and parmesan cheese.

Many traditional Niçoise menus offer delicious round zucchinis, tomatoes, or onions stuffed with pork mince called **petit farcis**—a name shared by the best cooking school in Nice, **Petits Farcis.** Cordon Bleu–trained chef Rosa Jackson (see p 173) taught this writer how to cook sea bass the right way, with fresh Provençal herbs bought during an early morning saunter that day around the bustling **Cours Saleya** food markets. *For more information on Nice, see chapter 6, p 164.*

From Nice, head west on the A8. Turn off at junction 36 (St-Tropez/ Ste Maxime/Les Arcs) and take the N555, the N7, and then the D10 (Les Arcs) to Taradeau. Distance: 96km (60 miles).

❸ ★ **Côte de Provence Wine Minitour.** Amid steep hills and sea views, the **Var** region is the land of rosé wine *par excellence.* This minitour takes you into the diverse, dramatic landscape of the Haut Pays (inlands), where gravelly, well-drained soils; generous sunshine; and winter showers yield some of France's best rosés. All these wineries are *premier cru. For the minitour, see p 33.*

Côte de Provence Wine Minitour

3A Château de Selle (Taradeau)
3B Château de St-Martin (Taradeau)
3C Château Roubine (Lorgues)
3D Jas d'Esclans
(La Motte-en-Provence)
3E Château de Bregançon
(Bormes-les-Mimosas)
3F Château de Mauvanne (Hyères)

An 18th-century bastide once owned by the counts of Provence, the **3A Château de Selle** in Taradeau, 5093 rte. de Flayosc (☎ 04-94-47-57-57; www.domaines-ott.com), now makes world-famous rosés, blending cabernet-sauvignon, grenache, and cinsaux grapes. For crisper rosé, visit nearby **3B Chateau de St-Martin,** rte. des Arcs (☎ 04-94-99-76-76; www.chateaudesaintmartin. com). This vineyard has a ruined 2nd-century B.C. Roman villa and a Gallo-Roman grape press on-site.

Take the D10 for 8km (5 miles) to Lorgues. **3C Chateau Roubine's** vines, route de vin, RD 562 (☎ 04-94-85-94-94; www.chateauroubine. com), yield light, fruity wines, yet date to Roman times. In 1307, the Knights Templar donated the site to the Order of St Jean. **Mas des Candeliers** is a lovely *gite* in the middle of the Roubine vines (www.masdes candeliers.com; from 76€/night in B&B, 195€ in the self-catering gîte).

From Lorgues, go back to the N7 in Les Arcs. Take the D555, and veer right on the D91 to La Motte. Stop briefly at the **3D Jas d'Esclans** for award-winning organic wines, route de Callas La Motte en Provence (☎ 04-98-10-29-29; www.jas desclans.com).

West along the coast (60km/37 miles on the N98, then take the D559 at La Garrigue), the **3E Château de Bregançon,** 639 rte. de Leoube, Bormes-les-Mimosas (☎ 04-94-64-80-73; www.chateaudebregancon. fr), is a lovely 17th-century château on 350 hectares (864 acres) of vines. The rosé is peach-hued, from cinsault, syrah, and grenache grapes.

From Bormes, take the D559 to La Garrigue and join the N98, and then (via Londe-les-Maures) join the D10 to Hyères (20km/12 miles). **3F Château de Mauvanne,** 2805 rte. de Nice, Hyères (☎ 04-94-66-40-25; www. mauvanne.com), has been making wine since the 1600s. Current owner Bassim Rahal produces some of the region's best rosés. ⏱ *2 days. Most wineries are open Mon–Sat 10am–noon, 2–6pm; call for details.*

Table (and a Room) with a View

For a gastronomic escapade just 15 minutes from Nice (east on D6007), serious foodies should head for the perched village of Eze. At the summit of its steep, narrow, medieval streets, you'll reach **Château de la Chèvre d'Or** (Golden Goat Castle)—a sumptuous hotel with Michelin-starred food, impeccable service, and views over jagged cliffs and the Côte d'Azur. Chef Didier Elena uses local produce to create magical dishes such as pigeon "Grémillon," cooked in a spicy salt crust with glazed eggplants. The place is so beautiful you may never want to leave, so don't. Splurge on a luxurious room (from 290€) and wake up to beautiful sea views. *Eze Village, 06360.* ☎ *04-92-10-66-66. www.chevredor.com. Menus from 130€. AE, MC, V. Open daily noon–2pm, 7:30–9pm (closed lunch May–Sept Mon–Thurs). Closed from late Nov–early Mar.*

From Hyères, join the A570 and follow signs to Toulon (via A57). Enter, then leave Toulon on the A50 and follow signs to Marseille. Distance: 85km (53 miles).

④ ★ Marseille. Fresh fruits of the sea define Marseillaise cuisine—most notably bouillabaisse, a fish stew as old as the city itself (from 600 B.C.). It's now expensive when prepared properly, but fishermen have been concocting it for centuries to make use of the least desirable portion of their catch. From the words *bouillir* (to boil) and *baisse* (to turn down the heat), genuine bouillabaisse is traditionally two dishes: a saffron-tinted broth, with orange zest and fennel seeds, followed by a variety of fish poached in the base.

Traditional bouillabaisse in Marseille.

Grapes awaiting harvest.

Servers present the fish first, to demonstrate its impeccable freshness, and then ladle more soup over it, served with *une rouille* (a sauce of red chilies, garlic, olive oil, egg yolk and cayenne). **Miramar** (see p 157) on the Vieux port is an excellent place to try it and learn to prepare it.

Other specialties to seek out in Marseille are *poupeton*—a soufflé made with the fish left over from bouillabaisse; *alibofis*—lightly battered sweet breads; and *oursinade,* a platter of sea urchins freshly caught from the ocean. Just behind the Cours d'Estienne d'Orves, **La Trilogie des Cépages,** 35 rue de la Paix Marcel Paul (04-91-33-96-03; www.trilogiedescepages. com), combines inventive, regional cooking with wine-tasting lessons. *For detailed information on Marseille, see chapter 5, p 144.*

Take the A7 from Marseille and, after 49km (30 miles), join the A54. Exit at junction 13 and follow signs to Les Baux-de-Provence. Distance: 87km (54 miles).

5 Les Baux. Too picturesque for its own good, Les Baux (see p 109) balances on the edge of the Alpilles

mountains. Sometimes it seems as though tourists may push it over the brink, yet it produces some of the most flavorful olive oils in the region. The oil's rich golden color has earned it the name *huile d'or* (golden oil); purist chefs swear that only oils from Les Baux can impart traditional Provençal flavor. **Terre des Huiles,** Grand-rue (04-90-54-37-62), sells a wide selection.

Les Baux is also a classified wine-growing region, and it specializes in organic and biodynamic wines. Reds and rosés dominate, but a few whites slip through. Ask the tourist office (04-90-54-34-39) about wine tours, or try the **Château Romanin** outside the village. Its cellar is in an eerie troglodyte cathedral, 13210 St-Rémy (04-90-92-45-87; www.romanin.fr).

If you can splurge, the culinary highlight of your trip could be **★★★ L'Oustau de Baumanière** (04-90-54-33-07; www.oustaude baumaniere.com). At this luxury hotel and restaurant in the heart of the village, Chef Sylvestre Wahid concocts wonders such as roasted blue lobster with asparagus and Morchella mushrooms. *Les Baux de*

Olives from the region surrounding Les Baux.

Provence tourist office, rue Porte Mage. ☎ *04-90-54-34-39. www. lesbauxdeprovence.com.*

From Les Baux, take the D27 for 2km (1¼ miles), and then join the D5 (left) for 8km (5 miles). At

A Provençal olive grower.

St-Rémy, take the D99a, then D99 for 16km (10 miles), and follow signs to Cavaillon.

6 Cavaillon. There's one reason not to miss this pretty but otherwise ordinary town: cantaloupe melons. The Cavaillon region has been cultivating them since the time when Avignon was the official papal residency, at least 5 centuries ago. Writer Alexander Dumas loved them so much, he donated all 194 of his published works to the town in exchange for a life annuity of 12 melons a year. Each July, during the 4-day melon festival, the whole town goes cantaloupe: A pyramid of melons dominates the marketplace, artists paint and sell melon-themed works, and minibus excursions take visitors to local melon farms.

Don't leave town without stopping at ★★★ **L'Auberge de Cheval Blanc,** 84460 Cheval Blanc (☎ 04-32-50-18-55; www.auberge-de-chevalblanc.com; menus 23€–68€; AE, MC, V; dinner Thurs–Sun; lunch Mon, Thurs–Sun). Talented chef Hervé Perasse prepares such dishes as turbot roasted in vanilla in a beautiful dining room, near Cavaillon. *Cavaillon tourist board, 79 pl. François Tourel.* ☎ 04-90-71-32-01. *www.cavaillon-luberon.com.*

Exit Cavaillon and take the D938, then the D99. After 1km (3/4 mile), turn right onto the A7 highway. Exit at junction 23, and then follow signs to Carpentras. Total distance: 45km (28 miles).

❼ Carpentras. This archetypal Provençal town hosts an exceptional Friday market along its tree-lined outer boulevards. Carpentras is particularly famous for its truffle market, which supplies France with more than half its black diamonds between November and March. Hard fruit-sweets called *berlingots* are another specialty. They come in every color under the sun at **Confiserie du Mont-Ventoux,** 288 av. N.D. de Santé (☎ 04-90-63-05-25. www.berlingots.net). Reserve in advance and you can watch as they're made (for free!). *Carpentras tourist board, pl. Aristide Briand.* ☎ *04-90-63-00-78. www.carpentras-ventoux.com.*

Exit Carpentras and take the D942. After 16km (10 miles), join the D225 (dir. Orange/Sourges); after 2km (1¼ miles), turn onto the D907 to Sourges, where you join the D17 to Châteauneuf-du-Pape. Distance: 32km (20 miles).

Black diamonds from the Carpentras truffle market.

❽ ★★ Châteauneuf-du-Pape. This small, scenic town produces heavy red Côtes du Rhone wines, first planted by the 14th-century Avignon popes, now famous the world over. Sample vintage selections at the **Domaine de la Roncière's** *caveau,* 3 rue de la République (☎ 04-90-32-57-96). *For more information, see p 84, in chapter 5. Châteauneuf-du-Pape tourist office, place Portail.* ☎ *04-90-83-71-08. www.ccpro.fr.*

Provence Wine Tours

Provence Wine Tours (6 impasse de la Goule, 13510 Eguilles; ☎ 04-91-49-58-87; www.provencewinetours.com) offers three oenological excursions in Provence: Wines from the Pays d'Aix (visit five estates and the city of Aix); Wines from the Pays de Cassis (discovery of the Cassis and Bandol A.O.C.s, plus a walk along the highest coastal cliffs in Europe); and Wine and Food (visit two estates and a liqueur producer before tasting calissons, olive oils, and tapenades).

Provence for **Art Lovers**

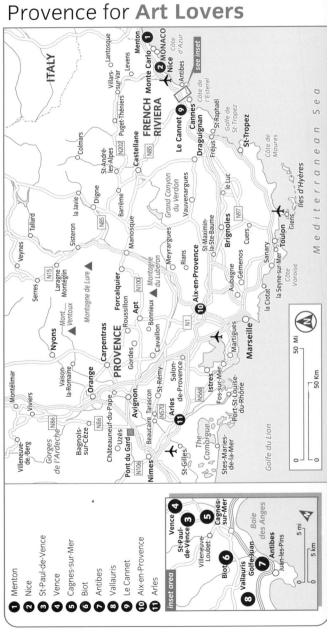

1. Menton
2. Nice
3. St-Paul-de-Vence
4. Vence
5. Cagnes-sur-Mer
6. Biot
7. Antibes
8. Vallauris
9. Le Cannet
10. Aix-en-Provence
11. Arles

Like moths to a flame, artists have gravitated toward Provence's vivid sunlight and vibrant landscape for centuries. Long before the rise of Impressionism for which Provence is most famous, the medieval Schools of Avignon and Nice were influential as well. Sculptor Pierre Puget (1620–94) was deemed Provence's answer to Michelangelo, and Provence's varied scenery inspired Grassois painter Jean-Honoré Fragonard's (1732–1806) romantic rococo style. Impressionists Claude Monet and Auguste Renoir eased the world into Modernism with their treatment of light, and Raoul Dufy, Pierre Bonnard, and Paul Signac carried the torch decades later. Both Paul Cézanne, a native Aixois, and Vincent van Gogh endlessly depicted sun-kissed Provençal landscapes. Pablo Picasso and Henri Matisse settled here, and Jean Cocteau spent much of his life on the Côte d'Azur, creating his own museum in Menton, the start of our tour. START: **Menton (30km/19 miles east of Nice). Trip Length: 7–10 days.**

Travel Tip

For hotels and restaurants, see chapter 6: Nice, p 171; St-Tropez, p 191; Aix-en-Provence, p 121; Arles, p 126.

❶ ★ **Menton.** Parisian born artist, dramatist, and surrealist filmmaker Jean Cocteau (1839–1963) was a big fan of Menton and left the town two important legacies: his sublime murals in the **Salle des Mariages,** Mairie de Menton, place Ardoïno (☎ 04-92-10-50-00), in Menton's City Hall, including the famous *Noce Imaginaire;* and the **Musée Jean Cocteau,** Bastion du Vieux Port (☎ 04-93-57-72-30; Wed–Mon 10am–noon, 2–6pm). The building Cocteau chose was a ruined 17th-century fort on the port. He oversaw all the restoration work, designing the floor mosaics on the ground level, the window mosaics on the first floor, and

the wrought-iron window decorations of his *zoomorphes.* He donated his tapestries, set designs, and drawings as well, but then he died before his museum opened in 1967. The **Musée des Beaux Arts** is set in the sumptuous 17th-century **Palais Carnolès** (former residence of Monaco's princes), a work of art in its own right. Its eclectic collections include primitive Italian works (12th–15th c.), Flemish and Dutch paintings from the 17th and 18th century, and Greek icons. The citrus groves surrounding the museum include some 400 lemon, lime, grapefruit, and kumquat trees, 3 av. de la Madone (☎ 04-93-35-49-71; Wed–Mon 10am–noon, 2–6pm). *Menton tourist office, 8 av. Boyer 06500.* ☎ *04-92-41-76-76.* *www.tourisme-menton.fr.*

A replica of Rodin's The Kiss *in Nice's Musée des Beaux Arts.*

MAMAC, the Museum of Modern and Contemporary Art in Nice.

From Menton, drive west onto the A8. Turn off at junction 55 and follow signs to Nice.

2 ★★★ Nice. The fifth biggest city in France attracted several 19th- and 20th-century artists, including Henri Matisse, who loved Nice's "crystalline, limpid" light. He lived at several addresses from 1917 until his death in Cimiez in 1954. Before he died, he bequeathed the city a vast collection of paintings, sculptures, drawings, engravings, paper cutouts, and illustrated books, visible today in the ★ **Musée Matisse** (see p 166). His iconic *Nu Bleu IV* (Blue Nude IV) and locally inspired *Tempête à Nice* (Nice in Storm) are here.

Russian-born Marc Chagall (1887–1985) lived in St-Paul-de-Vence, but his museum, the **Musée National Message Biblique Marc Chagall** (see p 168), is in Nice. He bequeathed the town paintings as well as sculptures, a mosaic, and three huge stained-glass windows. Chagall ordered the glass set amid cold-toned flora such as olive,

pine, and oak trees. Le Corbusier's disciple André Hermant designed the building. It's one of the world's most important Chagall collections.

Fauvist painter Raoul Dufy made revolutionary use of light and color in Nice, choosing the town as the background and inspiration for his works. A small but fine selection of paintings hangs on the walls of the ★ **Musée des Beaux Arts** (see p 169). One of the best contemporary art museums outside Paris is Nice's ★ **MAMAC** (Musée d'Art Moderne et d'Art Contemporain), which presents French and American avant-garde art from the 1960s onward. Both American Pop Art and French New Realism were very present on the Riviera, drawing inspiration from daily life. American Pop artists such as Andy Warhol appropriated objects from mass culture, while the work of the New Realists derived from manipulations of those same objects, often breaking them or putting them under glass. Examples of this can be found here. *For detailed information on Nice, see chapter 6, p 164.*

Exit Nice on the A8 toward Cagnes. Exit at junction 48 and follow signs for Vence/Cagnes-sur-Mer. Join the D2 as soon as possible (Route de Serres) to St-Paul. Distance: 28km (17 miles).

❸ **St-Paul-de-Vence.** This fortified medieval settlement—presiding over the Vence countryside amid orange and olive trees—is one of the most visited *villages perchés* in France. It was rediscovered by painters such as Amedeo Modigliani, Pierre Bonnard, and Paul Signac in the 1920s. Since then, hundreds of artists have followed suit, along with serious art dealers whose galleries flank the narrow cobblestone streets. No art buff should miss the **★★ Fondation Maeght** (☎ 04-93-32-81-63; www.maeght.com; daily 10am–7pm July–Sept; 10am–12:30pm, 2:30–6pm Oct–June). On a pine hill north of town, it's in a peach and white structure that epitomizes Mediterranean avant-garde architecture, designed by José Luis Sert. Marguerite and Aimé Maeght were art dealers in Cannes who hobnobbed with Chagall, Matisse, and Joan Miró. The couple's private collections form the basis of the museum. In the courtyard, marble statues by Miró and mosaics by

Fondation Maeght in St-Paul-de-Vence.

Chagall form a surrealistic garden. *St-Paul-de-Vence tourist office, 2 rue Grande.* ☎ *04-93-32-86-95.* www. saint-pauldevence.com.

Drive 4km (2½ miles) north along the D2.

❹ **Vence.** This resort town's historic core is charming enough, but don't miss the **★ Chapelle du Rosaire** (or Chapelle Matisse) on

The Matisse Chapel on the outskirts of Vence.

its outer edges, at 466 av. Henri Matisse (☎ 04-93-58-03-26; admission 3€, 2€ reduced; Mon, Wed, Sat 2–5:30pm, Tues, Thurs 10–11:30am, 2–5:30pm; closed Nov). Matisse designed it as a gift to the Dominican nuns who cared for him during the last years of his life. He called the chapel his "masterpiece," despite all its imperfections." It is his complete and final work—arguably the most exquisite piece of 20th-century art on the Riviera. The interior is made from Carrara marble and other reflective white materials, dazzling when dappled with colorful reflections from the stained-glass windows. *Vence tourist office, 8 pl. Grand Jardin. ☎ 04-93-58-06-38. www.ville-vence.fr.*

Take the D236 from Vence and, after 2km (1 mile), join the D36 to Cagnes. Distance: 10km (6 miles).

The seaside Picasso Museum in Antibes.

⑤ Cagnes-sur-Mer. Renoir deemed the perched old town of Cagnes-sur-Mer (see p 102) "the place where I want to paint until the last day of my life." He got his wish in 1919, when he died in his family home, Les Collettes—today's **Musée Renoir,** 19 Chemin des Collettes (☎ 04-93-20-61-07; admission 4€, 2€ reduced; May–Sept Wed–Mon 10am–noon, 2–6pm; Oct–Apr Wed–Mon 10am–noon, 2–5pm)—leaving a still life behind to dry. Les Collettes' house and olive groves have been restored to look as they did when Renoir lived here. Although crippled by arthritis, he began experimenting with sculpture in Cagnes, and the museum has 20 portrait busts and portrait medallions that constitute the largest collection of Renoir sculpture in the world. You can explore the drawing room and dining room on your own before going up to the artist's bedroom. In his atelier are his wheelchair, easel, and brushes. *Cagnes tourist office, place du Dr Maurel 06800. ☎ 04-93-20-61-64. www. cagnes-tourisme.com.*

Leave Cagnes on the D6007. After 4km (2½ miles), join the D4 to Biot. Distance: 10km (6 miles).

⑥ Biot. Famous for its bubble-flecked glass, known as *verre rustique,* Biot has also been known for its pottery since ancient times, when local merchants began exporting local earthenware jars to Phoenicia. It's also where Fernand Léger painted until the day he died. A magnificent collection of his work is on display at the ★★ **Musée Nationale Fernand-Léger,** Chemin du Val-de-Pome (☎ 04-92-91-50-30; www.musee-fernandleger.fr; admission 5.50€; open daily 10am–6pm, until 5pm Nov–May), a striking stone-and-marble building enhanced by Léger's mosaic-and-ceramic mural facade. The collection

In van Gogh's Footsteps

One of the most moving pilgrimages a van Gogh buff can make is to the **Monastère St-Paul de Mausole** asylum, outside St-Rémy (see p 183). After suffering from what was likely undiagnosed bipolar disorder, aggravated by absinthe and lead paint fumes, Vincent checked himself into Saint-Paul-de-Mausole in 1889 and stayed until 1890, the year of his death. In this sanctuary, he painted 150 canvases, including *Starry Night* and other masterpieces. St-Paul is still a functioning asylum, but visitors can tour the grounds, past hand-wrought signs that picture some of Vincent's most famous paintings on the very sites where he painted them.

includes paintings, ceramics, tapestries, and sculptures showing the artist's development from 1905 until his death. His paintings abound with cranes, acrobats, scaffolding, railroad signals, buxom nudes, casings, and crankshafts. *Biot tourist office, rue St-Sébastien.* 📞 *04-93-65-78-00. www.biot.fr.*

From Biot, take the D4 then at the island, the D6007 to Antibes: 6km (4 miles).

7 ★★ **Antibes.** This unpretentious port town with a bustling covered market is home to the Château Grimaldi, once the palace of the Grimaldi princes of Antibes, who ruled from 1385 to 1608. Nowadays, the castle shelters the world-class **Musée Picasso,** place du Mariejol (📞 04-92-90-54-20; Tues–Sun 10am–6pm, closed noon–2pm Sept–June; open until 8pm Wed and Fri July–Aug). When Picasso came to town after the war, he stayed in a small hotel at Golfe-Juan until the museum director at Antibes invited him to work and live at the museum. He spent the year 1946 painting here, and, upon his departure, donated all the work he'd created: paintings, ceramics, drawings, lithographs, oils on paper, sculptures, and tapestries. In addition, a

contemporary art gallery exhibits Léger, Miró, Max Ernst, and Calder. *Antibes tourist office, 11 pl. Gén de Gaulle.* 📞 *04-97-23-11-11. www. antibes-juanlespins.com.*

Leave Antibes on the D6107 and follow signposts to Vallauris. Distance: 7km (4 miles).

8 **Vallauris.** The tacky ceramics capital of the Riviera still attracts lovers of pottery and Picasso with its three-in-one **Musée National de Picasso, Musée Magnelli, and Musée de la Céramique,** in the village castle, place de la Libération (📞 04-93-64-71-83; admission 4€, 2€ reduced; free under 18; mid-June to mid-Sept Wed–Mon 10am–6pm; until 5pm mid-Sept to mid-June).

Picasso lived in Vallauris from 1948 to 1955, and created some 4,000 ceramic pieces. He also decorated a rough stone chapel with two fabulous contrasting paintings: *La Paix* (Peace) and *La Guerre* (War). In the main square, look out for Picasso's sculpture *L'Homme au Mouton* (Man with Sheep), which he created in just one afternoon. *Vallauris tourist office, av Frères Roustan 06220.* 📞 *04-93-63-21-07. www.vallauris-golfe-juan.com.*

From Vallauris, take the D135 to Le Cannet. Distance: 6km (4 miles).

9 Le Cannet. This town near Cannes offers eye-catching vistas over the bay and a sophisticated city center, the **Vieux Cannet,** which features 18th-century houses and tree-shaded squares linked by narrow alleyways. It is this singular charm that attracted 20th-century French artist Pierre Bonnard. Bonnard painted his most celebrated works in Le Cannet between 1926 and his death in 1939—and the town pays homage to him with the new **Musée Bonnard,** 18 bd. de Carnot (☎ 04-92-18-24-42), set to open in the stunning 20th-century Hôtel St-Vianney in 2011. *Le Cannet tourist office, place Benidorm, 73 av. du*

A sculpture of Paul Cézanne, native son of Aix-en-Provence.

Campon 06110. ☎ *04-93-45-34-27. www.le cannet.fr.*

From Le Cannet, take the D6285 to the A8 highway (dir. Aix-en-Provence). Exit at junction 31 and take the N7 to Aix. Distance: 147km (93 miles).

10 ★★★ Aix-en-Provence. Paul Cézanne and Aix-en-Provence are inseparable. Cézanne was a law student at his father's behest, but his real love was painting the countryside around Aix. Gradually he found recognition and friends among the circle of Impressionist painters in Paris. After outgrowing Impressionism, he began to juxtapose large patches of color in new ways and to exaggerate lines and relief. His most prolific works were inspired by Aix's outlying landscape, particularly the **Montagne St-Victoire,** visible from town. Today, visitors can see **Cézanne's atelier** as he left it when he died (see p 118). Contemporary art followers shouldn't miss the stellar collection at the **Fondation Vasarely** (p 119).

From Aix, take the D17 to the A8. After 23km (14 miles), join the A7 and follow the signs for Arles. Distance: 79km (49 miles).

11 ★★ Arles. In 1888, van Gogh attempted to overcome his gloomy temperament by settling in sunny Arles. Never one for good luck, he arrived to find the sunshine city covered with snow. Nevertheless, he went on to paint 200 canvases in fewer than 15 months here. But it

van Gogh's Café du Nuit.

Café van Gogh, depicted in the van Gogh painting Café du Nuit.

was in Arles that he notoriously lopped off his ear, after a fight with fellow artist Paul Gauguin. The **Espace Van Gogh** (see p 125) the **Café Van Gogh** (see p 127), and the **Fondation Van Gogh** all pay tribute to the tortured genius (see p 125, in chapter 6), who would die penniless, without recognition,

2 years later in Provence. If you'd like to stay the night, try the **Galerie Huit** (☎ 04-90-97-77-93; www.galeriehuit.com) an art gallery that doubles as a B&B, with luxurious rooms in the center of Arles. *For detailed information, see chapter 6, p 126.*

Best Historic **Architecture**

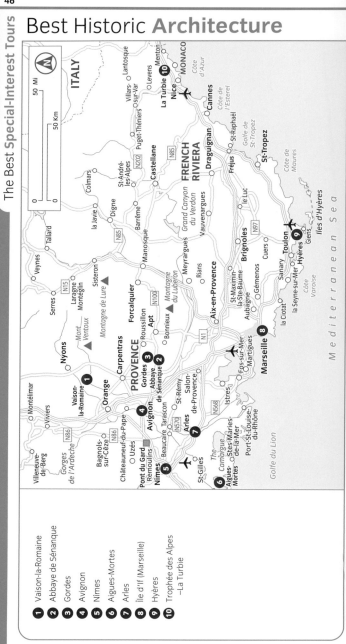

1. Vaison-la-Romaine
2. Abbaye de Sénanque
3. Gordes
4. Avignon
5. Nîmes
6. Aigues-Mortes
7. Arles
8. Île d'If (Marseille)
9. Hyères
10. Trophée des Alpes –La Turbie

As ancient Rome's first transalpine conquest, Provence has a wealth of ancient architectural wonders and ruins. Later, as Christendom took root and spread, the Middle Ages saw a surge in Romanesque abbeys and churches, followed by France's own home-grown Gothic style. From the 16th to the 18th century, the fortified walls and gates that protected many cities during the religious wars gave way to sumptuous châteaus and classical town houses. The wild 19th century, with its Belle Epoque villas and hotels, left behind some beautiful and extravagant *folies.* And although extensive tourism has spawned plenty of modern eyesores—particularly on the Riviera—a select few 20th-century buildings and art galleries are astonishing. START: **Vaison-la-Romaine is 56km (35 miles) north of Avignon. Trip length: 7–10 days.**

Travel Tip

For hotels and restaurants, see chapter 6: Avignon, p 134; Nîmes, p 179; Arles p 126.

① ★★★ Vaison-la-Romaine.

Built along the banks of the Ouvèze River, Vasio Vocontiorum (Vasion-la-Romaine) flourished under Roman rule for centuries. After the collapse of the Roman Empire and several years of flooding, however, all

evidence disappeared under layers of silt and sand. It wasn't until 1907 that the Roman ruins were rediscovered and excavated. Until then, Vaison was a small, amiable medieval village, high on a crag overlooking the river. Its Romanesque ★ **Cathédrale Notre-Dame-de-Nazareth** still has an 11th-century *chevet,* made from one solid block of stone. It is intricately decorated with cornices and friezes. The nave inside has pointed barrel vaulting

Roman artifacts in Vaison-la-Romaine.

and an octagonal dome covered with symbols of the evangelists. The adjacent **cloisters** are from the 12th and 13th century, wonderfully decorated with interwoven patterns, figures, and acanthus leaves. The **upper town (haute ville),** with its maze of alleyways, is surrounded by **14th-century fortifications,** the stones of which were taken from the Roman town ruins. There is a good view onto Mont Ventoux from the parvis of the 15th-century church. A dramatic **12th-century château,** built by the count of Toulouse, stands proud at the highest point of the hill. Back in the lower town, only 15 hectares (37 acres) of ★★★ kids **Roman Vaison** are accessible; the rest lies forgotten beneath modern buildings. The **Puymin** district is the first you'll see. It was the hub of Roman Vaison, containing the courthouse (praetorium), theater, temples, and shops. In Puymin, the **Maison des Messii** was home to a very important family. Remains of columns,

The Abbaye de Sénanque.

baths, a private temple, dining room, and living rooms are still visible.

One of the most impressive sites is the 34 semicircular rows of stone benches that make up the 1st-century **Antique Theatre.** It would have seated up to 6,000. The **Portico of Pompey** is a vast 65m (213-foot) array of columns that originally surrounded a garden and pool. You can view artifacts unearthed during excavations in the **Musée Théo Desplans,** where highlights include remarkable white marble statues presented in chronological order, the 3rd-century silver bust of a wealthy patrician, and a six-seater public latrine.

The ★ **bridge** linking the Haute Ville to lower town is 2,000 years old. It's one of the only constructions that survived torrential flooding in 1992, which killed 37 people and destroyed 150 houses. *Most sights are open Nov–Feb 10am–noon, 2–5pm; Mar, Oct 10am–12:30pm, 2–5:30pm; Apr–Sept 9:30am–6pm. Admission to all sites 8€; 3.50€ reduced. Vaison-la-Romaine, avenue Chanoine Sautel.* ☎ *04-90-36-02-11. www.vaison-en-provence.com.*

From Vaison, exit on the D938 and head for Carpentras. Leave Carpentras on the D4 and, after 12km (7½ miles), join the D177, the D224, and D15 to Gordes. The Abbey is signposted from the town center. Distance: 54km (33.5 miles).

❷ ★★★ **Abbaye de Sénanque.** The beauty, fragrance, and peacefulness of this gray-stone Luberon abbey, set in a valley of lavender fields, is not easily forgotten. It is an almost perfect example of Romanesque Cistercian architecture, with stone walls, plain windows, and barrel-vaulted ceilings. Certain parts of the roof are covered with limestone tiles called *lauzes,* also used on the

Vaulted stone huts, known as bories, outside Gordes.

unusual stone dwellings *(bories)* in nearby Gordes (see below). The dual-columned **cloister** shows superb craftsmanship with delicate, late-12th-century, floral-themed carvings. The barrel-vaulted **nave** leads to the eight-sided dome of the **transept,** in the corner of which lies the tomb of the abbey's 13th-century patron, the lord of Venasque. At its peak, the **chapter-house** was a hive of monastic activity. Here on the stone seats lining the walls, monks listened to the abbot's biblical sermons. The **cale-factory** was the only heated room in the abbey, enabling the monks to read and write without freezing. It is characterized by a beehive-shaped fireplace. ☎ 04-90-72-05-72. *www. senanque.fr. Guided visits only. Times change so call to verify.*

3 ★★★ Gordes. As chic as it is stunning, this dramatic perched village has a fine **Renaissance château,** built on the site of a 12th-century fortress. The 1541 chimney piece in the great hall is a decorative spectacle with ornate pediments, flowers, and shells. In the village, the labyrinth of paved streets are known as *calades*—recognizable by their steep incline, central gutters, vaulted passageways, and tall, old houses.

Just beyond the village, however, along the D2, lies an architectural conundrum dating back to the Bronze Age—the **Village des Bories** (☎ 04-90-72-03-48; daily 9am–sundown). Bories are peculiar, corbel-vaulted, dry-stone huts, used for 3,000-plus years for human housing, sheepfolds, wine cellars, cereal storage, and bakeries. Gordes has 400 of the 3,000 bories in Provence—many of which were inhabited until the 19th century. The village reconstructs the rural lifestyle of borie dwellers and shows a photo display of borie villages around the world. It's most atmospheric first thing in the morning. *Gordes tourist office, place Château.* ☎ 04-90-72-02-75. *www.gordes-village.com.*

Leave Gordes on the D2. After La Coustellet, join the D900 for 18km (11 miles), then D907 (for 200 yards/600 feet) before taking the N7 (near Noves) into Avignon. Distance: 40km (25 miles).

4 ★★★ **Avignon.** A jewel in Provence's sparkling crown, the Vaucluse capital can keep architecture enthusiasts busy with enough medieval streets, Renaissance mansions, and Romanesque churches to explore for a lifetime. However, you simply cannot miss the world's biggest Gothic palace—★★★ **Le Palais des Papes**—a testimony to the immense power of the papacy in the 14th century. Popes Benedict XII and Clement VI built it in fewer than 20 years (1335–1352). It soars 50m (164 feet) above the town in a massive ensemble of stone towers and sheer walls that hide a maze of passages, chapels, galleries, and halls. Two styles reign: Cistercian (by Benedict XII) and Gothic (by Clement VI). The most visible meeting point of these styles is in the **Cour d'Honneur,** with its machicolated conclave wing and irregular gothic openings across the facade. Below the **Tour des Anges,** the

treasury is a beautiful vaulted room with flagstones concealing the pope's secret hiding holes for gold, silver, and precious ornaments. More concealed compartments lie under the **Chamberlain's Bedchamber** on the third floor, which also shows a pretty 14th-century painted beam ceiling and some foliated scrollwork on the walls. The **Grand Tinel** banquet hall is the biggest in the palace, with a keel-vaulted roof that looks like a ship's hull, and 18th-century Gobelin tapestries. Frescos by Martini, brought from Notre-Dame-des-Doms cathedral, embellish the bare walls of the **Consistoire,** where the pope announced the names of his cardinals. It's stripped of most of its decoration, but some original frescos have resisted time. The **Chapels of St-Jean and St-Martial,** the **Pope's Bedroom,** and **Clement VI studium** all contain extraordinary paintwork (see p 129). The **Grande Audience** (Palace of the Great Causes), where 13 ecclesiastical judges formed the Tribunal de la Rota (named after the *rota,* or circular bench, they sat upon), has a vaulted ceiling, set off against a

Inside the Palais des Papes in Avignon.

Aigues-Mortes, a medieval fortified town in the Camargue.

deep-blue starlit sky and the **Fresco of the Prophets,** painted by master Matteo Giovanetti in 1352. *For more information, see chapter 6, p 128.*

Leave Avignon via the Porte de l'Oulle and join the N100. After 20km (12 miles), join the A9 and follow signs to Nîmes. Distance: 45km (28 miles).

5 ★★★ Nîmes. This ancient city wears its Gallo-Roman vestiges with proud nonchalance. The **Arènes** (arenas, also see p 175, chapter 6) are more complete than Rome's Colosseum. The name *arènes* derives from the sand used to soak up blood in the central oval space, *vomitorias* (exits), and corridors. This feat of engineering bears two small carvings of Romulus and Remus, the mythological founders of Rome who were raised by a wolf. You can still sit on the original stone benches and make out holes that would have held poles used to support awnings to shield the crowd from the sun. Medieval residents

sought protection within the arena's thick walls, using them as ramparts for a self-contained village. The village remained until the 19th century, when the buildings and trash (6m/20 ft. deep) were cleared to make way for bullfights. See chapter 6 for fuller coverage of the **Maison Carré,** Nîmes' tremendous Roman temple; the **Temple de Diane** ruins (part of a Roman sanctuary); the **Tour Magne,** with its panoramic viewing platform; and the **Castellum** water tower. **Porte Auguste** is the city's best-preserved Roman gate, measuring 6m by 4m (20 ft. x 13 ft.). *For more information, see chapter 6, p 174.*

From Nimes, head for the A9 toward Montpellier. Exit at junction 26 and follow signs for Aigues-Mortes. Distance: 42km (26 miles).

6 ★★★ Aigues-Mortes. South of Nîmes, this city of the "dead waters" (*aigues mortes,* in Provençal) stands alone in the middle of the Camargue's swamps and lagoons. Today it is France's best-preserved, medieval walled settlement, with **ramparts** (1272–1300) that still enclose the entire town. The 13th-century **Tour de Constance** (☎ 04-66-53-61-55; daily May–Aug 10am–7pm, Sept–Apr until 5pm) is a circular keep with walls 6m (20-ft.) thick. From the top, a sweeping panorama over the Midi salt marshes and the Camargue will get your pulse racing. In town, the religious centerpiece is the **Église Notre-Dame des Sablons** (rue Jean-Jaurès; no phone). Constructed of wood in 1183, it was rebuilt in stone in 1246 in the ogival style. Its modern stained-glass windows were installed in 1980 as replacements for the badly damaged originals. *Aigues-Mortes tourist board, place St- Louis 30220.* ☎ *04-66-53-73-00. www.ot-aigues mortes.fr.*

Leave Aigues on the D979 to the D46. At the second island, take the D58, turning off 3km (2 miles) later onto the D38c. After 5km (3 miles), turn left onto the D570. After 24km (15 miles), Arles is signposted along the N113. Distance: 47km (29 miles).

❼ ★★★ **Arles.** Known as the "the little Rome of the Gauls," Arles possesses some of France's best-preserved Gallo-Roman legacies. The 136m by 107m (446 x 351 yds) **Arène** is a complex structure of arches, corridors, vomitorias, seating for 20,000 spectators, and underground passages for machinery, animals, and gladiators. Mosaics furnished some floors, to facilitate cleaning after bloody battles (also see p 123). Other Roman architectural sites of interest are the **Thermes de Constantin** Roman baths, the **Musée d'Arles Antique,** the **Théâtre Antique** (the Roman theater), and the

The Chateau d'If, overlooking the Côte d'Azur near Marseille.

Alycamps cemetery. *See p 126, chapter 6, for details.*

If you're a fan of the Romanesque, you'll be mesmerized by the intricate detail on the **Église St-Trophime's** 12th-century portal, which displays an ancient classical arrangement that suggests a triumphal arch. *For more information, see chapter 6, p 125.*

Leave Arles on the N113/E80; join the A54 after 20km (12 miles). Continue for 24km (15 miles), and then join the A7 to Marseille. Distance: 93km (58 miles).

❽ ★★ **Île d'If—Marseille.** On the sparsely vegetated island of If, François I built a fortress to defend Marseille (1524–28). Later a bastioned curtain wall was added, but it was never attacked. The site later became a prison for Huguenots and political prisoners. A superb example of military Renaissance architecture, Alexandre Dumas used the château as a setting for the fictional adventures of *The Count of Monte Cristo* The château's most famous association—with the legendary *Man in the Iron Mask*—is also apocryphal. Today it makes for a fascinating visit, with austere prison cells and a viewing platform over choppy waters. *Marseille tourist board, 4 La Canebière.* ☎ *04-91-13-89-00. www.marseilletourisme.com.*

From Marseille, take the A50 to Toulon, then join the DN8 (av. Estienne d'Orves) and follow signs to Hyères (via A57, A570, N98). Distance: 83km (51 miles).

⑨ Hyères. Remnants of this seaside town's former life as a center for the Templar Knights live on in the **Tour Saint Blaise,** an impeccably restored 12th-century tower near the market place, and in the medieval hilltop **château** ruin. But Hyères's most distinctive architectural gems are more recent: Belle Epoque villas line the Godillot district—a throwback to Hyères's days as a winter resort for wealthy 19th-century English aristocrats—and the **Villa de Noailles,** Montée de Noailles 83400 (☎ 04-98-08-01-93; www.villanoailles-hyeres.com;), stands proud in cubist glory. In 1923, rich art patrons commissioned architect Robert Mallet-Stevens to build a villa bathed in sunlight. The result is this glorious, white structure—the scene of extravagant parties frequented by such artists as Salvador Dalí, Pablo Picasso, Jean Cocteau, and Man Ray. Today's artists still flock here to see cutting-edge art and photography exhibitions. *Also see Hyères, p 92.*

The Trophée des Alpes from 6 b.c.

From Hyères, take N98 to A570 (dir. Toulon) and then follow the A57 (dir. Nice). After 9km (5 miles) join the A57. After 45km (28 miles), join the A8, exit at junction 57 for Roquebrune, and then follow signs to La Turbie. Distance: 167km (103 miles).

⑩ ★ Trophée des Alpes. La Turbie has a ruined monument erected by Roman emperor Augustus in 6 b.c., to celebrate the subjugation of the French by the Roman armies. The trophy was originally 49m (160 ft.) high, topped by a statue of Emperor Octavius Augustus. Only the pedestal remains today, but the miniature replica in the **Musée du Trophée d'Auguste** (rue Albert-1er, La Turbie; ☎ 04-93-41-20-84) will help you imagine the grandeur of the original statue.

Provence & the Riviera **for Kids**

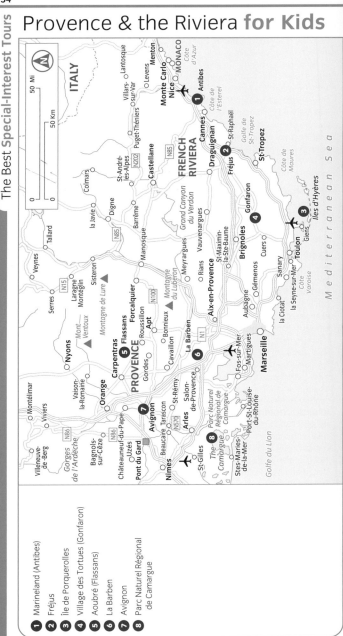

1 Marineland (Antibes)
2 Fréjus
3 Île de Porquerolles
4 Village des Tortues (Gonfaron)
5 Aoubré (Flassans)
6 La Barben
7 Avignon
8 Parc Naturel Régional de Camargue

Through a child's eyes, the castles and fortified hilltowns of Provence and the Riviera could have come straight from a Disney movie, which makes it easier to lure kids to "cultural attractions" (provided you don't call them that of course!). Then there's the great outdoors, which provides a host of activities, both on land and on sea, for the whole brood. The region is also known for its spectacular wildlife and flora, which gives kids a chance to learn about nature and have fun at the same time. With this tour, we have tried to provide a list of kid-specific attractions that can either be followed in order or mixed in with destinations on other tours. **START: Antibes. Trip length: 436km (270 miles).**

Travel Tip

For hotels and restaurants, see chapter 6, p 113.

1 Antibes. Just outside Antibes, near Biot, ★★ **Marineland** is an adventure park devoted to the ocean. Excellent live dolphin, killer whale, and sea lion shows reproduce the animal's natural behavior and give them a chance to show off their flips and turns. The 30m (32.5 yd) shark tunnel shows a variety of sharks, with their bristling jaws and streamlined bodies, and a huge stingray over 1.5m (1¾ yd) wide. **The Tropical Aquarium Gallery** has a vibrant display of seahorses, starfish, shrimp, and shoe crabs. The "touch" pool is particularly compelling to curious kids, who can caress skates and rays as they swim through the water.

Don't forget your swimwear. Adjacent to Marineland, **Aquasplash** is the Riviera's biggest waterslide park, with 13 giant toboggans; a "lazy river," where you can relax in a rubber ring; and a wave pool. **La Petite Ferme du Far West** will amuse kids under 13 with cowboy-themed pony rides, an Indian teepee

The Ferris wheel at Marineland, near Antibes.

Aquasplash near Antibes.

full of distorting mirrors, and a labyrinth of obstacle courses. Finally, the **Adventure Golf** section is a crazy Jurassic-themed golf course with giant dinosaurs—including a mean-looking tyrannosaurus. Combined tickets with Marineland are sold for all attractions. *RN 7, Antibes. ☎ 08-92-30-06-06. www.marineland.fr. Open Feb–Mar 10am–6pm daily; Apr–Jun & Sept 10am–7pm daily; Jul–Aug 10am–11pm daily. Admission from 36€ adults; from 28€ kids 3–12.*

From Antibes, join the D35 (toward Cannes) to the A8. Exit junction 38 and follow signs to Fréjus. Distance: 50km (31 miles).

➋ **Fréjus.** Fréjus is home to great beaches, a Roman Ampithéâtre (see p 93), and a 20-hectare (50-acre) safari-style ★★ **Parc Zoölogique,** zone du Capitou, off A8 (☎ 04-98-11-37-37; www.zoo-frejus.com; daily 10am–6pm June–Aug, until 5pm Mar–May, Sept; and until 4:30pm Nov–Feb; admission 14€, 9.50€ kids 3–9). More than 150 different species from five continents roam the park, including Asian elephants, wild cats, wolves, birds, and reptiles. The park runs a permanent breeding program to help maintain its many endangered animals, so

you might be lucky enough to see newborns, particularly lion or tiger cubs. On a hot day, take a good bottle of sunscreen to Fréjus's ★ **Aqualand,** Quartier le Capou, RN98 (☎ 04-94-51-82-51; www.aqualand.fr; admission 25€ adults, 19€ children 3–12; open daily June–Sept 10am–6pm). It's a veritable outdoor kingdom of fast-flowing water slides for the whole family. The park's most popular ride is the *Twister*—a triple whammy slide that twists and turns like a corkscrew. For smaller kids, the *Mini Parc Jungle* provides tame slides and a shallow pool. Your teenagers might want to hang out at *Surf Beach,* where they can lounge around a swimming pool.

From Fréjus, take the N7 to the A8 (toward Marseille). After 30km (19 miles), join the A57 and follow signs to Hyères. Distance: 91km (56 miles).

➌ ★★ **Île de Porquerolles.** Most kids will love the boat trip to this island jam-packed with beaches, forests, and cycle paths. Porquerolles is the largest and westernmost of the Îles d'Hyères (off the shores of Hyères)—a land of rocky capes, pine forests twisted by the mistral, sun-drenched vineyards, and pale ocher houses.

The south coast is rugged, but the north strand, facing the mainland, has sandy beaches bordered by heather, scented myrtles, and pine trees—excellent spots for a family picnic. The 8 by 2km (5 x 1¼ mile) island is best explored on bike. Several companies rent them, but we recommend **Le Cycle Porquerollais,** 1 rue de la Ferme (☎ 04-94-58-30-32; www.cycle-porquerollais.com; from 14€/day, 9€ children). Outside the village, cycle paths are often bumpy but well-marked and great fun for kids with a sense of adventure. The ancient **Fort Ste-Agathe,** built in 1531 by François I, will fire young imaginations. Boats to the island, run by **TLV-TVM** (☎ 04-94-58-95-14; from 17€; daily from 7:30am–6pm; times are subject to change), depart south of Hyères at the Tour Fondue on the peninsula of Gien.

From Hyères, take the A570 (toward Toulon). Join the A57 (toward Gonfaron). Exit junction 11 and follow signs to Gonfaron (along N97). Distance: 46km (29 miles).

Marineland near Antibes.

④ ★★ Village des Tortues-Gonfaron. At the foot of the Massif des Maures mountains, amid fields of lavender and oak, this sanctuary cares for 2,500-plus species of tortoise—particularly the Hermann tortoise, which is almost extinct in France. Here staffers nurse sick tortoises back to health before releasing them into the wild. Babies are on view in the hatching room and nursery, and a series of enclosures present the different species, from the most fierce and exotic, to water tortoises and terrapins. Staffers

A turtle from Village des Tortues-Gonfaron.

Food on the Farm

Graine & Ficelle is a wee farm, in the flower-strewn hills behind Vence, offering excellent vegetarian lunches on weekends. Small kids can feed the donkeys and fawn over the baby rabbits and hens, while you admire the vegetable patch and wait for Isabella Sallusti to prepare the delicious food. Guests eat on communal tables, and, in the spring, baby lambs run around your legs as you dine. Your budding little chefs can also take a cooking class. *670 Chemin des Collets, 06640 St-Jeannet.* ☎ *06-85-08-15-64. Daily, upon advance reservation by telephone or e-mail. graine.ficelle@wanadoo.fr. Lunch and farm visit 35€ adults; 19€ under 18. 2-hour farm visit 11€ adults; 8€ children. Cooking classes 25€. No credit cards.*

mostly are passionate volunteers who offer guided tours that showcase their protection programs. *Gonfaron.* ☎ *04-94-78-26-41. www.villagetortues.com. Daily 9am–7pm Mar–Nov (until 6pm Dec–Mar). Admission 8€ adults; 5€ children.*

From Gonfaron, take the D39 (rte. de Flassans) to Flassans-sur-Issole and follow signs for Parc des Cèdres. 9km (5½ miles).

⑤ ★★★ Aoubré—Flassans. Within this 30 hectare (74-acre) cedar forest, the whole family can pretend to be primates for the day and move from tree to tree between platforms hoisted high above the forest floor. Routes range in difficulty, but all are highly secure. The **Mowgli Path,** 1m (3 ft.) above ground level, has been specially created for 5- to 7-year olds. Older children and brave adults can try the 120m (394-foot) high death slide **(Tyrolienne des Cimes).** Suspended from a harness, you slide down to ground level along a rope. To calm everybody's nerves, the **Petite Ferme** (small farm) provides plenty of cooing opportunities with cute rabbits, guinea pigs, chickens, and dwarf goats. The **Parc**

Animalier (animal park) contains larger deer, wild boar, and donkeys; if your French is good, you can follow an educational tour: The **Jardin des Papillons** (butterfly garden) tour takes you into a .8-hectare (2-acre) park with over 1,500 species of flora that attract caterpillars and butterflies. *Parc des Cèdres, Flassans.* ☎ *04-94-86-10-92 or 06-12-58-02-26. www.aoubre.fr. By reservation only. Open Sat–Sun, public holidays, and school holidays 9am–8pm. Closed Nov–Feb. 19€ adult, 16€ ages 8–11, 11€ age 5–7. No credit cards.*

Leave Flassans on the N97 and follow signs to the A8 (via Le-Cannet-des-Maures). At the island, join the A57 (dir. Aix-en-Provence); then, after 1 mile, the A8. After 81km (50 miles), take the N296 (dir. Celony). At Celony, take D7N; then, at St-Cannat (dir. Salon), join the D572 to La Barben for 123km (76 miles).

⑥ ★★★ La Barben. On a plateau halfway between Marseille and Avignon, more than 600 animals (120 species) live together harmoniously under the watch of a medieval castle. Visitors will see wolves, giraffes, elephants, llamas, leopards, tigers, and baboons in habitat. A small farm provides petting opportunities for smaller kids, and a minitrain runs to and from the park entrance.

A fascinating reptile house is set within the humid warmth of a restored 12th-century sheepfold. The château's square turrets are visible from most areas in the zoo. Good King René built it just before the 11th century, and it is period furnished. *La Barben.* ☎ 04-90-55-19-12. www.zoolabarben.com. Daily 10am–6pm (until 5:30pm Dec–Jan; until 7pm July–Aug). Admission 14€ adults, 8€ children, free kids under 3. MC, V.

From La Barben, take the D22a to Pélissanne, and then head for Salon-de-Provence (via D572 and A54) to the A7. Follow signs to Avignon. Distance: 65km (40 miles).

⑦ ★ Avignon. Avignon makes for a jam-packed family day. The Pont d'Avignon, stretching only halfway across the river, is particularly fun for kids who might know the famous children's song "Sur le Pont d'Avignon." The streets themselves present an atmospheric and eclectic array of 15th- to 18th-century mansions, characterized by big doors with ornate doorknockers.

From Avignon, take the N570 (dir. Arles) and pick up the D570N at Rognognas bridge. Still following Arles, take the N113 and follow signs for Stes-Maries-de-la-Mer.

⑧ ★★ Parc Naturel Régional de Camargue. The Camargue, where French cowboys ride the range, is an alluvial plain inhabited by wild horses, fighting black bulls roaming gypsies, pink flamingos, lagoons, salt marshes, and

An elephant and giraffe from the zoo in La Barben.

wetlands. The area is known for its colonies of pink flamingos *(flamants roses)* and some 400 other bird species. Bring a pair of binoculars and head for the area around **Ginès,** a hamlet on N570, 5km (3 miles) north of Camargue's capital, Stes-Maries-de-la-Mer. A memorable way to explore is on the back of a Camarguais horse, which will take you to otherwise inaccessible places. Numerous stables dot the road from Arles to Stes-Maries de la Mer. They all charge around 85€ to 95€ a day and cater to beginners. Helmets are not traditionally worn in the Camargue; if you're worried, ask for a helmet beforehand. The visitors' center *(Maison du Parc)*, with parking and picnic areas, is 4km (2½ miles) south of Stes-Maries de la Mer, at Pont de Gau. *RD 570, Pont de Gau.* ☎ 04-90-97-86-32. www.parc-camargue.fr. Open Apr–Sept daily (except May 1) 10am–6pm; Oct–Mar Sat–Thurs (closed Dec 25, Jan 1) 9:30am–5pm. Admission free.

Best **Gardens & Fragrant Sites**

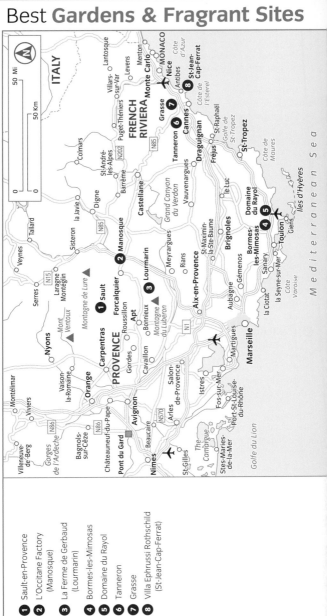

1. Sault-en-Provence
2. L'Occitane Factory (Manosque)
3. La Ferme de Gerbaud (Lourmarin)
4. Bormes-les-Mimosas
5. Domaine du Rayol
6. Tanneron
7. Grasse
8. Villa Ephrussi Rothschild (St-Jean-Cap-Ferrat)

Intense sunshine has penetrated the Provençal landscape for millennia, creating perfect growing conditions for all sorts of aromatic herbs, flowers, fruits, and exotic plants. A 400-year-old perfume industry thrives in Grasse, owing to Queen Catherine de Medici's penchant for perfume-scented leather gloves. As the region's popularity burgeoned among 19th-century aristocrats, so did their desire to create elaborate gardens in which to impress fellow socialites. These floral legacies still stimulate the senses and enrich every visitor's stay today. START: **Eygalières**. Trip length: 466 km (289 miles).

Travel Tip

For hotels and restaurants, see chapter 6.

1 Sault-en-Provence. When the lavender blooms in July and August, this hillside town, with its pale buildings and peach roof tiles, looks like an island protruding from a purple sea Sault's tourist office (see below) has a detailed list of lavender paths you can follow. Lavender lovers should spend time at ★★ **La Ferme-aux-Lavandes** (rte. du Mont Ventous; ☎ 06-82-93-52-09; by appointment only), a working lavender farm that will take you on an aromatic journey into the heart of lavender culture. *Sault en Provence tourist office, avenue Promenade.* ☎ 04-90-64-01-21 www.saultenprovence.com.

Exit Sault on the winding D954 and, at Fourcalquier, take the

Provence's hallmark lavender.

N100 to Mane. Then take the D13 for 10km (6 miles) to the D4096 (via Voix) to Manosque. Distance: 73km (45 miles).

2 Manosque—L'Occitane Factory: L'Occitane is a cosmetics company that uses Provence's fragrant herbs, flowers, and fruits to make its products. In the ★ **L'Occitane factory,** 21 St-Maurice, 04100, Manosque (☎ 04-92-70-19-50; www.loccitane.com), visitors can take a sweet-scented trip through oil extraction, candle-making, soap manufacturing, and more.

In nearby Mane (23km/14 miles via D13), you'll find L'Occitane's only French hotel and spa, the luxurious ★★ **Le Couvent des Minimes,** Chemin des Jeux de Mai, 04300, Mane (☎ 04-92-74-77-77; www. couventdesminimes-hotelspa.com; doubles from 170€; 3-course meal from 50€), set inside a medieval

Products from the L'Occitane factory in Manosque.

convent. The hotel is home to Cloître, a gourmet restaurant, and a spa that uses L'Occitane products. Heaven! *Manosque Tourist Office. 16 rue du Docteur Joubert.* ☎ *04-92-72-16-00. www.manosque-tourisme.com.*

From Manosque, follow the D4096, then D907 to the A51 (dir. Aix/Marseille). Exit at Junction 15, and follow signs to Pertuis (along D556 and D596). Exit Pertuis on D973 and, 13km (8 miles) later, cross Cadenet and take the D139. After Puyvert, join the D27 to Lourmarin. Distance: 61km (38 miles).

❸ ★★ **La Ferme de Gerbaud (Lourmarin).** Join farm owner Paula Marty in Lourmarin for a guided tour through her remote fields. She'll teach you how to recognize the *herbes de Provence* in their natural habitat. Paula also sells her own products (oils, dried herbs, honey, lavender, and herb-flavored cookies) in the farm shop (daily 2–7pm). *Lourmarin.* ☎ *04-90-68-11-83. www.plantes-aromatiques-provence.com. Guided visits Apr–Oct Tues, Thurs, Sat 5pm; Nov–Mar Sun 3pm. Admission 5€ adults, children free.*

From Lourmarin, take the D139 and head for the N7 and N296 toward Aix-Encagnane, to the A8 (toward Fréjus). After 12km (7½ miles), join the A52 to Toulon. From Toulon, take A57 to Hyères, then the N98 to Bormes. Distance: 156km (97 miles).

❹ **Bormes-les-Mimosas.** Its name gives it all away: Bormes-les-Mimosas is a center for the fluffy,

A stroll through the blooming streets of Bormes-les-Mimosas.

sweet-scented yellow balls of the mimosa flower (in bloom Jan–Mar). This gorgeous, 12th-century village tumbles delicately down the steep hillside. Each February, the village bursts alive with the *Corso fleuri*—a parade of innovative mimosa sculptures on floats. Fans should also head to France's leading mimosa cultivator *(pépinerie)*, ★ **Gérard Cavatore,** avenue André Del Monte (☎ 04-94-00-40-23; www.pepinierescavatore.fr), where over 400 varieties are for sale. *Also see p 92. Bormes-les-Mimosas tourist office, 1 pl. Gambetta.* ☎ *04-94-01-38-38. www.bormeslesmimosas.com.*

From Bormes, take the D559 (via Pramousquier) to Rayol. Distance: 12km (7½ miles).

⑤ ★★★ **Domaine du Rayol.** This vast protected domain is one of the most magnificent sites on the coast. Ten gardens re-create plant life from Mediterranean-type climates across the world: agaves from Central America, eucalyptus trees from Australia, proteas from South Africa, and bamboo from China. Wild dolphins spend most of the spring in the bay below the gardens. Equipped with snorkel gear, you can observe the aquatic plant life at the bottom of the domain with a guide (18€). *Avenue des Belges, Rayol-Canadel-sur-Mer.* ☎ *04-98-04-44-00. www.domaine durayol.org. Admission 9€; 6€ reduced. Daily 9:30am–sundown or 7:30pm, depending on the season.*

From Rayol, take the D27 and join the N98 to Ste-Maxime, where you join the D1098 for 21km (13 miles) (dir. Fréjus. then A8). Join the A8 as soon as possible and exit at junction 39 to the D37 After 4km (2½ miles), turn right onto D38 into Tanneron. Distance: 85km (52 miles).

Domaine du Rayol on the Côte d'Azur.

⑥ **Tanneron.** Between January and March, the hilltop village of Tanneron blooms with bright yellow mimosa flowers. During the mimosa season, visit ★★ **La Forcerie Vial,** Les Carreiros, Tanneron (☎ 04-93-60-66-32; www.vial-tanneron.com; open daily Dec–Mar 9am–noon and 2–6pm), an old-fashioned farm where you can buy mimosa flowers. Don't leave Tanneron without dining on Mediterranean fusion cuisine at ★ **La Champfagou,** 53 Chemin de la colle d'Embarque, Tanneron (☎ 04-93-60-68-30; www.lechampfagou.fr), which also doubles as an excellent hotel with rooms from 55€, including dinner. *Tanneron Tourist Office, place de la Mairie, 83440, Tanneron.* ☎ *04-93-60-71-73. www.tanneron.fr.*

Leave Tanneron on the D38; after 7km (4 miles), at Auribeau-sur-Siagne, join the D509. At the island, take the third exit and join the D9; follow signs for Grasse-Centre. Distance: 16km (10 miles).

⑦ **Grasse.** The capital of the perfume industry since the Renaissance, Grasse produces three-quarters of the world's essences. The most fragrant town on the Riviera is redolent with jasmine, roses, violets, wild lavender, and other blooms.

The Grasse Perfume Museum.

As you gape in sticker shock at the price of perfume sold here, remember this: It takes 10,000 flowers to produce 1kg (2⅕ pounds) of jasmine petals and nearly a ton of petals to distill 1 liter (¼ gallons) of essence. To learn about scents and the history of the perfume industry, visit the ★ **Musée International de la Parfumerie,** 2 bd. du Jeu de Ballon, Grasse (☎ 04-97-05-58-16; www.museesdegrasse.com; 3€ adults, children 18 and under free; Dec–June and Sept–Oct open daily 11am–6pm, July–Aug daily 11am–7pm). If you want to create your own perfume, visit ★ **Fragonard Parfumeur,** 20 bd. Fragonard (☎ 04-93-36-44-65; www.fragonard. com; free admission; open Feb–Oct daily 9am–6:30pm, Nov–Jan daily 9am–12:30pm and 2–6:30pm). *Also see chapter 5, p 100.*

From Grasse, go back to the A8 in the direction of Cannes. Once on the A8, head for Nice, then Promenade des Anglais and Cap. Leave Nice towards Ville-franche-sur-Mer, and take D25 to St-Jean-Cap-Ferrart. Distance: 50km (31 miles).

8 ★★★ **Villa Ephrussi Roth-schild—St-Jean-Cap-Ferrat.** Known as the Riviera's most perfect villa, this nest of opulence has themed gardens designed to resemble the prow of a ship, suited to the fine sea views over Villefranche-sur-Mer and Beaulieu. Fountains, gargoyles, columns, and statues adorn the stone garden; a waterfall splashes over into a rockery next to a replica of Versailles's Temple of Love; and the French, Japanese, and tropical gardens complement each other beautifully. Inside the house, art treasures litter every room, including an unrivaled collection of drawings by namesake Jean-Honoré Fragonard. *Avenue Denis-Séméria.* ☎ *04-93-01-33-09. www.villa-ephrussi.com. Admission 10€; 7.50€ reduced. Mid-Feb to mid-Oct daily 10am–6pm; July–Aug daily 10am–7pm; Nov–Jan Mon–Fri 2–6pm, Sat–Sun 10am–6pm.*

Blooming Calendar

Provence is stunning year-round, but it can take your breath away when flowers are in bloom and fruit is on the tree. Look for **mimosas** and **lemons** in January and February, **roses** in June, **lavender** and **jasmine** in July and August, and **grape vines** heavy with fruit ripe for harvest in September. ●

The Great Outdoors

Best **Beaches**

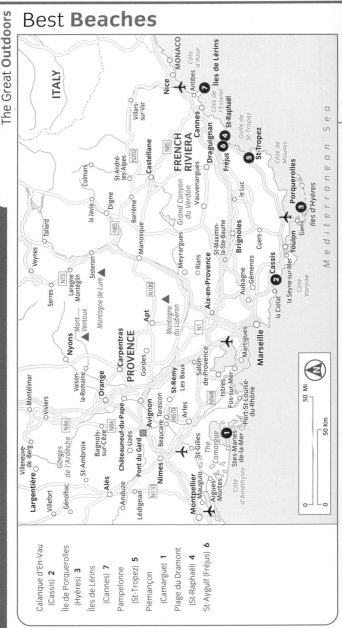

Previous page: A wild horse in the marshy Camargue region.

Contrary to the French Riviera's film and tabloid image, it's not just about bronzing stick figures and celebrities hiding behind Chanel shades. The coastline from the Camargue to Nice is lengthy and varied enough to satisfy a range of beachcombers—whether you seek solace and tranquillity in a secluded cove, wild nature, family activities, or a hotspot in which to see and be seen. The region has fabulous shorelines not mentioned here; this list was designed to accommodate a host of needs, tastes, and interests.

Tip

In busy resort areas, restrooms and watering holes usually line the shores. Remote beaches, however, are often without any public facilities, including restrooms and fresh water. Before setting out, be sure to pack food, water, and plenty of sunscreen, and prepare to water the seaweed when nature calls.

Calanque d'En-Vau (Cassis). The Calanques form some of the prettiest and most spectacular beaches in the South of France. Though the name stems from the Provençale word *cala,* meaning steep slope, calanques are actually creeks carved from the chalk cliffs, for 20km (12 miles) between Cassis and Marseille, by now-dry rivers and centuries of weathering. Flora and fauna flourish here: You'll find a semi-arid environment of viburnum, rosemary, heather, sea lavender, oak, and Allepo pine, plus Europe's largest

A plunge from the cliffs of the Calanques.

The Calanque d'En-Vau.

lizard, the Ocellar (up to 60cm/24 in. long), and Europe's largest snake, the Montpellier Grass Snake (up to 2m/7 ft.). **Le Calanque d'En-Vau** is by far the most picturesque, encircled by tall, spiky rocks called *doigts de Dieu* (fingers of God). The small beach is pebbly, but the sea is a beautiful shade of emerald green, and the overall effect is enchanting. You can access the beach on foot or by boat from the port in Cassis. The **Bateliers Cassisains** (☎ 04-42-01-90-83; www.cassis-calanques.com; no credit cards) run a variety of excursions to 3, 5, or 8 *calanques*. Tickets are sold on the boat (from 13€); reservations aren't required. Walking takes 2 hours from Cassis. You can hire a guide via the Cassis Tourist Office (see p 194), or obtain a map. If you go it alone from Cassis, walk past Port Miou and Port-Pin calanques. Make sure you have decent footwear and water. The route can be steep

The sands of St-Tropez.

and uneven, with little shade on sunny days. Be warned, access to the Calanques is limited and often prohibited between July and August, to protect the fragile ecosystem from sun-seekers who come here in droves.

Île de Porquerolles (Hyères). A short boat crossing from the Hyères Peninsula leads you to an island of pine trees, vineyards, walking and cycling trails, plus several small, sandy beaches—the landscape that reportedly inspired Robert Louis Stevenson to write *Treasure Island*. Hire a bicycle and choose a route to either the silvery sands of the Plage d'Argent; Plage de la Courtade, ideally situated by the Ste-Agathe Fort; or the beautiful Plage Notre Dame—the island's biggest beach, bordered by pines and furnished with a seasonal restaurant. Maps are available at the information center in the village. To hire a bike, try **Le Cycle Porquerollais** (1 rue de al Ferme; ☎ 04-94-58-30-32; www.cycle-porquerollais.com; 14€ day, 11€ children). **TLV-TVM** runs boats to the island (☎ 04-94-58-21-81; from 17€; daily from 7:30am–6pm; times are subject to change). Embark south of Hyères, at the Tour Fondue on the peninsula of Gien, at the bottom of the D97.

Îles de Lérins (Ste-Marguerite & St-Honorat beaches). Away from the glitter and the glitterati of Cannes, two offshore islands called the Îles de Lérins offer sanctuary to those wishing to escape the Riviera's glamor queens and kings. **Île St-Honorat** is the smallest of the two, dominated by a fortified Cistercian monastery, still occupied by monks today. Its remote creeks and beaches are peaceful and inviting, but tourists are expected to dress appropriately while swimming and sunbathing (no nipples or privates). If hours of sunbathing aren't for you, head for **Île Ste-Marguerite,** where you can break up the beach time with nature hikes. Throughout the island, trails run through pine and eucalyptus woods and lead to several small beaches, many of which look out onto Cannes. Certain spots can only be reached by scaling steep cliffs, however, so wear suitable footwear. An old fortress, built by Richelieu and reinforced by Vauban in the early 18th century, contains a marine museum. Pack food and drink, if you're visiting either island. Ste-Marguerite has several cafes and restaurants near the port, but little elsewhere, and St-Honorat has practically nothing in the line of refreshments. **Trans Côte d'Azur** boats run to both islands from Quai Maubeuf (04-92-98-71-30; www. trans-cote-azur.com; tickets 12€ adults; 6€ children 5–10; MC, V; first departure from Cannes 9am; last return boat to Cannes 6pm, subject to change and weather).

Pampelonne Beach (St-Tropez).

St-Tropez's public image was forged and burnished on this 9km (5.5 miles) stretch of white sand. A galaxy of stars have bronzed their busts and butts to perfection on this beach, and the mega-wealthy and famous continue reserving places in the exclusive beach clubs. Certain stretches are reserved for nudists. Gays and families also have their own designated areas. The most exclusive beach clubs are **Le Club 55** (04-94-55-55-55; www.leclub55. com), and **Nikki Beach** (04-94-79-82-04; www.nikkibeach.com). To get there, head eastwards from St-Raphaël along the N98.

Piémançon Beach (Camargue).

This flat, golden stretch of sand, bordered by lonely salt lagoons and magnificent bird reserves, draws mostly *Camargian* residents and Riviera refugees looking for a peaceful moment away from the crowds. Although the sand can get more populated in warmer months, the beach's relative seclusion keeps the hoards at bay. The Camargue's reputation for virulent mosquitoes is also daunting (see p 107). If you plan to bring children here, be warned that part of this beach has designated areas for nudists perfecting their full-body tans. To get there, head for Salins de Giraud (D36), and then look out for a sign marked "La Mer." The beach is 1km (⅗ mile) from the road.

Plage du Dramont (St-Raphaël).

It was on this sand, on the 15th of August 1944, that the 36th Division of the U.S. Army landed at the end of World War II.

Nowadays, the beach is attractive and less commercial than St-Raphaël's other shorelines, and you can watch the French Navy float by on a variety of military boats (there are military bases nearby). When you've made one sandcastle too many, stretch your legs and follow the signposted, 1-hour walk up to the **Sémaphore du Dramont,** which provides excellent views along the coastline. A second path leads to the **Port of Agay,** a family resort with plenty of watersports and another sandy beach. The nearby **Pointe du Dramont** provides the best view of the tiny, private Île d'Or (Golden Island), where a 19th-century mock medieval tower stands proudly.

St-Aygulf Beach (Fréjus).

Just outside of Fréjus, St Aygulf beach is encircled by rocks inside a nature preserve—a world apart from the commercialized, often tacky beaches on this shoreline. A haven for more than 217 species of birds, it protects both fresh and sea water lagoons called Les Etangs de Villepey. The most exciting time to visit is spring, when pink flamingoes and gray herons fly overhead as you soak up the sun. The beach affords a lovely view over the Fréjus Bay.

St-Honorat Island.

Hiking the **Vaucluse & the Lubéron**

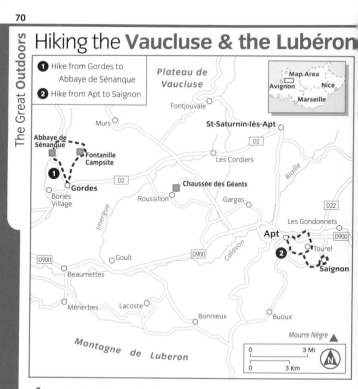

1 Hike from Gordes to Abbaye de Sénanque

2 Hike from Apt to Saignon

If you're looking to freshen up your town tours with a dose of country air, consider this hiking route. This two-day hiking trip will take you from postcard-perfect Gordes to the market town of Apt, with an overnight stay in Gordes. You will need a car to travel between Gordes and Apt, and then you can proceed on these hikes on foot. For more walking tours in the Vaucluse, contact Cèdres (3 Grand'rue, La Bastidonne; ☎ 04-90-07-54-02; www.cedres-luberon.com), which specializes in Luberon nature hikes and offers English-speaking guides. If you wish to hoof it farther afield, you can contact local tourist offices or the **Fédération Française de la Randonée Pédestre** (64 rue du Dessous des Berges, Paris; ☎ 01-44-89-93-90; www.ffrandonnee.fr), which covers France's main GR routes (long-distance trails). START: Gordes. Trip length: 17 km (11 miles). Time: 2 days; each day's hike is about 3 hours (excluding picnic time).

Travel Tip

For more information, see "Vaucluse & the Lubéron," in chapter 5, p 84. Also contact the Gordes tourist office at ☎ 04-90-72-02-75 or www.gordes-village.com, or the Apt tourist office at ☎ 04-90-74-03-18 or www.ot-apt.fr.

❶ Hike from Gordes to Abbaye de Sénanque.

Gordes is one of France's spectacular *villages perchés*—medieval towns that look as though they're growing from the hilltops where they were built to stave off invaders (for more information, see p 88).

On day 1, park your car early, pack a picnic, and start your hike in the **Place du Château** in Gordes. Take the second road to the right of the **Le Provençal** cafe (not the D15 to Murs), which leads past **La Poste** (post office) on your right.

Bear right at the Y-junction, with the cemetery on your left. Continue straight until you turn left down a road lined with dry-stone walls—this leads to the D15. Go straight, then turn left uphill at the signpost marked FONTA-NILLE. (By this point, you should have walked around 30 minutes.) Bear left by the Fontanille campsite, and look for some mailboxes; then turn right. When you reach another fork, take the rocky path to the right. It eventually skirts left, but continue straight along a narrow path, with the fields to your right. When you reach a T-junction with a huge pine tree, turn right. (You should have been walking for about an hour.) After 150m (492 ft.), turn left down a wide, uneven

path. Cross the valley, keeping a farm entrance to your right. At the next fork, stay left along a stony path. Near the Sénanque hamlet you'll reach a crossroads. Turn right and head downhill into a wood. At the next crossroads, head straight along the vehicle-friendly road, which comes out on the D177. Cross the road to climb the GR6/97, a path (30m/33 yds. downhill on the left) that leads to a crossroads with red and white marks. This path turns left downhill toward the Abbey.

Founded by Cistercian monks in the 12th century, the **Abbaye de Sénanque** saw much death and destruction before becoming the tranquil retreat it is today. **Note:** The abbey is closed for lunch from noon to 2:30pm, so you may want to find a picnic spot nearby. See p 88.

On the D177, look out for traffic and bear right to follow the sign to COTE DE SÉNANQUE. Just after, turn right and descend a pebbly track with a view onto Gordes. Back on the D177, fork left down a street after 200m (656 ft.). Once you're back in Gordes, turn left back into the center where you'll spend the night. The **Hôtel Les Bories** (☎ 04-90-72-00-51; www.hotellesbories.com) is Gordes's best accommodations, a

Hikers with a plum view of Gordes.

A Detour to Bories Village

Located 3km (2 miles) southwest of Gordes, the **Village des Bories** is home to mysterious structures called *bories,* which are composed of thin layers of stone that spiral upward into a dome. Their origin and use is a mystery—some sources claim they're Neolithic. What is known is that they were inhabited until the early 1800s. Their form suggests they were developed by shepherds and goat herders as shelter for themselves and their flocks. To get here, take D15, veering right beyond a fork at D2. A sign marks another right turn toward the village, where you must park and walk 45 minutes to visit the site. The village is open daily from 9am to 7:30pm. Admission is 5.50€ for adults and 3€ for children. For more information, call ☎ 04-90-72-03-48.

modern hotel clad in rough stone and built around the core of an old Provençal mas. After your long hike, dine at **Les Cuisine du Château** (☎ 04-90-72-01-31), a charming restaurant in Gordes's *épicerie* (food market), originally built in the 1850s.

Early the next morning, drive from Gordes to Apt. By car, head north on D102 toward rue André Lhote. Turn left at D2, and follow the road for 6km (4 miles). Turn right at D4, and follow the road for 6km (4 miles), then turn left at D210. At the traffic circle, take the third exit to D900, and follow that road into the town of Apt.

❷ Hike from Apt to Saignon. Apt's history goes back to Roman times when it was a prosperous ancient city. Remnants of its days as a Christian bishopric are also visible in its gorgeous 11th-century Saint-Anne Cathedral. Today the town is loved for its crystallized fruits, jams, lavender essence, and truffles, and a colorful market that teems with Provencal produce on Saturday mornings.

When you arrive in Apt, park your car in the cours Lauze-de-Perret car park in the east of town, and then set out on your hike.

On foot, take the avenue de Saignon onto the D48. Continue walking along the D48, until you see the Auriane track on the left, where you will turn left and cross the bridge over the Rimayon River. As the road sweeps left, go straight ahead along the path that climbs the hill, then bear left and follow a tarmac path for 50m (164 ft.) until you get to the Ginestière crossroads. Here, bear right and walk for 30m (100 ft.), and then go up the track on the left, which turns into a cobbled road leading to the bottom of Saignon. Bear right and follow the D174 to get to the village entrance, which leads to the pretty place de la Fontaine.

Saignon is little known by tourists, yet it has 3 château ruins and a wonderful lookout point. To get there, turn left on **rue du Bourget** and walk for 100m (330 ft.) until you reach a cobbled path, on your left, that leads to a square by a parking lot. At the bottom of the car park, you'll find a path winding around the village's ramparts. After the last house, huff and puff your way up the steps to the main castle ruins and marvel at the vistas from the lookout point. Then go back

Outdoors in Luberon National Park

Apt lies at the gateway to the vast Luberon National Park. The area covers 1,200 sq. km (463 sq. miles) encompassing several villages and many desolate forests. The information office for the park is in an 18th-century house, La Maison du Parc, 1 pl. Jean-Jaurès (☎ 04-90-04-42-00). The office provides maps, details of hiking trails in the park, and other outdoor activities in the area. Otherwise, the tourist office in Apt (see p 194) will provide information as well as useful maps. Much of the land in the Luberon area is privately owned, but trails in the park are open to the public. Admission is free, and it's open May to October Monday to Saturday from 8:30am to noon, and the rest of the year Monday to Friday from 1:30 to 6pm. No buses or taxis serve the area. To reach the park from Apt, take D48 southeast to the village of Saignon.

down around the ramparts, before turning left to join the D174.

From place de la Fontaine, backtrack to the Ginistère crossroads, and turn right. After the bend, keeping Tourel (a settlement) on your left, take the shortcut at the next bend and continue straight for 200m (650 ft.). At the next bend, turn left along a dirt track and head straight through an oak forest and then a residential area. Continue

straight, and then cross the old N100, using the steps to join the cycle path. Keep going over the Cavalon River, and then head up a ramp on the right to follow the D22 back to Apt, where refreshments await. Finish your hike with a hearty French meal at **Auberge du Luberon** (☎ 04-90-74-12-30; http://francemarket.com/auberge-luberon), located in a century-old building in the city's historic center.

The town of Apt.

Cycling Between **Mont Ventoux & Dentelles de Montmirail**

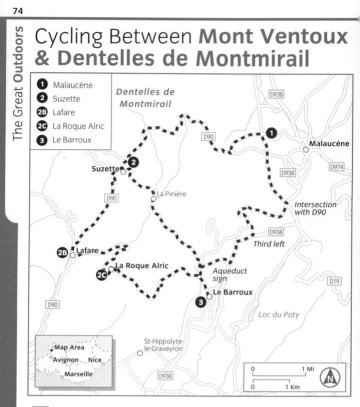

1 Malaucène
2 Suzette
2B Lafare
2C La Roque Alric
3 Le Barroux

Dentelles de Montmirail

D938

D90

1 **Malaucène**

D974

Suzette
2

D938

La Pinière

Intersection with D90

D90

D938
Third left

2B **Lafare**

La Roque Alric
2C

Aqueduct sign

D19

D90

Le Barroux
3

Lac du Paty

Map Area
Avignon Nice
Marseille

St-Hippolyte-le-Graveyron

D938

0 ——— 1 Mi
0 ——— 1 Km

This cycling trip is for those unafraid of a challenge. The terrain is steep, but the unrivaled views make it one of the most rewarding tours around. There are several viewpoints of the **Dentelles de Montmirail** between **Malaucène** and **Suzette**; look behind you as you ride. Once you get to Suzette, you will have to decide whether to return to Malaucène via the pretty perched hamlet of **Le Barroux**, or take a detour through the villages of **Lafare** and **La Roque Alric** in the Dentelles Massif, where the views are breathtaking. START: Malaucène. Trip length: 22 km (14 miles). Time: 3–4 hours (excluding picnic time).

Travel Tip

For more information, contact the **Malaucène tourist office** at ☎ 04-90-65-22-59 or http://village malaucene.free.fr.

1 **Malaucène.** The gateway to Mont Ventoux is a pleasant town with a 14th-century fortified church that was once part of the ramparts. The small streets are filled with fountains and wash houses. The path to the left of the church leads to a viewpoint over the Drôme mountains and Mont

Detour from Suzette

At the viewpoint table in Suzette, follow signs for "Le Village." Continue on the main road to the D90a, which leads to the market village of **2B Lafare,** laced with steep, charming lanes. Turn left out of the village to **2C La Roque Alric.** Perched on its rocky outcrop, right in the heart of Les Dentelles, it's a world apart from urban noise and haste. Cross the village and head to **Le Barroux** via the D90a, from where you continue your tour back to Malaucène.

Ventoux. Start your tour in front of the tourist office, on **Place du Mairie.**

Head in the direction of Vaison-La-Romaine. At the small island on the edge of Malaucène, turn left toward Suzette. Follow this road until you get to Suzette, where you will have a choice of routes.

2 Suzette. This tiny village, located 410m (459 ft.) above sea-level amid rolling hills, exudes charm. Its church is a Romanesque gem, and it has a huge, ceramic viewpoint table, indicating directions for both nearby settlements and faraway cities such as Geneva and Milan. Spend time wandering the pleasant streets. See the box **"Detour**

The jagged peaks of Les Dentelles.

A bakery in Malaucène.

A vineyard in Suzette.

from Suzette," if you wish to lengthen your ride (p 75).

Travel Tip

Don't embark on this tour—or any of the outdoor tours in this chapter—without sufficient water, food, sun protection, and suitable clothing and footwear. In the summer, weather can get very hot, so don't push yourself too hard. For this tour, and other cycling tours, we recommend a 21-speed mountain bike.

Take the C2 downhill to your left toward the perched village of Le Barroux.

❸ **Le Barroux.** Come off season and you could easily be in a ghost town. Le Barroux is an exquisite village, with sloping streets, that is dominated by its 12th-century château. The whole village was burned down in WWII, before being restored to what you see today.

Return to Route de Suzette and turn right toward Monastère (a monastery). Continue along the

Organized Bike Tours

For cycling tours around France, contact the **Fédération Fran-çaise de Cyclotourisme** (12 rue Louis-Bernard, Ivry-sur-Seine; ☎ 01-56-20-88-88; www.ffct.org). The official tour operator for the Tour de France, **Cyclomundo** (La Chatelaine; 18 rue Rene Cassin, 74240 Gaillard; ☎ 04-50-87-21-09; www.cyclomundo.com) offers guided and self-guided tours for cyclists of all levels, from novices to seasoned riders. **Come to France** (17 Rue des Martyrs, Paris; ☎ 01-48-74-05-10; www.cometofrance.com) organizes 3- or 4-day bike tours along the Luberon's verdant wine routes.

Pony Trails

Some of the best places to go horseback riding are in the Luberon and Bouches-du Rhône. Try **Provence à Cheval** (☎ 04-42-04-66-76; http://perso.orange.fr/provence.cheval), which offers 2-day excursions with overnight accommodations in such villages as **Saignon** (see p 72), or **La Sariette** (Route du mas des Mauniers 13810 Eygalières; ☎ 04-90-95-94-50; www.lasarriette.com) near St-Rémy. If you dream of riding a white horse from the Camargue, call **La Bergerie de Maguelonne** (rte. d'Arles, 13460, Les Saintes-Maries-de-la-Mer; ☎ 06-26-39-54-00; www.camargue-a-cheval. com). Many schools don't require you to wear a helmet. If you want one, ask when you book. The **Fédération Française d'Équitation** (9 bis bd. MacDonald, 75019 Paris; ☎ 01-53-26-15-50; www.ffe. com) also has useful addresses for riding vacations.

The Camargue's wild horses.

main road, and follow signs for AQUEDUC (aqueduct). Take the third left (1.5km/1 mile after the intersection); at the yellow signpost indicating a hiking trail, choose the right-hand dirt track leading back to Malaucène. Go past the aqueduct, and come to a tarmac surface. Continue on past the monastery and onward to the intersection with the D90. Take the path on the left of the bend, and go straight on to the D90. Turn right at the stop sign and cycle back into Malaucène.

Cycling Around
Vaison-la-Romaine

If you're looking for Roman heritage, medieval villages, and vineyards with views onto the Dentelles de Montmirail, this loop will suit you. **START: Vaison-la-Romaine. Trip length: 42 km (26 miles). Time: 3–4 hours (excluding picnic time).**

Travel Tip

For more information on Vaison-la-Romaine, see "Best Historic Architecture," in chapter 3, p 47; or contact the **Vaison-la-Romaine tourist office** at ☎ 04-90-36-02-11 or www.vaison-la-romaine.com.

❶ Vaison-la-Romaine. The ruins of the old Roman town make for a wonderful visit, before you climb up the medieval part of town that dominates the hillside. Park opposite the

Office de Tourisme in Vaison-la-Romaine (av. Chanoine), and begin your tour in front of the Jardin des 9 Damoiselles. For more information, see p 47.

Take the D975 to St-Quentin's chapel (before the cooperative wine cellar), then join the Route de Villedieu on the left. After 700m (766 yds), turn left down a little road just before Palis (toward Baud). Turn left at the intersection, then right. At the next junction, turn left, then go

A fountain in Vaison-la-Romaine.

straight at the crossroads. *Note:* Use caution; the road is very busy. Turn right at Roaix's Island and enter the village.

2 Roaix is a tiny place, dominated by its château, which is privately owned. It is renowned for its Côte du Rhônes wines.

Cross the village and head straight toward Rasteau. Turn right at the island in front of Rasteau's wine cellar. Turn right at the bend to get to the village square.

3 Rasteau is another small wine village, producing Côte du Rhônes and a dessert wine, aptly named Rasteau. Its wine museum, **Musée du Vigneron** (☎ 04-90-46-11-75), contains a collection of vintage Châteauneuf-du-Pape.

After visiting the village, turn right at the stop sign to return to the D69. Turn right down the path behind the signpost. Turn right at the fork in the road and right at the intersection, on an uphill path that leads to a dirt track. Go straight ahead at the junction of three roads (veer to the right, then left); then cycle straight ahead along the hillside. At the crossroads, go straight ahead. At the next crossroads, turn left and cycle down toward the center of Cairanne.

4 Cairanne is another pretty wine village located on the Côtes du Rhône wine route. Wander through the old village, which has many buildings that date from the 18th century.

Turn left at the stop sign, go straight at the island, and then make the first right toward Travaillan. At the next intersection, turn left under an alley of plane trees. Continue to the intersection with the D975. Go straight ahead (Memorial Plan de Dieu). Cross the D24 and head straight to

5 Violès. This peaceful vine-encircled village is home to a few historic churches. Stroll along the picturesque banks of the Ouvèze River.

Upon leaving the village, take the small road on the left. Cross the D8 and take the Chemin St-André, leading to the wine estate Domaine St André. Cross the estate, and then go straight. At the intersection near the tennis courts, go straight. At the next intersection, turn right up a road leading to the village of Sablet, before you head downhill to the D7. Turn left, then, at the island, turn right toward Séguret.

6 Séguret. From this picturesque town on a steep hill with a ruined castle, you can marvel at the Dentelles from a scenic overlook. Walk through the steep streets lined with old houses.

From Séguret, follow signs for Vaison-la-Romaine. Go straight ahead (toward Roaix) and, after 600m (656 yds.), turn right onto the Chemin de Bel Air. Cross the bridge over the Ouvèze River, head past the industrial estate, then, at the next island, go straight toward the Jardin des 9 Damoiselles, where you began.

Best Golfing

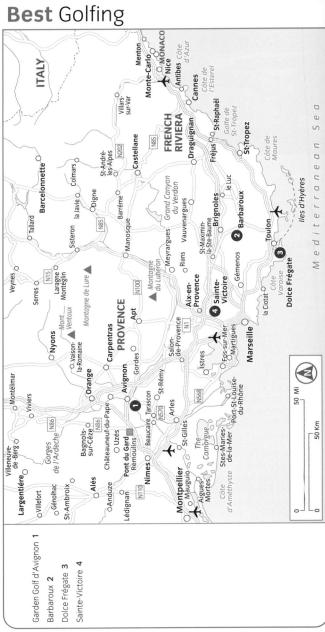

Whether you're looking for a sea view, a backdrop of mountains, or an ultrachic clubhouse, you'll find a course nonpareil on which to plant a tee and improve your handicap. An excellent destination for golfers, Provence has many courses for all budgets and all levels of play. If you want to play multiple courses, buy the **Golf Pass Provence,** which allows you to play 16 golf courses. The packages, which vary from 135€ to 275€ for 3- or 5-greens passes, are reserved for golfers visiting from outside of France and can be used in all clubs mentioned in this chapter. For more information, visit www.golfpass-provence.com.

Garden Golf d'Avignon. French golf star Géry Watine and golf-course architect Thierry Sprecher devised this challenging and technical course, characterized by gentle curves, 30 bunkers, small greens (the 6th, 14th, and 15th holes are perched on an embankment), and lots of water—in ditches, ponds, reservoirs, and a series of interconnected lakes. No less than 12 holes lie on the water's edge, but you'll only actually have to hit the ball over a lake at hole 3. (Watch out for the ducks and Florida turtles!) If you want to practice your swing, there are 24 berths in the driving range. There are also several putting greens and a clubhouse that serves hearty Provencal fare at lunchtime. *Garden Golf 'Avignon is 10 minutes from Avignon's centre-ville. Take the N100 from Avignon, then at Le Pontet, join the N107. At the island take the third exit and join the D910 to Morières-lès-Avignon. 1596 rte. de Châteaublanc, 84310, Morières les Avignon.* ☎ *04-90-33-39-08. www. gardengolfavignon.com. 9 and 18 holes.*

Barbaroux. This prestigious course near Brignoles is one of Europe's top-50 golf clubs. Eighteen holes unfold over 87 hectares (215 acres) of pine-covered hills, encompassing the biggest green in Europe (69m/75 yds. long). In one area, you have to drive your balls over a working vineyard to reach the fairway. Three of six lakes are on the same hole. The course was created by Pete and PB Dye, two of America's most renowned golf architects, in a traditional American design. One of their trademarks is the use of wooden beams to retain the lake. The 4th hole is particularly remarkable, where you have to pass under the green through a tunnel. A special practice area allows you to play off grass. The pro shop sells all the latest golf-world merchandise. Don't pass by without dining in the club house, with two restaurants that serve excellent French cuisine.

The hotel is unpretentious with 24 rooms and five apartments, an independent terrace, a swimming pool, and tennis courts. *Barbaroux is 10 minutes from the Brignoles highway exit (jct. 35), 35 minutes from Aix, and 50 minutes from St-Tropez. Route Cabasse, Brignoles, 83170.* ☎ *04-94-69-63-63. www. barbaroux.com. 18 holes.*

Dolce Frégate. Designed by American architect Ronald Fream, this course near Toulon is renowned as one of the prettiest courses in Europe. It affords sea views, a salty breeze, vineyards, pines, rock gardens, and aromatic shrubbery. The 18 holes are varied enough to accommodate players of all levels.

The clubhouse adjoins a large, modern hotel, often reserved for weddings and private functions so be prepared to smile for the bride. Three restaurants fill hungry golfers' bellies, including the gastronomic Le Mas des Vignes, one of the best Provençal restaurants in the region. *From Toulon and Hyères, Dolce Frégate is accessed via the A50. From Marseille via the A7. Route de Bandol, RD 559, 83270, St Cyr sur Mer. ☎ 04-94-29-39-39. www.dolcefregate-hotel.com. 18 holes.*

Sainte-Victoire. Between Marseille and Aix, this 18-hole golf course stands out from the crowd by virtue of its views: Every hole looks onto the majestic Mont St-Victoire—the mountain prized by Cézanne. The beautiful 17th-century ocher Château de l'Arc is the proud centerpiece of the grounds. It used to belong to the painter Bernard Buffet, who painted the chapel. Today it's a four-star hotel with two decent restaurants. The fairways, surrounded by Mediterranean pines, are somewhat of a challenge, with several ponds and three levels of greens, sunken below a multitude of bunkers. The practice areas include putting and pitching zones, plus a driving range on carpet or grass. *To get to Sainte-Victoire from Aix, take A8 toward Nice, exiting at*

Every hole at Sainte-Victoire affords a view of the mountain peak for which it's named.

Le Canet, and then head toward Trets on the D6. At the island with the level crossing, turn right. From Marseille, take the A51. Take the Gardanne exit and follow the D6 to the island and level crossing. Domaine Château l'Arc, 13710, Fuveau. ☎ 04-42-29-83-43. www. saintevictoiregolfclub.com. 18 holes. ●

Vaucluse & the Lubéron

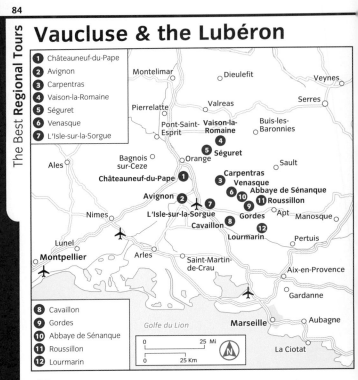

Perched villages spring up like mushrooms around many a bend in the hills of Provence's northernmost region. It's an idyllic, kaleidoscopic landscape, adorned by grape vines and fields of lavender and poppy, with bountiful village markets that specialize in truffles, melons, and other seasonal produce. Avignon, capital of the Vaucluse and briefly the seat of Christendom, is a fine cultural center with a world-famous annual theater festival. Some of Provence's best wines come from Châteauneuf-du-Pape, near Avignon. Vaison-la-Romaine is rich with Roman ruins. L'Isle-sur-la-Sorgue is a mother lode for antiques lovers, and don't miss the pretty village of Fontaine la Vaucluse, with its mysterious water source and castle ruin.
START: **Châteauneuf-du-Pape. Trip Length 7–10 days.**

A Note on Hotels & Restaurants

For a full list in Avignon, see p 134, in chapter 6.

1 ★ Châteauneuf-du-Pape.

This village gave the most famous Côte du Rhône wine its name. Some 350 domains now constitute the *appellation contrôlée*. The tastefully restored medieval village rolls up a

Previous page: A classic Provençal landscape near Les Baux.

hill toward the old ruin of the **Château des Papes.** Built in 1317 by Pope John XXII, who first planted the surrounding vineyards, it was destroyed during the wars of religion in the 16th century, but it still commands a wonderful view of Avignon and the surrounding countryside. Besides the pretty streets, the main attraction here is the **Musée du Vin,** Le Clos (☎ 04-90-83-70-07; www.brotte.com; daily). Its displays are relatively interesting, but the highlight is undoubtedly the tasting at the end of the tour. *Châteauneuf-du-Pape tourist office, place Portail;* ☎ *04-90-83-71-08.*

Leave Châteauneuf on the D17, then join the D507 at the island (2nd exit) and follow signs to Avignon (via D225). Distance: 17km (11 miles).

❷ ★★★ **Avignon.** Stunningly beautiful Avignon is dominated by the **Palais des Papes,** formerly inhabited by the 14th-century popes who fled here to escape political infighting in Rome. The town's famous 12th-century half-bridge, the Pont d'Avignon, is deservedly one of France's top tourist magnets. For detailed information about Avignon, see chapter 6.

Leave Avignon on the D225 (rte. Touristique du Docteur Pons). After 5km (3 miles), take the D942 to Carpentras. Distance: 27km (17 miles).

❸ **Carpentras.** Ruled until 1791 by the Catholic church via Avignon, as part of the **Comtat Venaissin**—a tax-free, military-free papal territory—Carpentras became a haven for Jews expelled by France during the Middle Ages. The town walls crumbled long ago, but the streets still follow their original medieval pattern, which is difficult to drive but a joy to walk. Carpentras is particularly famed as the site of France's oldest synagogue, dating to 1367, opposite the **Hôtel de Ville. Cathédrale St-Siffrein** (pl. St-Siffrein), has a special entry for converted Jews, the *Porte des Juifs.* The cathedral itself is far more attractive on the outside than on the inside, displaying a mixture of styles. Near the cathedral, look out for a **Roman Arc de Triomphe.**

Despite the historic setting, contemporary Carpentras is down to earth, with a bustling population of 30,000, some of France's most excellent markets (most notably the winter truffle market), and rich Provençal atmosphere. *Carpentras tourist office; 97 pl. du 25 Août 1944;* ☎ *04-90-63-00-78; www.carpentras-ventoux.com.*

A wine store in Châteauneuf-du-Pape.

Vaison-la-Romaine dates to Roman times.

From Carpentras, take the D938 via Malaucène to Vaison-la-Romaine. Distance: 30km (19 miles).

❹ ★★★ **Vaison-la-Romaine.** This town is a symbiosis of ancient Rome, the Middle Ages, and modernity. For a full list of attractions, see p 47, in chapter 3. *Vaison-la-Romaine tourist office, pl. du Chanoine Sautel;* ☎ *04-90-36-02-11; www.vaison-la-romaine.com.*

Leave Vaison and take the Ave Ulysse Fabre along the D977. After 5km (3 miles), join the island and take the D88 (3rd exit) to Séguret. Distance: 9km (5½ miles).

❺ ★★ **Séguret.** After Vaison, spend an hour in this exquisite, quintessential Provençal village. Built into a steep hill, a rabbit's warren of sloping streets lead to a ruined castle. From the village entrance, enter the main street and head toward the **12th-century St-Denis church,** past a **14th-century belfry** and a **15th-century fountain.** A viewing table provides sweeping vistas over **Les Dentelles** and even the **Massif Central.** *Séguret Mairie (City Hall*

deals with inquiries), rue Poterne; ☎ 04-90-46-91-06.

From Séguret, head to the D23 (via Sablet) then, at the island, join the D7 (past Gigondas). After 17km (11 miles), enter Carpentras, leaving via the D4 to Venasque. Distance: 35km (22 miles).

❻ ★ **Venasque.** On a warm afternoon, a stroll through Venasque's tranquil streets, past painters and potters, is enchanting. Before Carpentras, Venasque was the seat of the Avignon Comtat bishopric (thus its name, Comtat Venaissin). The village has a **baptistery** (☎ 04-90-66-62-01) dating from the Merovingian period, from the mid–5th to the mid–8th century. Though it was remodeled in the 11th century, it remains one of France's oldest religious edifices. *Venasque tourist office, Grande Rue;* ☎ *04-90-66-11-66; www.venasque.fr.*

Leave Venesque on the D28 and pick up the D4, then the D1 to Pernes-les-Fontaine. Leave Pernes on the D938 (Route de Carpentras) to L'Isle-sur-la-Sorgue. Distance: 22km (14 miles).

❼ ★ **L'Isle-sur-la-Sorgue.** This wealthy, attractive town owes its name to the Sorgue River, whose crystalline source starts at nearby **Fontaine de Vaucluse** (see p 88). Seventy watermills once pressed the grains and oil that made the town so prosperous. Only nine inoperable wheels remain, but the money rolls in from the antiques industry. More than 300 dealers make it an international center for fine old stuff. But it's expensive. Shops are concentrated around avenue de la Libération, avenue des Quatres Otages, and the station. On Sundays, *brocanteurs* join in, plying their wares along the water's edge.

The **Collégiale Notre Dame des Anges** is worth visiting just to

Fontaine de Vaucluse.

snap a photo of its cherub-clad, baroque interior. Devoted to the French surrealist poet who was born here, the **Maison Rene Char,** 20 rue du Dr. Tallet (☎ 04-90-38-17-41), is a stately 18th-century mansion that hosts temporary modern art exhibitions. *L'Isle-sur-la-Sorgue tourist office, place de la Liberté;* ☎ *04-90-38-04-78; www.oti-delasorgue.fr.*

Exit l'Isle-sur-la-Sorgue on the D938 (Route de Cavaillon) to Cavailllon (via Velorgues). Distance: 12km (7½ miles).

⑧ Cavaillon. Juicy melons are the fruit most associated with this sweet little town. In fact, the area around Cavaillon is used to cultivate a wide range of fruit and vegetables, which adorn stalls here on market days.

Cavaillon began life at the top of the looming St-Jacques hill, but moved down to the current level when the Romans took over the region. A 1st-century **Roman arch** stands proud in place Duclos. Other ancient finds are in the small **Musée Archéologique,** Hôtel Dieu, Porte d'Avignon (☎ 04-90-76-00-34).

Cavaillon's **synagogue** in Hébraïque dates from the 18th century. Like the one in Carpentras, however, it has roots in the 14th

century. The **Musée Juif Comtadin,** rue Hébraïque (☎ 04-90-76-00-34), recounts the history of Judaism in the region. *Cavaillon tourist office, 79 pl. François Tourel;* ☎ *04-90-71-32-01; www.cavaillon-luberon.com.*

Leave Cavaillon on the D15 (rte. de Gordes). After 12km (7½ miles), join the D2 (via Les Imberts). After 5km (3 miles), turn left onto the Chemin de la Calade,

L'Isle-sur-la-Sorgue.

View from the Top

The Lubéron region of the Vaucluse is particularly hilly and green year-round. The rocky limestone massifs abound with crags, gorges, rolling hills, and perched villages. Much of the area is a national park, protected by dedicated mountain rangers and foresters. It is a fine destination for walking and cycling. **Fontaine de Vaucluse** (D25) is a pretty village with a waterwheel, decent restaurants, and an eerie panoramic castle ruin. It is encircled by a seemingly impenetrable green wall of cliffs, from which springs the Sorgue River in a cascade called the *fontaine* (fountain). Strangely, no one has ever determined the source of the water. To reach the spring, follow the Chemin de la Fontaine uphill. Vast white-capped **Mont Ventoux** rises 1,912m (2,091 yds.) above sea level. During the Tour de France, hundreds of professionals huff and puff up the steep slopes to the top. Because it's windy year-round, moisture doesn't have time to condense, which means the views from the summit are often unobstructed by clouds. From a distance, the mount is recognizable by its white limestone tip, covered with snow in winter. **Les Dentelles de Montmirail** are the region's most picturesque mountain ranges, formed by three chalk ridges, topped by ragged crowns, that look more like sharp teeth than the lace *(dentelle)* suggested by their name. Séguret makes for a good stop-off point when you're visiting the Dentelles.

and enter Gordes on the D102. Distance: 20km (12 miles).

⑨ ★★★ Gordes. Quite possibly the most fashionable place in which to have a holiday home if you're a wealthy Parisian, Gordes is a startlingly steep perched village, with prices to match. Its beauty has attracted many a film director—including Ridley Scott, who used Gordes as the setting for his romantic comedy, *A Good Year,* starring Russell Crowe. The village is best viewed from afar, from where the houses seem to spill higgledy-piggledy down the rock face. The village is crowned by the 16th-century **Château de Gordes** (☎ 04-90-72-02-75), which houses a collection of Pol Mara paintings. West of Gordes, you should see the strange

Bories Village, made up of beehive-shaped, dry-stone huts. For more information, see p 72. *Gordes tourist office, place Château;* ☎ *04-90-72-02-75; www.gordes-village.com.*

From Gordes, follow signs to the nearby Abbaye de Sénanque.

⑩ ★★★ Abbaye de Sénanque. In the height of summer, this tranquil Cistercian abbey is engulfed by a carpet of purple, perfumed lavender, rendering it one of the most photographed sites in Provence. But don't be put off; it is for good reason that the abbey's harmonious yet austere Romanesque architecture and lovely gardens are so famous. Founded in 1148, it was torched in 1544 during the antiprotestant

Vaudois Massacre—Provence's bloodiest event, during which men, women, and children were burned alive. Then, in 1580, it was hit by the plague, before the French Revolution in 1789 and the subsequent antimonastic movement almost sealed the abbey's fate for good. Restored by a wealthy industrialist in the 1980s, some monks moved back in to cultivate the lavender and sell other homegrown products to the public. *4km (2½ miles) north of Gordes on D15/D177;* ☎ *04-90-72-05-72; www.senanque.fr.*

Leave Gordes on D102. After 7km (4½ miles), turn left onto Chemin de Joucas and left again onto the D169. Next, turn right onto the D105 (rue de la Fontaine) to Roussillon.

⓫ **Roussillon.** If it weren't for the traditional Provencal houses, all painted a bright peachy hue, Roussillon would look more at home on the red planet Mars than in Provence. The ochre soils and strangely eroded red outcrops surrounding this village lend it an otherworldly romanticism. The town center is enjoyable to wander. Note the belfry-sundial of the Eglise St-Michel.

The real fun is to be had at the ★ **Sentiers des Ocres** (left of the village cemetery, above the car-park; closed Nov–Mar)—an educational path through an old ochre quarry, which takes you past weird and wonderful rock formations, and affords some peculiar views. *Roussillon tourist office, place Poste, 84220;* ☎ *04-90-05-60-25; www.roussillon-provence.com.*

Exit Roussillon on the D105, then take the D104, turning right at the island onto the D149. Turn right onto the D900, then at the island, left onto D36 to the D943 to Lourmarin. Distance: 26km (16 miles).

⓬ ★ **Lourmarin.** Just when you think you can't take another darling village, Lourmarin eases into view to change your mind. It is easily one of Provence's most charming towns, dominated by its **château,** built high on a crag. Part 15th-century, part Renaissance, it has wonderful chimneys, ornamented with Corinthian columns. The main staircase is a splendid work, ending abruptly with a thin stone pillar and a cupola. Literary buffs might want to visit the town cemetery where lie the remains of former resident Albert Camus, author of *The Stranger* and *The Plague.* *Lourmarin Marie (City Hall, which fields tourist inquires), av. Philippe de Girard;* ☎ *04-90-68-10-77.*

The ochre cliffs of Roussillon.

The Var & Haute-Provence

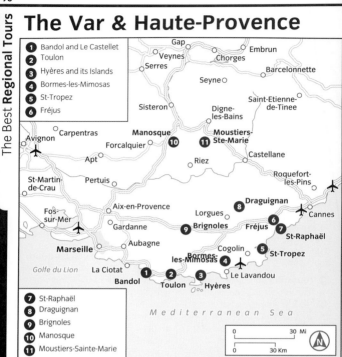

1 Bandol and Le Castellet
2 Toulon
3 Hyères and its Islands
4 Bormes-les-Mimosas
5 St-Tropez
6 Fréjus

7 St-Raphaël
8 Draguignan
9 Brignoles
10 Manosque
11 Moustiers-Sainte-Marie

The Var's rocky outcrops, mountain brooklets, dense forests, luscious vineyards, undulating hills, and beaches speckled with bronzing bodies make for a patchwork of a landscape; no two areas look alike or offer the same attractions. The Var is home to some of the Côte d'Azur's most famous port towns—St-Tropez, St-Raphaël, and Fréjus. But if you tire of seaside frivolity, head north to mountainous Haute-Provence, where the chocolate-box capital of faience pottery, Moustiers-Sainte-Marie, provides a dramatic gateway to the Gorges du Verdon and ever-rolling lavender fields and olive groves. This regional tour can be covered in reverse order.
START: **Bandol. Trip Length 10–12 days.**

A Note on Hotels & Restaurants

For a full list in St-Tropez, see p 191, in chapter 6.

1 **Bandol and Le Castellet.** If you're looking for a laid-back resort, come to Bandol (Bandol tourist office, all Alfred Vivien; ☎ 04-94-29-41-35; www.bandol.org). Unlike most Provençal vintages, Bandol wines are red, full-bodied, and high in tannin, with subtle notes of

pepper, cinnamon, and vanilla. The town itself is a popular tourist destination, thanks to four sandy **beaches:** Le Lido, Rènecros, Centrale, and Casino. On Fridays and Sundays, a cheerful market enlivens the center and, in warmer months, boat trips run every 30 minutes from the harbor (☎ 04-94-10-65-20; www.bendor.com) to the tiny offshore island of **Île de Bendor,** noted for its excellent beaches and Provençal craft village.

North of Bandol (11km/7 miles), don't miss the perched village of **Le Castellet** (tourist office, Hôtel de Ville; ☎ 04-94-98-57-90; www. tourisme83.com). This former stronghold of the Lords of les Baux has remarkably in-tact **ramparts, a 12th-century church,** and a **castle.** There are numerous arts and crafts shops here.

Head back to Bandol, then leave on D559 towards the A50 highway, and follow signs to Toulon. Distance: 16km (10 miles).

2 Toulon. France's second largest naval port is stately, distinguished by its nautical heritage. Antisubmarine, antimissile frigates, and minesweepers line the port. The best way to take it in is via a **boat tour** from quai Cronstadt.

Contact the tourist office for more details, or call **Bateliers de la Côte d'Azur** (☎ 04-94-93-07-55). You can also retrace Toulon's naval history in the **Musée de la Marine,** place Monsenergue, quai de Norfolk (☎ 04-94-02-02-01), next to the stunning old arsenal entrance—one of the only historical sites to have survived WWII.

In the Old Town, you'll find the 900-year-old **Cathédrale Sainte Marie de la Seds** (rue Emile Zola), with its baroque altar and works by Puget; narrow streets lined with shops, fountains, and cafes; and pretty squares, such as **place Victor Hugo,** dominated by Toulon's Opera House. The 19th-century part of town, designed by Paris planner Baron Haussmann, is characterized by wide, tree-lined boulevards, cafe terraces, and grand Empire-era fountains such as the **Fontaine de la Fédération** (1889), which spurts proudly on **Place de la Liberté.** If you're looking for a seaside holiday atmosphere, head to the **Mourillon** district, which has several beaches. Look out for **Fort St Louis** on the way, another one of Vauban's 17th-century military constructions. *Toulon tourist office, 334 av. de la*

The landscape around Port Grimaud.

Bormes-les-Mimosas.

République; ☎ 04-94-18-53-00; www.toulontourisme.com.

Leave Toulon on the N8 and follow signs to Hyères along the A57. After 3km (2 miles), it becomes the A570. Enter Hyères on N98 (toward Hyères airport and St-Tropez). Distance: 19km (12 miles).

❸ ★★ Hyères and its Islands. The oldest winter resort on the coast has 35km (22 miles) of sandy beaches and a charming town center lined with palm trees. The best way to see the sights is to attack the town in three sections: the steep and scenic streets of the **old town,** which leads to the ruined **Château des Aires** and the 1920s artists' haunt, **Villa de Noailles** (p 53; be sure to wear comfortable shoes); shopping around **rue Massillon;** and strolling past the sumptuous 19th-century villas of the **modern town** and **Godillot district.**

Hyères's unspoiled islands, Les Îles de Hyères, make for an excellent day trip. The largest, ★ **Porquerolles,** is famed for its pine forests, beaches, wines, and bumpy cycle paths (for details, see p 56, in chapter 3). **Port-Cros** is a national park with marine life and walking routes through lush forests. If you have snorkel equipment, you can follow an underwater swimming route and observe the sea creatures in their natural habitat. For more details, inquire in Hyères's tourist office (see p 194).

Île de Levant was formerly inhabited by Cistercian monks. Nowadays, the French Navy prohibits access to much of the island. In the west, however, the village of Héliopolis is coveted by nudist bathers. Inquire at the tourist office in Hyères.

For places to stay and dine in Hyères, see p 97. *Hyères tourist board, avenue Ambroise Thomas; ☎ 04-94-01-84-50; www.hyeres-tourisme.com.*

Leave Hyères on the N98. After 2km (1¼ miles; La Garrigue), take the D559 via La Lond-les-Maures to Bormes. Distance: 20km (12 miles).

❹ ★ Bormes-les-Mimosas. As its name suggests, Bormes-les-Mimosas is famous for mimosa flowers, which it cultivates for export all over the world. Each year in February, a colorful street festival celebrates the harvest (see p 197). The old town twists and turns through cobbled slopes, covered passages, and a precipitous lane with 83 steps, known in Provençal as *rompicuo,* or neck-breaker. If you're into churches, visit the 16th-century **Chapelle St François** (next to Wed's market place). The **Église St-Trophime** is also interesting for its trompe l'oeil frescoes around the choir. If you fancy a tipple in a working winery, stop by the **Château de Bregançon** (see p 33), which offers samples of its Côte de Provence rosés. *Bormes Les*

Mimosas tourist office, 1 pl. Gambetta; ☎ 04-94-01-38-38; www. bormeslesmimosas.com.

Exit Bormes on the D559. At La Garrigue, turn right onto the N98. After 30km (19 miles), turn left onto D98a, then immediately right to the D61. At Gassin, rejoin the D98a to St-Tropez. Distance: 40km (25 miles).

⑤ ★★ St-Tropez. Some consider St-Tropez the birthplace of Riviera glamour; others regard it as an epicenter of hedonism. But for the locals, especially out of season, it's still a winning, old fishing village with a market and traditional craftsmen. For detailed information on St-Tropez, see chapters 6 and 2, p 186 and p 26.

From St-Tropez, take the D98 to Sainte-Maxime, and then join the N98 (on the right) to Fréjus. Distance: 36km (22 miles).

⑥ ★★ Fréjus. Once an important center for Roman merchants, Fréjus still has a **Roman amphitheater** and the remains of an **aqueduct.** The upper town, painted in ochre and peach tones, houses small boutiques, cafes, restaurants, and artists' ateliers. Make sure you set aside an hour to visit the unusual, fortified **Groupe Episcopal** (baptistery, cathedral, cloisters, and archaeological museum) in the old town. Other unique buildings are linked to Fréjus' military role as a center for colonial troops from Africa and Asia at the start of the 20th century. Exotic architectural legacies include a redbrick **Mosquée de Missri** (leave Fréjus on av. de Verdun and take the D4 toward Fayence for 3km/2 miles', built by Senegalese soldiers as an exact replica of the Missiri de Djenne mosque in Mali; and the **Hông Hiên Buddhist pagoda,** along the N7 (☎ 04-94-53-25-29),

A street in Fréjus.

surrounded by an Asian garden with sacred animals and mythological guardians. Less colorful, but equally worthy of your attention is the **Lanterne d'Auguste,** a landmark in the old port for sailors entering the harbor. The beach area of Fréjus is a long stretch of fine sand known as **Fréjus-Plage,** bordered by tacky bars and amusements. Families are welcome here. For full detailed information, see chapters 2 and 3. *Fréjus tourist office, 249 rue Jean Jaurès; ☎ 04-94-51-83-83; www. frejus.fr.*

The avenue du Maréchal de Lattre de Tassigny (D98c) in Fréjus leads to rue Anatole France (D37) in St-Raphaël. Distance: 3km (2 miles).

⑦ St-Raphaël. A continuation of Fréjus-Plage, the resort of St-Raph (as the locals call it) has 36km (22 miles) of coastline—30 beaches and creeks. It also lies at the foot of the magnificent **★★ Massif de l'Estérel**—a red, porphyry (volcanic rock) mountain. For watersports, check out the following companies:

Terrescale (☎ 04-94-19-19-79; www.terrescale.com; Jun–Sept) runs sea kayaking and diving trips from Dramont beach. **Club Sous l'Eau** (☎ 04-94-95-90-33; www.clubsousleau.com) offers diving from the pleasure port of Santa Lucia. **Les Bateaux de Saint-Raphaël** (☎ 04-94-95-17-46; www.tmr-saintraphael.com) runs boat trips to St-Tropez and Les Iles de Lérins near Cannes. To discover the Massif de l'Estérel, ask the tourist office for information or try **Autres Regards** (☎ 06-08-33-00-68), which provides themed walks on volcanism, astrology (at night), and local geology. In summer, access to the Massif can be restricted due to the threat of forest fires. Check before you travel by calling the tourist office or the Forest Commission (☎ 04-98-10-55-41, French only). *St-Raphaël tourist office, quai Albert 1er; ☎ 04-94-19-52-52; www.saint-raphael.com.*

Go back into Fréjus and take the N98. At the Rond-point de la Miougrano island, take the D98b.

Docks in St-Raphaël.

At the Rond-point du Harkis island, take the N7 to join the A8. Exit at junction 36 toward St-Tropez, and take the N555 via Le Muy and Trans-en-Provence. Enter Draguignan on the D562. Distance: 34km (21 miles).

8 Draguignan. This pleasant market town is a gateway to the Var's inland gorges, wild truffle woods, vineyards, and hilltop settlements. The best way to walk through the old town is along the **Montée de l'Horloge** towards the clockless 17th-century tower. Continue to **Place du Marché,** where you'll see charming ramshackle houses and a food market on Saturdays and Wednesdays.

The **Musée des Traditions Provençales,** 15 rue Joseph-Roumanille (☎ 04-94-47-05-72), is a fine little museum that reconstructs scenes of regional rural life. The **Musée Municipal,** 9 rue de la République (☎ 04-98-10-26-85), is also worth a visit for its Rubens and Renoirs. Don't miss the **Église St-Michel** (place de la Paroisse), which contains a statue of St-Hermentaire, first bishop of Antibes, famed for having slain the dragon that gave Draguignan its name. *Draguignan tourist office, av. Lazare Carnot; ☎ 04-98-10-51-05; www.dracenie.com.*

From Draguignon, go back to the A8 (toward Hyères/Aix-en-Provence). Exit at junction 35 and follow signs to Brignoles. Distance: 60km (37 miles).

9 Brignoles. Ignore the unattractive new town and head straight for medieval Brignoles, a labyrinthine village with narrow streets that twist and turn within thick 13th-century ramparts. If possible, visit on a market day (Wed on **place Carami;** Sat at **place Général de Gaulle** and **pl. du 8 Mai**), when locally grown peaches, honey, olives, and oils are sold in abundance. **Église St-Sauveur** has an ornate Romanesque wooden doorway. Admire it on your way up the covered stairway of **rue du Grand Escalier,** which leads to the atmospheric 13th-century Counts Palace, today's **Musée du Pays Brignolais,** place des Comptes de Provence (☎ 04-94-69-45-18). *Brignoles tourist office, carrefour Europe; ☎ 04-94-72-04-21; www. museebrignolais.com.*

From Brignoles, follow signposts to join the A8 (dir. Aix en Provence/Nice). After 57km (35 miles) leave the A8 (dir. Gap) to join the N296. After 7km (4 miles), join the A51 for 48km (30 miles), and follow signs to Manosque. Distance: 116km (72 miles).

The rooftops of Fayence.

🔟 **Manosque.** The largest town in Haute-Provence is industrial and sprawling. There are some quaint medieval streets in the old center, but its main attraction is the ★ **L'Occitane factory** (ZI Saint Maurice; ☎ 04-92-70-19-50; www. loccitane.com), where you can watch workers mixing, labeling, and packaging L'Occitane products such as perfumes and creams.

After a whirl around the shop, follow your nose 26km (16 miles) northeast (along D4096 and N100) to the medieval village of ★ **Forcalquier** (crowned by the octagonal 19th-century **Notre Dame de Provence** chapel) where the **Couvent des Cordeliers,** a former Franciscan convent and home to the UESS (European Scent and Flavor University), offers fragrance workshops (☎ 04-92-72-50-68; www. uess.fr). *Manosque tourist office, place du Dr Joubert; ☎ 04-92-72-16-00; www.manosque-tourisme.com.*

Other Villages near Draguignan

It would be a waste to travel as far as Draguignan without visiting the picture-perfect villages that freckle the countryside. Visit **Lorgues,** for its wine and olives; **Barjols,** famed for its numerous stone fountains; **Aups,** for its winter truffle market, old streets, and plane trees; and **Fayence,** for weaving and pottery. Also worth a detour is the **Abbaye de Thoronet** (Le Thoronet; ☎ 04-94-60-43-90), a Cistercian abbey in the Var. The acoustics in the abbey church are remarkable: a single sound resonates for 14 seconds!

The streets of Fayence.

From Manosque take Allée de la Ponsonne, then head left on the D4096. At the island join the D907, then, at the next island, take the first exit onto the D4. Join the D554, then after Vinon-sur-Verdon, take the D952 to Moustiers. Distance 57km (35 miles).

⓫ **Moustiers-Sainte-Marie.** Moustiers is an idyllic medieval town that clings to a gorge-torn cliff. The steep labyrinthine streets are watched over by the eerie 13th-century **Notre-Dame** chapel. The town is known for a golden star that hangs from a cord that connects both sides of the gorge. According to a legend, the knight Bozon de Blacas was held captive by the Saracens in the 10th century and pledged to hang a star above Moustiers, if he returned home safely—but no one actually knows the star's true origins. Since the 17th century, the village has been a center for faience pottery, and today several artists still sell their original designs in the village shops. *Moustiers tourist office, place de l'église;* ☎ *04-92-74-67-84; www. moustiers.fr.*

Les Gorges du Verdon

Reputedly the most beautiful canyon in Europe, the Verdon's clear turquoise waters and theatrical gorges provide an awe-inspiring backdrop for hiking, cycling, and water sports (ask the Moustiers tourist office for information; ☎ 04-92-74-67-84). Nearby, the 22km-(14 mile) long man-made Sainte-Croix Lake is breathtaking, especially when seen from Sainte-Croix village, which juts out of a rocky promontory above the azure water.

Where to **Stay & Dine**

★★★ L'Hostellerie de l'Abbaye de La Celle LA CELLE

Alain Ducasse manages the restaurant in this 18th-century Benedictine abbey-turned-country inn. Chef Benoit Witz's Provencal cuisine earned a Michelin star in 2006, and the verdant gardens contain 80 varieties of vine. *10 pl. du General de Gaulle, 83170.* 📞 *04-98-05-14-14. www. abbaye-celle.com. 10 units. Doubles 250€–450€. Menus 40€–82€; entrees 27€–43€. AE, MC, V. Lunch & dinner daily.*

Hotel du Soleil HYERES

The decor is simple and old-fashioned, but the welcome is warm, the location is central (in the old town). Wi-Fi is free, and rates are reasonable. *Rue du Rampart.* 📞 *04-94-65-16-26. www.hoteldusoleil.com. 22 units. Doubles 59€–125€. MC, V.*

★★★ Le Couvent des Minimes

MANE Set in a former medieval convent this chic hotel has sumptuous rooms, two excellent restaurants frequented by locals, and the world's first Occitane spa. *Mane, 04300.* 📞 *04-92-74-77-77. www.couvent desminimes-hotelspa.com. 46 units. Doubles 170€–415€. AE, MC, V.*

★★ L'Aréna FREJUS

The villa's decor is tastefully Provençal, with yellows and blues throughout. The turquoise pool is inviting. The restaurant serves delicacies such as fricassee of lobster and fois-gras. *145 rue Général de Gaulle.* 📞 *04-94-17-09-40. www.arena-hotel.com. 36 units. Doubles 85€–150€. AE, MC, V.*

★★★ Le Bastide de Moustiers

MOUSTIERS You likely won't find a more gorgeous setting than this country *auberge.* Service is 5-star, the rooms an ode to comfort, and the cuisine—created by another Alain Ducasse protégé, Alain Souliac—deeply, deeply satisfying. *Chemin de Quinson, 04360, Moustiers-Sainte-Marie.* 📞 *04-92-70-47-47. www.bastide-moustiers.com. 12 units. Doubles 190€–400€. Meals from 55€. AE, MC, V. Lunch & dinner daily.*

★★ Le Haut du Pavé HYERES

Think perfectly cooked fish, Provençal specialties, fine wine, medieval vaults, and friendly service. Think one of the best restaurants in Hyères. *Place Massillon.* 📞 *04-94-35-20-98. Menu 20€–30€. MC, V. Lunch & dinner Wed–Sun.*

L'Hostellerie de l'Abbaye de La Celle.

The Riviera & Monaco

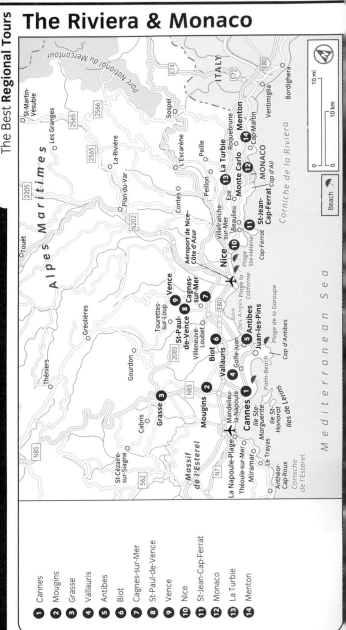

ITALY

Parc National du Mercantour

Alpes Maritimes

Mediterranean Sea

Corniche de la Riviera

St-Martin-Vésubie

Les Granges

2566

2565

Sospel

Ventimiglia

Bordighera

Menton

Roquebrune

Martin

La Turbie

Monte Carlo

MONACO

Cap d'Ail

La Rivière

L'Escarène

Peille

Peillon

2565

Èze

Beaulieu

St-Jean-

Cap-Ferrat

Plan-du-Var

Contes

Villefranche-

sur-Mer

Cap-Ferrat

N202

2205

Touët

Aéroport de Nice–

Côte d'Azur

Nice

Plage

Ste-Hélène

Greolières

Tourettes-

sur-Loup

Vence

St-Paul-

de-Vence

Cagnes-

sur-Mer

Villeneuve-

Loubet

Plage la

California

Baie

des Anges

Plage

Thenier

N85

Gourdon

2085

Biot

Vallauris

Golfe-Juan

Juan-les-Pins

Palm-Beach

Plage de la Garoupe

Cap d'Antibes

Antibes

Cabris

Grasse

Mougins

Mandelieu-

la-Napoule

Cannes

St-Cézaire-

sur-Siagne

562

N85

Massif

de l'Esterel

La Napoule-Plage

Théoule-sur-Mer

Miramar

Le Trayas

Anthéor-

Cap-Roux

Corniche

de l'Esterel

N7

Île Ste-

Marguerite

Île St-

Honorat

Îles de Lérins

Beach

10 mi

10 km

E74

E72

E80

E80

1 Cannes
2 Mougins
3 Grasse
4 Vallauris
5 Antibes
6 Biot
7 Cagnes-sur-Mer
8 St-Paul-de-Vence
9 Vence
10 Nice
11 St-Jean-Cap-Ferrat
12 Monaco
13 La Turbie
14 Menton

The Riviera and Monaco encompass the best and the worst of the south of France. On the one hand, there are all those tall, concrete, post-War constructions monopolizing sea views along some of France's most spectacular coastline. On the other, there's the definitive glamour of towns such as Cannes and Monte Carlo; there's the legacy of artists such as Henri Matisse, Auguste Renoir, Jean Cocteau, and Pablo Picasso; and there's a subtropical climate that supports extraordinary gardens and citrus groves. When the coast gets to be too glitzy and expensive, relief is a brief trip inland, in villages such as Haut de Cagnes, Mougins, St-Paul-de-Vence, or the perfume capital, Grasse. START: **Cannes. Trip length 7–10 days.**

A Note on Hotels & Restaurants

For a full list, see chapter 6: for Cannes, see p 142; for Nice, see p 171; for Monaco, see p 163.

① ★ **Cannes.** The legendary film festival has fixed Cannes on the map as an epicenter of wealth, fame, and adulating stargazers and paparazzi. You could spend a day looking around town, shopping, and salivating over designer merchandise, before winding down over a cocktail in a trendy bar or hotel. Once you've explored the city center, you could embark on a day trip to Cannes's offshore islands, the **Îles de Lérins,** with their nature trails, pebbly beaches, and breathtaking views

across the sea onto Cannes; or visit the fairytale Château de la Napoule (see p 141) in nearby Mandelieu. Cannes is also an ideal base from which to explore nearby villages such as **Mougins** (see below) and the town of **Grasse** (see below). For more on Cannes, see p 136, in chapter 6. For more on the islands, see p 68, in chapter 4.

Leave Cannes via Le Cannet district on the D6285. At the rond-point Winston Churchill, join the D3 and follow signposts to Mougins. Distance: 7km (4 miles).

② ★ **Mougins.** As with most of the Riviera's hilltop villages, Mougins was adopted by artists (Surrealists Francis Picabia and Cocteau, in the case of Mougins). Picasso also came here with

A view of Cannes.

Pottery from Vallauris.

Man-Ray, and the Spaniard was so short of money, he resorted to painting the walls of his room just to pay his rent. He came back a wealthier man in 1961, and he and his last love, Jacqueline Roque, bought a house they named **L'Antre du Minotaur** (the Minotaur's Lair). You can still see it today, opposite the pretty **Notre-Dame-de-Vie** chapel just southeast of the village. Mougins collects a lot of elite runoff from Cannes—a mon-eyed population responsible for restoring the village's wonderful medieval houses, all built upon the lines of ancient ramparts. Art lives on here inside the numerous art galleries. The **Musée de la Photographie André Villiers,** 67 rue de l'Église/Porte Sarrazine (☎ 04-93-75-85-67), exhibits lesser-known works by celebrated photographers such as Robert Doisneau. For refreshments in Mougins, head for the elm-shaded **Place du Commandant Lamy,** lined with restaurants and cafes. *Mougins tourist office, 96 av. Moulin de la Croix;* ☎ *04-93-75-87-67; www.mougins.fr/tourisme.*

Leave Mougins on the Ave du Moulin de la Croix, and then turn left onto the D35. At the rond-point de Tournamy, turn right onto avenue St-Martin. After 100m (328 ft.), take the D6185 and follow the signs to Grasse (D9 and D4). Distance: 13km (8 miles).

❸ Grasse. The fragrance capital of the world has been making scents since the Renaissance. You could easily spend a languorous half-day in the famous perfume factories of **Fragonard** (see p 64 in chapter 3) and **Molinard** (60 bd. Victor-Hugo; ☎ 04-93-36-01-62; www.molinard. com; free admission; May–Sept daily 9am–6pm, Oct–Apr Mon–Sat 9am–12:30pm and 2–6pm), where you can watch *parfumiers* extract the essence of flowers, and you can learn to make your own scent. The revamped **Musée Intérnational de la Parfumérie (MIP),** 8 pl. du Cours (☎ 04-97-05-58-00; www.musees degrasse.com; late Dec–Apr and Oct Wed–Mon 11am–6pm, May–Sep daily 10am–7pm, closed Nov–early Dec), recounts the history of perfume and cosmetics over the last 1,000 years. Just outside the museum, catch the bus to the MIP's lovely new aromatic gardens in nearby Mouans-Sartoux, where you can discover the jasmine, lavender, and roses used in perfume extraction. Wander the narrow streets of Grasse's colorful *centre-ville,* linked by old arches, steep ramps, and staircases, before entering the **Cathédrale Notre-Dame-du-Puy**—a magnificent example of Lombard-influenced Romanesque architecture. The **Musée d'Art et d'Histoire de Provence,** 2 rue Mirabeau (☎ 04-93-36-80-20; www. museesdegrasse.com; late Dec–Apr and Oct Wed–Mon 11am–6pm, May–Sep daily 10am–7pm, closed Nov–early Dec), is set inside the magnificent 18th-century Clapier-Cabris mansion—former home to Revolutionary politician Honoré Mira-beau's sister. Its collections portray 19th-century life in Provence. The

Villa Musée Jean-Honoré Fragonard, 23 bd. Fragonard (☎ 04-97-05-58-00; www.museesdegrasse.com; late Dec–Apr and Oct Wed–Mon 11am–6pm, May–Sep daily 10am–7pm, closed Nov–early Dec), is the mansion where the 18th-century artist sought cover when he fell out of favor with powerful Revolutionaries. Today it is a cultural center devoted to art, with a stairwell that displays Masonic allegories painted by Fragonard's 13-year-old son. For more on Grasse, see p 63 in chapter 3. *Grasse tourist board, 22 cours Honoré Cresp;* ☎ *04-93-36-66-66; www.grasse.fr.*

Retrace your steps to the D6185 and enter St-Basile, bypassing Cannes. At St-Basile, take the D35 toward Vallauris and follow the signs. Enter Vaullauris on the D135. Distance: 20km (12 miles).

❹ **Vallauris.** Despite standing out for its rare grid plan, conceived in the 16th century after the town was razed in 1390, tacky Vallauris would have little to offer were it not for Picasso, who took up pottery here Indeed, don't put aside more than an hour, unless you visit the ★ **Musee National de Picasso** and adjacent **Musée Magnelli** and **Musée de la Céramique** (see p 43), or live and die for ceramics—a tradition that continues here, although most workshops qualify as tourist traps. *Vallauris tourist board, av. Frères Roustan 06220;* ☎ *04-93-63-21 07; www.vallauris-golfe-juan.com.*

Leave Vallauris on the D135. After 2km (1 mile) turn left onto D6007. Turn left at the first island, then right. At the next island, take the D6107 to Antibes. Distance: 9km (5½ miles).

❺ ★★ **Antibes.** The largest pleasure port on the Riviera is an ideal base for visiting the smaller villages of Biot, Haut-de-Cagnes,

St-Paul-de-Vence, and Vence. As a result, you could spend 2 nights here—more if you plan to sunbathe (the main beach is La Gravette). Antibois (Antibes) began life around 500 B.C. as a Greek trading post. After Ligurian assaults, a tremulous spell under the Romans, and further barbaric invasions, it eventually fell to the Lords of Grasse, then the bishops of Antibes, and, in the 14th century, the Grimaldis of Monaco. Henry IV of France bought it back in 1608 as a defense post against the kingdom of Savoy. Today the **Château Grimaldi** houses the **Musée Picasso** (also see p 43), which displays a collection of works donated by the artist. The picturesque streets of old Antibes are lively year-round. One of the region's best produce markets, **Le Marché Provençal** (Tues–Sun), is on cours Masséna. While you're there, don't miss **Balades en Provence** at N 25 (☎ 04-93-34-93-00)—a wonderful boutique selling olive oils, pesto, honeys, and the favored drink of all hedonists, absinthe. Try it in the bar downstairs, but don't count on a meeting with the Green Fairy: Absinthe lost its hallucinogenic properties years ago. To best rub shoulders with the

The market in Antibes.

yachterati, head to **Port Vauban,** where you'll see some of the grandest vessels on the coast. Over the port, the **Fort Carré,** av. du 11 Novembre (☎ 04-92-90-52-13; www.antibes-juanlespins.com; Tues–Sun 10am–4:30pm winter, until 5:30pm June 15–Sept 15), is a fine example of the star-shaped defenses designed in the 17th century by Marquis de Vauban, Louis XIV's military genius. Guided tours are available in English.

Inside the ramparts, the **Église Notre-Dame de l'Immaculée Conception** was built over a Roman temple devoted to Diana. It's decorated in ochres, reds, and penetrating blues. The belfry is a converted 12th-century watchtower. South of the marina, the small **Musée Archéologique,** Bastion St André (☎ 04-92-90-53-31), covers 4,000 years of Provençal history. Within an old 19th-century school building, the **Musée Peynet,** Place Nationale (☎ 04-92-90-54-30) contains hundreds of works by Raymond Peynet (1908–1999), one of France's most successful cartoonists. For shopping, **rue Sade,** between cours Masséna and place Nationale, is lined with quaint shops. If you're in Antibes with kids,

A glassblower in Biot.

don't miss the sea life at **Marineland** just outside the center (see p 55). *Antibes tourist board, 11 pl. Gén de Gaulle; ☎ 04-97-23-11-11; www.antibesjuanlespins.com.*

From Antibes, take the D6007 (bd. du Général Vautrin) and turn right onto the D704 (rte. d'Antibes) to Biot. Distance: 6.5km (4 miles).

6 Biot. Biot is a tiny perched village famous for its flowers (roses, carnations, and mimosa) and blown glass, strewn with pretty bubbles. It's easy to circumnavigate, and the tourist office publishes a very good self-guided map. Once you've taken in the sights, head out of the village along the D4 (Chemin de Combes) to watch live glassblowing at the **Verrerie de Biot** (☎ 04-93-65-03-00; www.verreriebiot.com; daily), which has a shop and adjacent art gallery that showcases contemporary glass-themed pieces. Farther along the D4, the ★ **Musée National Fernand Léger** is a treat for fans of cubism. *Biot tourist office, rue St-Sébastien; ☎ 04-93-65-78-00; www.biot.fr.*

Leave Biot via the D4. After 3km (2 miles), turn left onto the D6007. After another 3km (2 miles), turn right onto the D241, and then continue on the D6098. After 2km (1 mile), turn left onto the D341. Distance: 10km (6 miles).

7 Cagnes-sur-Mer. This town is in fact three separate divisions: **Cros-de-Cagnes,** which covers the seafront, is of little interest aside from a crowded pebbly beach, tacky restaurants, and watersports rentals. **Cagnes-sur-Mer,** farther inland, contains the former home of artist Renoir, whose estate, **Les Collettes,** is now a moving museum. **Haut-de-Cagnes**—a gem of a village perched high above the coast in medieval, chocolate-box glory—is a magnet for contemporary art, thanks

to the UNESCO-sponsored International Painting Festival that takes place here each summer. The village's fortified **Château-Musée-Grimaldi** (☎ 04-92-02-47-30; www.cagnes-tourisme.com; Wed–Mon) is home to an olive tree museum, a modern art museum, and the fabulous **Donation Suzy Solidor,** a collection of more than 40 portraits by Raoul Dufy, Cocteau, and Tamara de Lempicka. *Cagnes tourist office, place du Dr Maurel;* ☎ *04-92-02-85-05; www.cagnes-tourisme.com.*

Leave Cagnes via D136. At the first island, take D336. At the second, turn left onto the D436. Continue on D2 for 3km (2 miles), and after a short stint on D7, rejoin D2 on the right into Saint-Paul de Vence. Distance: 7km (4 miles).

The streets of St-Paul-de-Vence.

⑧ **St-Paul-de-Vence.** Picture-perfect St-Paul is another delightful village full of pretty, medieval streets lined with art galleries, and crafts and antiques shops. Visit on market day to soak up Provençal life: **Marché d'Yvette** sells fruit and vegetables at the village entrance in the old washhouse (Tues, Thurs, Sat); every Saturday morning, the **Marché aux Fleurs** peddles flowers here too. Every Wednesday, a country market sells regional produce on place de Gaulle. Art lovers come especially to see the spectacular ★★ **Fondation Maeght** (see p 41). *Saint-Paul-de-Vence tourist office, 2 rue Grande;* ☎ *04-93-32-86-95; www.saint-pauldevence.com.*

Take the D2 out of St-Paul and follow signs to Vence. Distance: 6km (4 miles).

⑨ **Vence.** This former Episcopal town, loved dearly by writer D. H. Lawrence, who died here in 1930, has retained much of its medieval charm. Part-ruined rampart walls still encircle the old town. You can take in sweeping views over the Alps from boulevard Paul André, which follows the old ramparts. **Porte Peyra,** one of five original gates, leads to **place Peyra,** the site of the former Roman forum, today a lovely square with an urn-shaped fountain. The old 17th-century **Château de Villeneuve,** 2 pl. du Frène (☎ 04-93-58-15-78), with its 13th-century watchtower, contains the **Fondation Emilie Hughes,** which shows works by 20th-century masters and holds regular temporary art exhibitions. The town's centerpiece is the **Cathédrale Notre-Dame de la Nativité,** built on top of a Roman temple to Mars. Don't miss the Matisse-decorated ★ **Chapelle du Rosaire,** just north of the center. See p 41. *Vence tourist office, 8 pl. Grand Jardin;* ☎ *04-93-58-06-38; www.vence.fr.*

From Vence, take the D36 to Cagnes-sur-Mer, where you can join the A8 autoroute to Nice. Exit junction 50. Distance: 23km (14 miles).

⑩ **Nice.** Thanks to its stunning setting in the Baie des Anges, a climate to die for, and wonderful culinary and cultural traditions, Nice is one of the most charming cities on the Riviera. Allocate at least 2 days for the town—more if you plan to use it as a base for exploring the region. For complete coverage of Nice, see chapters 3 and 6.

From Nice, follow the D6098 for 8km (5 miles) via Villefranche-sur-Mer. Join the D125, then the D25 to Cap-Ferrat. Distance: 11km (7 miles).

⑪ **St-Jean-Cap-Ferrat.** Snuggled between the resorts of Beaulieu and Villefranche, the Cap-Ferrat peninsula affords some of the best views over the sea from its coastal roads and footpaths. The main town, **St-Jean-Cap-Ferrat,** is a former fishing village with old houses that smile down over the pleasure boats in harbor. For the best views walk up to the 19th-century chapel at **Pointe St-Hospice,** or drive round to the **Phare** (lighthouse). Once you've climbed the 164 steps to the top, you can see as far as Italy, the Alps, and the Esterel. The peninsula is lined with some of the grandest villa's on the coast—the highlight of which is the astoundingly beautiful ★★★ **Villa Ephrussi-de-Rothschild** and gardens (see p 64).

Leave St-Jean-Cap-Ferrat on the D25, and at avenue Jean Monnet, join the D125 to Beaulieu. Leave

Beaulieu on the D6098 to Monaco. Distance: 15km (9 miles).

⑫ **Monaco.** Governed by the Grimaldi family since the 13th century, the principality of Monaco is the tax-free playground of the mega-rich and famous. You needn't worry about crime here: Big Brother is watching from practically every street corner, and there is 1 cop for every 55 inhabitants. Monte Carlo, with its fancy casino and shops, is where much of the action goes down, but you'll find excellent museums, an aquarium, and the Grimaldi family château to visit just across the port on La Rocher. *For complete coverage of Monaco, see chapter 6.*

Leave Monaco via D6098. Join the D51 and enter Beausoleil. Leave Beausoleil on the D53 and after 4km (2½ miles) turn left onto D2564 to La Turbie. Distance: 7km (4 miles).

⑬ ★★ **La Turbie.** Built upon the Grande Corniche road, at the base of the Tête de Chien (dog's head) headland over Monaco, this hilltop village is mainly famous for the **Trophée des Alpes** (Alpine Trophy), one of the tallest and most spectacular Roman ruins in the region (see p 53). If possible come late afternoon to

La Turbie's Roman Trophée des Alpes.

Where to Stay & Dine

In addition to Cannes, Nice, and Monaco, Antibes makes for a fine base. Stay at the wonderful **La Jabotte:** a gem of a hotel with exquisite, personalized decor. It's a 10-minute walk from the old town, opposite the beach, and Tommy the dog is the star of the house (13 av. Max Maurey, Cap d'Antibes; ☎ 04-93-61-45-89; www.jabotte.com; doubles from 69€–201€). For lunch or dinner, dine at **Le Comptoir de la Tourraque,** where you will find textbook gourmet French cuisine for around 35€ (1 rue Tourraque; ☎ 04-93-95-24-86).

Relaxing outside La Jabotte.

climb the trophy, and then stay for sunset when the lights of Monaco begin to twinkle over the jagged coastline. *La Turbie tourist office, place Detras; ☎ 04-93-41-21-15; www.ville-la-turbie.fr.*

Perched Village Hopping

If Provence's hilltop settlements compel you to see more, whip out your map and drive from La Turbie to the stunningly attractive villages of **Contes, Coaraze, Eze, Peillon, Peille,** or **Roquebrune.**

Leave La Turbie on the D2564 to the A8 and follow signs to Menton. Distance: 17km (11 miles).

⓮ ★ **Menton.** The warmest spot on the Riviera is the lemon capital of France, with an annual lemon festival in February, which draws in crowds of festive onlookers. The streets of the old town are colorful and inviting. Shops, cafes, and houses with Belle Epoque facades

along the main pedestrian thoroughfare, **rue St-Michel,** are intermingled with citrus trees. A stroll through the bustling **covered market** will stimulate your senses with luscious local produce. The **Basilique St-Michel-Archange,** with its fine medley of Baroque ornamentations, is the largest church of its kind in the region. Jean Cocteau is associated with Menton, thanks to the **Salle des Mariages** he decorated in the City Hall, and to the **Musée Jean Cocteau,** devoted to his art. The **Musée des Beaux-Arts** (see p 39), inside the **Palais Carnolès,** showcases works from the 12th to the 15th century, and has a sumptuous citrus garden. Another fine garden is the **Jardin du Val Rameh** (from Promenade de la Mer, take the Chemin de St-Jacques), which has a startling array of subtropical flora that thrive on panoramic terraces with views over the town and the sea. *Menton tourist office, 8 av. Boyer; ☎ 04-92-41-76-76; www.menton.fr.*

Bouches du Rhône & the Rhône Delta

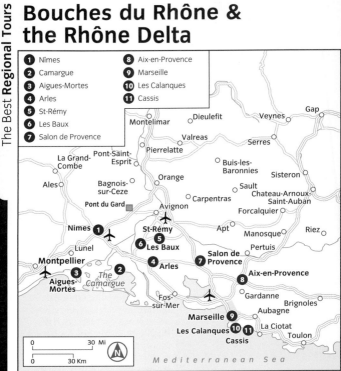

1 Nîmes
2 Camargue
3 Aigues-Mortes
4 Arles
5 St-Rémy
6 Les Baux
7 Salon de Provence
8 Aix-en-Provence
9 Marseille
10 Les Calanques
11 Cassis

Most of the Bouche du Rhône's attractions lie inland, on the Rhône River, which fans into the sea via the saltwater marshes of the Camargue, French cowboy country. In ancient times, the Romans inhabited much of the Rhône Valley. Their legacy endures in cities such as Arles, Aix-en-Provence, and Nîmes. Farther inland towards the Alpilles mountains, St-Rémy is quintessentially Provençal, and nearby Les Baux teeters atop a rocky outcrop. Back along the coast, Marseille and the fishing town of Cassis are popular destinations, linked together by dozens of stony creeks called Calanques. This tour can also be covered in reverse order. START: **Nîmes. Trip length: 7–10 days.**

1 ★★★ **Nîmes.** An incredibly sturdy set of Roman ruins will be the highlight of this tour for many historical architecture lovers. Geographically situated in the Languedoc-Roussillon *département,*

Nîme's traditions and proximity to the Rhône make it thoroughly Provençal in spirit. While you're there, don't miss the ★★ **Pont du Gard** (25km/16 miles northeast along the N86, then D6086), the tallest of all

Roman aqueducts (48m/157 ft.). *For more details on Nîmes, see p 174, in chapter 6, and p 51, in chapter 3.*

A Note on Hotels & Restaurants

For a full list in these towns, see the following pages in chapter 6: in Nîmes, see p 179; in Arles, see p 126; in St-Rémy, see p 184; in Aix-en-Provence, see p 121; and in Marseille, see p 156.

From Nîmes, join the A54 autoroute (toward Arles) and leave at junction 4 to follow signs to Stes-Maries-de-la-Mer, capital of the Camargue. Distance: 65km (40 miles).

❷ ★★★ **Camargue.** Unique to the region in every way, the Camargue has its own traditions, and it's home to *gardians*, France's only cowboys. They herd and care for white horses and black bulls, and live in distinctive, low, whitewashed *mas*, or farmhouses. A haunting, flat region of rice paddies and salt marshes, it attracts rare birds, including pink flamingos. One of the best places to observe our feathered friends is in the **Parc Ornithologique du Pont-de-Gau,** off the D570 (☎ 04-90-97-82-62; www.parcornithologique.com;

The Camargue police station.

▲ *Camargue cowboy.*

daily), where more than 400 species of migrating birds visit annually. While you're there, check out the **Centre d'Information du PNRC** (☎ 04-90-97-86-32; Apr–Sept daily; Oct–Mar Sat–Thurs), also in Pont-de-Gau. It commands excellent views over the lagoon and chronicles the history of the Camargue. Just 4km (2½ miles) south of here is the region's capital, ★ **Saintes-Maries-de-la-Mer.** It is named after three Marys: Mary Magdalene, her sister Mary Jacobea, and Mary Salome, mother of the apostles James and John. According to legend they set sail after the crucifixion, landing with their servant Sarah in Saintes-Maries, where they built a shrine. Their arrival is celebrated in May and October, when residents carry a statue to the sea for a blessing. Despite the crowds in summer, cheery Saintes-Maries feels like a traditional fisherman's town year-round. The local Gypsy population's presence is most evident in the town center, where you will find shops strewn with colorful Romany souvenirs. The Romanesque **Église de Notre-Dame-de-la-Mer** is a gem of a fortified church. Climb up to the rooftop walkway encircling the church for a view over the sea, the town, and the Camargue plains. Back inside the church, on the north side of the nave above the altar, you can see the Three Marys' boat, which locals parade around town in May and October during the celebrations. In the crypt lie the relics of St. Sarah.

Along the D570, 10km (6 miles) southwest of Arles, the **Musée de la Camargue,** Parc Naturel Regional de Camargue, Mas du Pont de Rousty (☎ 04-90-97-10-82; www. parc-camargue.fr; Apr–Sept daily, Oct–Mar Wed–Mon), a fabulous museum, is set inside an old 19th-century *mas*. It is devoted to traditional Camargue life and the plants and animals that thrive in the delta. The museum is also affiliated with a 3.5km (2 mile) educational trail that allows you to observe local husbandry and agricultural activities.

The main roads through the Camargue are the D36, D36C, D570, and D37. The **Salin de Giraud,** just off the D36, provides a viewing point over the salt pans in the east. The only way to fully appreciate the strange beauty of this region, however, is to go off the beaten track on

foot, bike, or horseback. Ask for detailed maps at the tourist office in Nimes, Arles, Aigues-Mortes, or Sainte-Maries. The wonderful **Le Mas de Peint** hotel and working farm in Le Sambuc (see "Where to Stay," below), offers excellent horseback riding excursions across their land, where they raise horses and bulls used in local bullfights. *For more information, see chapter 3 and chapter 4.*

Leave Saintes-Maries and join the D570 via La Brouztière. Turn left onto D85, then right onto the D38, and left again onto the D38a. Join the D58 and after 12km (7½ miles), at the island, join the D46. At the next island, take the D979 to Aigues-Mortes. Distance: 31km (19 miles).

❸ ★★ **Aigues-Mortes.** The turreted silhouette of Aigues-Mortes is impressive any time of day, but it's especially beguiling at sunset. The medieval town's defensive curtain wall rises gallantly from the flat plains of the Camargue. Built to stave off outsiders, it now welcomes them into the town's grid-patterned streets via a series of ancient *portes* (gates). You

The rooftops of Stes-Maries-de-la-Mer.

could easily spend an entire lazy day here. Start by touring the **ramparts,** and then take a break in one of the many cafes around **place St-Louis.** The tourist office runs excellent 2-hour guided tours. Once you've taken in the towers and chapels, try a boat trip along the **Grau-du-Roi canal.** The Pescalune Barge leaves at the foot of Tour de Constance (☎ 04-66-53-79-47; www.peniche-aiguesmortes.com) *For more information, see p 18 in chapter 2.*

Leave Aigues-Mortes on the D979 and join the D46. At the second island, join the D58 and then the D38c. After 5km (3 miles), turn left onto the D570 toward the N113. From here, follow signs to Arles. Distance: 46km (29 miles).

④ ★★★ **Arles.** The Romans and Vincent van Gogh put this little town on the map. The Romans left behind an **arena,** a **theater,** relics, and ruined baths. Van Gogh left behind more than 200 paintings and drawings of Arles and its surrounding countryside. *For a full list of attractions, see chapter 6; p 15, in chapter 2; and p 44, in chapter 3.*

Leave Arles on the D570n and after 15km (9 miles) turn right onto the D99 to St-Rémy. Distance: 25km (16 miles).

⑤ ★★★ **St-Rémy.** This quintessentially Provençal market town was the birthplace of Nostradamus, who later lived in Salon-de-Provence (below, p 110). Its streets are lined with 15th- and 16th-century mansions, including the Marquis de Sade's family home, now a museum displaying local Roman finds. The nearby settlement of **Glanum** is another trove of Roman and Greek artifacts, a short drive or 30-minute walk from the town center along the D5. Van Gogh's presence is felt nearby here too, in the **Monastère St-Paul-ce-Mausolée** (5km/3 miles along D5,

A sidewalk cafe in St-Rémy.

where he convalesced after cutting off his ear in Arles. *For full listings, see chapter 6, and p 13, in chapter 2.*

Leave St-Rémy on the D5. After 7km (4 miles), join the D27 to Les Baux. Distance: 10km (6 miles).

⑥ ★★ **Les Baux.** Possibly the most dramatic fortified village in France, Les Baux commands spectacular views across **the Val d'Enfer, Les Alpilles** mountains, and, on a good day, the **Camargue.** This vantage, coupled with the town's beautiful, winding streets, attracts hoards of visitors each summer. Visit off-season or develop nerves of steel, but, whatever you do, don't miss it. Set amid vineyards and olive groves, it is famous for its wines and oils, all sold in typical Provençal boutiques. At the 10th-century ruined **Château de Baux** (☎ 04-90-54-55-56; www.chateau-baux-provence.com), you can watch reenactments of medieval sieges and visit a museum devoted to Les Baux's history. The village emblem is the Star of Bethlehem, thanks to a Lord of Baux who claimed to be the descendant of one of the Three Wise Men, King Balthazar. Back in the main village, two contrasting churches are the 12th-century **Église St-Vincent** and next door

Chapelle des Pénitents Blancs.
Just opposite the village, an old quarry stands proud as the site where the mineralogist Pierre Berthier discovered bauxite (the principle component of aluminum) in 1822, naming it after the town. Today, part of the quarry has become the spectacular **Cathédrale d'Images**—an eerie light and sound show inside an old tunnel, route de Maillane D27 (☎ 04-90-54-38-65; www.cathedrale-images.com). Cars cannot drive up to the village, so leave your vehicle near the Porte Mage gate. *For more information, see chapter 2, p 14, and chapter 3, p 35.*

Leave Les Baux on the D27. After 2km (1 mile), turn right onto the D5 and enter Maussane-les-Alpilles. Leave the town on the D17, regaining the D5 after Mouriès. At the island, join the D113 toward Salon-de-Provence. Distance: 32km (20 miles).

❼ Salon-de-Provence. Salon's most famous inhabitant was the physician and astrologer Nostradamus, who wrote his celebrated book of predictions, *Les Centuries.* Published in 1555, it attracted much attention. The Vatican banned it for foretelling the downfall of the papacy. After its publication, King Charles IX appointed Nostradamus as his personal physician. An audio-guided tour leads you through a series of kitschy waxwork tableaux at the **Maison de Nostradamus,** rue Nostradamus (☎ 04-90-56-64-31), the house in which the seer spent the last 19 years of his life. You can also pay a visit to his tomb, just outside the city wall, in the Gothic **Collégiale de St-Laurent.** Another pretty church is the 13th-century **Église de St-Michel,** with its five-bay arcaded tower. Shadowing over Salon is the kids **Château de l'Emperi**, Montée du Puech

(☎ 04-90-56-22-36; Wed–Mon). Built between the 10th and 13th centuries by the Bishops of Arles, it houses a military museum, covering the history of the French Army from the reign of the Sun King to 1918. **City Hall** (Hôtel de Ville), the shops on **cours Gimon,** and the cafes on **place Croustillat** are the hub of modern life.

The town is particularly famous for its olives and soap. Most of the *savon de Marseille* actually comes from Salon. Around the station, look out for Belle Epoque follies, built by Salon's prosperous soap barons in the 1900s. *Salon de Provence tourist office, 56 cours Gimon 13300; ☎ 04-90-56-27-60; www.visitsalondeprovence.com.*

From Salon, leave along the D538, heading towards the A54 (toward Aix). Join the A7 for 10km (6 miles), then the A8. Exit at junction 31 and follow signs to the center. Distance: 40km (25 miles).

❽ ★★★ Aix-en-Provence. This former Roman spa-town, nestled beneath the Mont St-Victoire, was once the capital of Provence. Now it's best-known as the home of Emile Zola and Paul Cézanne. Cézanne, in particular, immortalized Aix and the mountain in his paintings. Today, the town is a chic jamboree of fountains, Renaissance mansions, medieval streets, cafes, restaurants, and boulevards shaded by plane trees. *For full listings, see chapters 6, 2, and 3.*

From Aix, join the A8, and then follow signs to Marseille (via A51 and A7). Distance: 35km (21 miles).

❾ ★★★ Marseille. France's oldest city has been a trading hub and center for immigration for millennia. It's split into quarters you could liken to urban villages, and you need at least 2 days to get a feel for the place, longer to get your bearings, and a lifetime to see and understand the ancient town and its chalky coastline. Make sure you grab a boat from the **Vieux Port** on Quai des Belges to visit the **Îles de Frioul** offshore. The main island is the **Île d'If,** dominated by the 16th-century fortress that inspired Alexandre Dumas to write *The Count of Monte Cristo. For more information see p 144, chapter 6; p 20, chapter 2; and p 52, chapter 3.*

The direct route from Marseille to Cassis is along the D559. Along the coastline, you will notice the Calanques, access to which is signposted. Marseille and Cassis are 30km (19 miles) apart.

⑩ ★★ Les Calanques. These spectacular slashes in the limestone cliffs between Marseille and Cassis are the craggy sea edges of a 5,000-hectare (12,355 acre) national park—home to rare flora and fauna (including Europe's largest snake and lizard) and a wealth of birdlife. In the coves, some locals are lucky enough to have family *cabanons*—tiny, old fisherman's huts passed down from generation to generation. The only way to access most of the Calanques is on foot, but pack plenty of water and wear decent shoes before you set out. The only Calanque fully accessible by car on the Cassis side is **Port Miou.** It has the longest beach, and it's nearly always invaded by pleasure boats. The Calanques close to Marseille are flatter and wider, with some limited parking facilities. From Marseille toward Cassis, the best Calanques are **Les Goudes,** a tiny fishing village set amid impressive cliffs, with a few local restaurants; **Callelongue,** with its many cabins and *cabanons;* **Sormiou,** widely considered the best Calanque, with a tiny port, beach, and seafood restaurants; **Morgiou,** separated from Sormiou by the **Cap Morgiou,** which has a wonderful viewing point; **Sugiton,**

Marseille's city hall and port.

with its turquoise water (coveted by nudists); **En-Vau,** the prettiest of them all (see p 67); **Port-Pin,** surrounded by pines; and Port Miou. At sunset, don't miss the heart-stopping views over the Calanques along the **Route des Crêtes.** (See p 25; take D559 east from Cassis and watch for a signposted road on your right, then turn left at Pas de la Colle.) If you fancy diving around the Calanques, contact the **Centre Cassidain de Plongée** (3 rue Michel Arnaud; ☎ 04-42-01-89-16; www.centrecassidaindeplongee. com); for walking and rock climbing, ask the Cassis tourist office (quai des Moulins; ☎ 08-92-25-98-92; www.ot-cassis.com). *To see the Calanques by boat, see En Vau on p 67 in chapter 4.*

⑪ ★★ Cassis. This fishing port, sheltered by the Cap Canaille outcrop, is famous for its pretty streets and excellent seafood. A summer resort coveted by artists such as Dufy and Matisse, it continues to inspire artists today. *For more information, see chapters 2 and 4.*

Where to **Stay & Dine**

★★ **Château de Cassis** CASSIS
Every nook and cranny is charmed in this beautifully restored château, where old armor stands alongside contemporary art. The views over Cassis and the coast will stay etched in your memory. Rooms are sublime. *Traverse du Château.* ☎ *04-42-01-63-20. www.chateaudecassis.com. 9 units. Doubles 220€–690€. Lunch 45€; dinner 75€. MC, V.*

Hôtel Angleterre SALON DE PROVENCE The decor here can be kitschy (check out the frescoes in the lobby); but the price is right, the service friendly, the rooms comfortable, and the location central. *98 cours Carnot.* ☎ *04-90-56-01-10. www.hotel-dangleterre.biz. 26 units. Doubles 54€–66€. MC, V.*

★★ **Le Mas de Peint** CAMARGUE White horses, bulls, and genuine *gardians* wander around this beautiful 500 hectare (1,235 acre) property, which organizes excellent horseback excursions into the Camargue. The great country kitchen–diner combo churns out lip-smacking gourmet food, and the chef gives cooking lessons. *Le Sambuc via D570 and D36.* ☎ *04-90-97-20-62. www.masdepeint.com. 11 units. Doubles 235€–435€. Half-board available. MC, V.*

★ **L'Eau à la Bouche** SALON DE PROVENCE The fruits of the sea served here come straight from the fishmongers next door. The veranda is an agreeable spot in summer. *Place Morgan.* ☎ *04-90-56-41-93. Menus 25€. MC, V. Tues–Sun lunch.*

★ **Nino** CASSIS Smack bang on the pretty port, Nino serves some of the best seafood and Provençal cuisine in town. The three bedrooms feel like the inside of a luxury yacht. *1 quai Jean Jacques Barthélemy.* ☎ *04-42-01-74-32. www.nino-cassis.com. 3 units. Doubles 100€–200€. Menu 30€. AE, MC, V. Tues–Sat breakfast, lunch & Dinner; Sun breakfast & lunch.* ●

A room at the farmstead Le Mas de Peint.

Aix-en-Provence

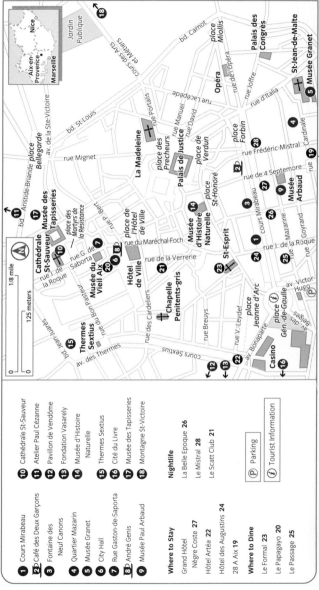

Previous page: The streets of St-Rémy.

Provence's former capital, demi-Parisian Aix is chic and contemporary, save for its elegant 17th- and 18th-century setting. Its tree-lined avenues, stately *hôtels particuliers,* graceful fountains, and exquisitely detailed facades have long inspired artists and writers. Both Paul Cézanne and author Emile Zola lived here, and visitors can follow in their footsteps via themed walks organized by the tourist office. For more than 600 years, the University of Aix-en-Provence has infused the town with intellectual energy; today, the large student population congregates on busy cafe terraces, soaking up the sun between classes. Aix is also a renowned spa town, built over a natural spring, and the largest center in France for processed almonds, used to make the delicious local specialty, Calissons d'Aix. **START: Aix is 80km (50 miles) southeast of Arles and 32km (20 miles) north of Marseille.**

Tip

Aix's tourist office (☎ 04-42-16-11-65) runs excellent themed walking tours, including tours entitled "Unexpected Aix," "In the Steps of Cézanne," and "Libertines and Courtisanes."

❶ ★★ Cours Mirabeau. Built in the 1650s as a promenade for the wealthy, this boulevard is the social hub of Aix. The once privately owned aristocratic mansions *(hôtels particuliers),* with finely carved doorways and wrought-iron balconies, are now official buildings or banks, but their splendor endures. Each *hôtel* has a story; the most bloodthirsty goes to the **Hôtel d'Iosard de Vauvenargues** (No. 10), where in 1784, Bruno d'Entrecasteaux murdered his wife. The largest mansion is **L'Hôtel de Forbin** (No. 20). Built in 1656, it is remarkable for its simplicity and symmetry.

In complete contrast, the opulence of the **Hôtel d'Espagnet** (No. 38), reflects the social success of its owner, Pierre Maurel, whose booming textile business allowed him to climb the social ladder and join France's noble classes. The balcony, supported by giant Atlases, is typical of Aix's baroque architectural style.

The right-hand side has fewer mansions but more cafes, and it catches the sun. Next to passage Agard, you'll find **Cézanne's childhood home** (today a shop called La Plume d'Or).

Take a Break

❷ Café des Deux Garçons. Once a hangout for Cézanne, Zola, and their chums, this cafe is an essential stop in Aix. *53 cours Mirabeau.* ☎ *04-42-26-00-51. $.*

❸ Fontaine des Neuf Canons. Built over a natural hot spring, Aix has always been associated with

The main plaza in Aix.

The Atlas figures that support the Hôtel d'Espagnet.

water; the word *aix*, in fact, means "water source." Over time, the whole town was ornamented with graceful fountains *(fontaines)*, three of which adorn the Cours Mirabeau. The **Fontaine des Neuf Canons** (rue Clémenceau) marks the center of the Cours and dates from 1691. Water from the moss-coated **Fontaine Moussue** (rue de Nazareth and rue Laroque) issues forth at a steaming 34°C (93°F). **Fontaine du Roi René** (just before Place Forbin) is a 19th-century ode to Good King René (sculpted by David d'Angers), who introduced the Muscat grape to the region in the 15th century.

❹ ★★ **Quartier Mazarin.** Archbishop Mazarin designed this grid-patterned district in the 17th century as a "luxury housing estate" for Aix's haute bourgeoisie and Parliament members. As you saunter through the restful squares and exquisite facades, you'll come across hidden art galleries, atmospheric antiques shops, and Aix's first Gothic building, the late 13th-century ★ **St-Jean-de-Malte Priory.** Built in honor of the Knights

of Malta, it was the burial site of the counts of Provence and is now part of the Musée Granet (see below). *Rue Cardinale and rue du 4 Septembre.*

❺ ★ **Musée Granet.** The former commander's palace, the *Palais de Malte* (1676) houses major painting collections from the great European schools of the 16th to 20th centuries. The Masters' A-list includes Rubens, Van Loo, Ingres, Rembrandt, and Cézanne. Fabulous temporary painting exhibitions frequently enhance the collections, too. 🕐 *1 hr. Place St-Jean-de-Malte.* ☎ *04-42-52-88-32. www.musee granet-aixenprovence.fr. Admission 4€; free under 18. Oct–May Tues–Sun noon–6pm; June–Sept 11am–7pm, closed Mon.*

❻ **City Hall.** The Hôtel-de-Ville is a 17th-century masterpiece by Pierre Pavillon. Step through the wrought-iron gate into a pretty paved courtyard with classical pilasters separating the buildings. The square is dominated by a stunning 16th-century belfry with an astronomic clock, built in 1661 and embellished by four wooden statues that represent the seasons. *Place de l'Hôtel-de-Ville.*

❼ ★★ **Rue Gaston-de-Saporta.** In ancient times, this bustling semi-pedestrian street was a road. Today it heaves with commerce. Between shops are several sumptuous mansions: No. 23, the Hôtel Maynier-D'Oppède, was rebuilt in 1730 and holds summer concerts in its courtyard; No. 21, the Hôtel Boyer de Fonscolombe contains wonderful frescoed ceilings; Louis XIV stayed at No. 19, the Hôtel du Chateaurenard, in 1660; and No. 17, the 17th-century mansion of the Estienne de St-Jean family, has elegant Corithian Pilasters and houses the **Musée du Vieil Aix** (Museum of old Aix;

Aix Markets

An orgy for the senses, from 8am until noon, Aix's vast street markets take over **Place des Prêcheurs** and **Place de la Madeleine** every Tuesday, Thursday, and Saturday. On the same days, a wonderful flower market showers color onto the square in front of the **Hôtel de Ville** (city hall), and an antiques fair fills **Place Verdun**. A daily farmers market, selling fresh local produce, also sets up beneath the plane trees on **Place Richelme**.

☎ 04-42-21-43-55; www.mairie-aixenprovence.fr; Apr–Oct Tues–Sun 2:30–6pm, Nov–Mar 10am–noon and 2–5pm). The museum wows visitors with intricate friezes and majestic staircases, paintings, screens, ceramics, wooden puppets, and *santons*.

Take a Break

🍵 **André Genis.** For four generations, the Genis family has satisfied sweet-toothed locals with their crunchy *biscotins* (grilled hazelnuts in a biscuit coating, flavored with orange-flower) and their divine Calissons d'Aix. Legend says Good King René of Aix concocted this almond dessert to win the trust of

his young second wife, Jeanne on their wedding night in 1473. Until she was ready, he sublimated his own advances with a symbolic, petal-shaped *calisson*—which literally means "sweet caress." Like the dessert, the name endured. 1 *rue Gaston de Saporta.* ☎ 04-42 23-36-64. *$.*

● **Musée Paul Arbaud.** Located in the heart of the Mazarin quarters, this intimate museum, with its paneled ceilings and dark wooden cabinets, houses a small but rich collection, which includes 18th-century faience pottery from Moustiers Sainte-Marie (see p 96). Visit the dusty library, home to a

The calissons d'Aix, made from a medieval recipe.

The streets of Aix.

wealth of ancient intricately decorated Provencal manuscripts. ⏱ *45 min. 2a rue du 4 September.* ☎ *04-42-38-38-95. Admission 3€; free under 18. Tues–Sat 2–5pm; closed Sun and public holidays.*

⑩ ★★★ Cathédrale St-Sauveur. According to legend, this architectural hodgepodge was built between the 5th and the 18th century on the site of a temple to Apollo. To the south, a 12th-century Romanesque gate joins a Roman wall; to the north a colossal 14th-century bell tower flanks a richly carved gothic gate (15th–16th c.). Inside, cross the chancel to the

stirring 12th-century cloisters, with pillared galleries casting dramatic shadows on the floor. ⏱ *30 min. Place de l'Université.* ☎ *04-42-23-45-65. Free admission. Daily 7:30am–noon and 2–6pm.*

⑪ ★ Atelier Paul Cézanne. The major forerunner of Cubism, Cézanne lived and worked in this unassuming house uphill from the cathedral. It remains much as he left it in 1906; even his coat still hangs on the wall. Here he painted his celebrated *The Bathers.* ⏱ *50 min. 9 av. Paul-Cézanne (head north along rue Pasteur).* ☎ *04-42-21-06-53. www.atelier-cezanne.com.*

Aix's Christmas Figurines

Since the 18th century, Provençal families have traditionally hand-crafted Christmas nativity scenes. The figurines, called *santons,* represent the holy family, the magi, oxen, asses, and ordinary tradesfolk. Aix is a center for this craft, and the **Santons Fouque workshop,** 65 cours Gambetta (☎ **04-42-26-33-38;** www.santons-fouque. fr), is an institution.

Admission 5.50€ adults, 2€ ages 13–25, free under 12. Open Apr–June, Sept daily 10am–noon, 2:30–6pm; July–Aug daily 10am–6pm; Oct–Mar daily 10am–noon, 2–5pm. Closed public holidays and Sun in Dec–Feb.

⑫ Pavillon de Vendôme. When the duke of Vendôme was forced to enter the clergy in 1665, he built this sumptuous palace and gardens as a secret love nest for his mistresses. The entrance is supported by two well-muscled Atlases, and the rooms contain interesting Provençal furniture and paintings. ⏱ *40 min. 32 rue Célony.* ☎ *04-42-21-05-78. Admission 3€; under 25 free. Wed–Mon 10am–6pm.*

⑬ ★ Fondation Vasarely. Much of Aix's charm derives from its old buildings, but this modern structure is refreshing, made from black and white metal, shaped like honeycomb. Designed by Hungarian artist Victor Vasarely in the 1970s, it houses his avant-garde collections (often wild geometric tableaux), explores the boundaries between art and architecture, and promotes Aix's art on a national and international scale. ⏱ *1 hr. 1 av Marcel Pagnol.* ☎ *04-42-20-01-09. www.fondationvasarely.fr. Admission 9€; 6€ youths 7–26. Tues–Sun 10am–1pm and 2–6pm (closed Tues Jan–Mar).*

⑭ Musée d'Histoire Naturelle. In the Jurassic era, Aix-en-Provence was a breeding ground for Megaloolithid dinosaurs. Fossil lovers should visit just to admire 553 of the 1,000 Titanosaurus eggs found in Aix—the greatest number in the world ⏱ *45 min. 6 rue Espariat.* ☎ *04-42-27-91-27. www.museum-aix-en-provence.org. Admission 3.10€, free under 25. Open daily including public holidays 10am–noon and 1–5pm.*

⑮ ★★★ Thermes Sextius. Aix lies on the site of a 10,000-year-old hot spring, enriched in calcium and magnesium, which served as the baths of Aix's founder, Roman Emperor Augustus Sextius, in 122 B.C. If you're feeling flush, pamper yourself at the modern spa, where remains of the original thermal pool are visible at the entrance. *55 av. des Thermes.* ☎ *04-42-23-81-82. www.thermes-sextius.com. Basic treatments: 30€–156€. Mon–Fri 8:30am–7:30pm, Sat until 6:30pm, Sun 9:30am–2:30pm (autumn/winter); 9am–8pm spring/summer.*

⑯ Cité du Livre. In an old match factory, the Méjanes library holds some 80,000 tomes left by the marquis de Méjannes in 1786. It also seconds as the official headquarters of the contemporary Preljocaj Ballet (www.preljocaj.org). *8–10 rue des Allumettes.* ☎ *04-42-91-98-88. www.citedulivre-aix.com. Opening hours vary.*

⑰ Musée des Tapisseries. This former archbishop's palace houses three series of important tapestries from the 17th and 18th

Aix cathedral.

The modern spa built on the grounds of the Roman Thermes Sextius.

centuries, including the world's only example of *The History of Don Quixote,* by Natoire (1735). 🕐 *40 min. 28 pl. des Martyrs de la Résistance.* 📞 *04-42-23-09-91. Admission 3€. Wed–Mon 10am–12:30pm, 1:30–5pm. Closed public holidays.*

⑱ ★★★ Montagne St-Victoire. It's easy to understand why this limestone range, 1,011m (3,297 ft.) tall and 7km (4 miles) wide, obsessed Cézanne. He painted it more than 60 times. Picasso, however, got the final word: The Spaniard is buried on its north slopes at the Château de Vauvenargues, where he lived until his death in 1973. *From Aix, Vauvenargues is 15km (9 miles) northeast along the D10.*

Aix After Dark

La Belle Epoque, bar 29 cours Mirabeau (📞 04-42-27-65-66), is popular for its large terrace and attractive happy hour. Pretty people (Aix has plenty) flock to **Le Mistral** nightclub, 3 rue Frédéric-Mistral (📞 04-42-38-16-49; www.mistralclub.fr), for a late-night bop (open at midnight). For a variety of live music, **Le Scat Club,** 11 rue de la Verrerie (📞 04-42-23-00-23), is a crowded den in medieval vaults that maintains notoriously late hours.

Where to **Stay & Dine**

★ Grand Hôtel Nègre Coste

COURS MIRABEAU This 17th-century town house is popular with musicians who flock to Aix for the summer festivals (see p 198). Rooms are excellent value and parking is available. *33 cours Mirabeau.* ☎ *04-42-27-74-22. www.hotelnegre coste.com. 37 units. Doubles 85€– 145€. MC, V.*

Hôtel Artéa HISTORIC CENTER

The best budget hotel in town is in a stately 19th-century house with bright, clean rooms. *4 bd. de la République.* ☎ *04-42-27-36-00. www.hotel-artea-aix-en-provence. com. 42 units. Doubles 78€–118€. AE, MC, V.*

★ Hôtel des Augustins COURS

MIRABEAU History lovers enjoy this quirky hotel—first a 12th-century chapel, then an auberge where Martin Luther stayed after his excommunication from Rome. *3 rue de la Masse.* ☎ *04-42-27-28-59. www.hotel-augustins.com. 29 units. Doubles 99€–250€. AE, MC, V.*

★★★ Le Formal COURS MIRA-

BEAU *FRENCH* Join the local gastronomes for Chef Jean-Luc's succulent foie-gras, locally produced cheeses, fresh lobster, and solid wine list. *32 rue Esplariat.* ☎ *04-42-27-08-31. Menus: 36€– 65€. AE, MC, V. Lunch Tues–Fri, dinner Tues–Sat.*

Le Papagayo HISTORIC CENTER

SALADS Cheap food and copious salads are served with a smile on this bustling, sun-filled square. *22 pl. Forum des Cardeurs.* ☎ *04-42-23-98-35. Menus 14€–18€, salads 10€. Lunch daily year-round;* *May–Aug lunch & dinner daily. No credit cards.*

★ Le Passage QUARTIER MAZA-

RIN *FRENCH FUSION* This converted warehouse is Aix's most fashionable address, combining fun design with great food (there's an organic menu too), art exhibitions, live music, and even cooking classes. *10 rue Villar.* ☎ *04-42-370- 900; www.le-passage.fr. Menus 13€–35€; a la carte 40€. AE, MC, V. Lunch & dinner daily; closed some public holidays.*

★★★ 28 A Aix COURS MIRABEAU

This chic B&B, set in an 18th-century Aix mansion, has charming rooms richly infused with the decorative traditions of Aix, a tea-room, art gallery, and a decorating workshop. *28 rue du 4 Septembre.* ☎ *04-42-54- 82-01. www.28-a-aix.com. 4 units. Doubles 200€–500€. AE, DC, MC, V.*

Le Passage.

Arles

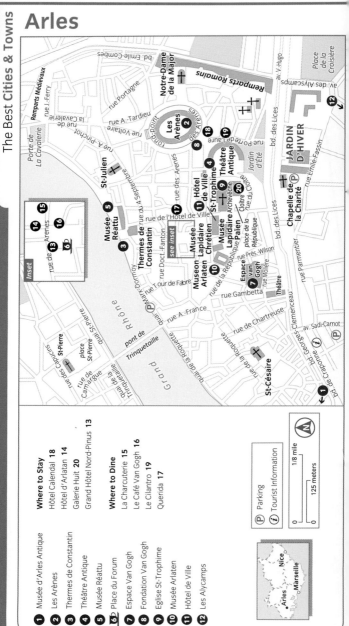

1 Musée d'Arles Antique
2 Les Arènes
3 Thermes de Constantin
4 Théâtre Antique
5 Musée Réattu
6 Place du Forum
7 Espace Van Gogh
8 Fondation Van Gogh
9 Église St-Trophime
10 Museon Arlaten
11 Hôtel de Ville
12 Les Alyscamps

Where to Stay
Hôtel Calendal 18
Hôtel d'Arlatan 14
Galerie Huit 20
Grand Hôtel Nord-Pinus 13

Where to Dine
La Charcuterie 15
Le Café Van Gogh 16
Le Cilantro 19
Querida 17

P Parking
i Tourist Information

0 — 1/8 mile
0 — 125 meters

Nice
Marseille
Arles

Arles is the gateway to the Camargue delta, French cowboy country. Once a Greek trading post and then a Roman colony, Arles is one of Europe's best-preserved Gallo-Roman cities, with ancient monuments casually woven into the town fabric of narrow medieval alleys, several superb Romanesque structures, modest homes with blue-shuttered windows, and cafes you may recognize from the paintings of Vincent Van Gogh. Residents are generally friendly, with a strong identity influenced by the nearby Catalan regions of France and Spain. Bullfights and paella are common, and locals often wear traditional Arlésian costume during Arles' frequent festivals and the *course camargue* START: **Arles is 32km (20 miles) southeast of Nîmes, 36km (22 miles) south of Avignon, and 80km (50 miles) west of Aix-en-Provence. TRIP LENGTH: 1 or 2 days.**

Money-Saving Travel Tip

Buy a **Pass Monument** (14€; 12€ students 18–25) from the tourist office and enter all Arles' sites and museums for free.

1 ★ **Musée d'Arles Antique.** Although it's away from the old center, visit this museum before the rest of Roman Arles: A series of model replicas show how the ancient city would have looked, which will help you to visualize the ruins later. Collections include Roman Christian sarcophagi, sculptures, mosaics, inscriptions from the Augustinian period to the 6th century A.D., and a rare bust of Julius

Ceasar found in the Rhône River. 🕑 *45 min. Presqu'île du Cirque Romain.* ☎ *04-90-18-88-88. www. arles-antique.cg13.fr. Admission 7.50€, 5.50€ students 18–25. Wed–Mon 10am–6pm. Closed some public holidays.*

2 ★★★ **Les Arènes.** Built at the end of the 1st century, this oval, UNESCO-protected arena measures 136 by 107m (149x117 yds.). With space for 20,000 spectator seats, it was the largest Roman monument in Gaul. Today, Provençal and Spanish bullfights have replaced the Romans' bloody affrays. Amazingly, it was transformed into a fortress during the early Middle Ages and contained 200 houses and two

An aerial view of Arles.

Say Olé!

Arles' ties to Spain are strong, and polemical bullfights (*corridas*, or *course camarguaise*) take place between Easter and late September. The bull is only killed during the Easter *corridas*; otherwise, fighters *(raseteurs)* use long forks to grab trinkets hanging from a cord between the bull's lyre-shaped horns. Seats range from 15€ to 85€ (see contacts below).

chapels. You can still see three of the four watchtowers that surveyed the city. ⏱ *45 min. Rond point des Arènes.* ☎ *08-91-70-03-70. www. arenes-arles.com. Admission 6€; 5€ concession. Nov–Feb 10am–4:40pm; Mar–Apr and Oct 9am–5:30pm; May–Sept 9am–6pm.*

Travel Tip

Tickets for Les Arènes and the Thermes de Constantin may be combined.

❸ **Thermes de Constantin.** These ruins of 4th-century baths were the Romans' preferred meeting place. *Rue Dominique Maïsto.* ☎ *04-90-49-59-05.*

❹ **Théâtre Antique.** In the 1st century B.C., pantomimes and

mimes would have played to audiences of 12,000 here. It was almost lost forever when medieval folk used its stones as a quarry. The remaining parts—twin marble columns, seats, stage, and orchestra— are still impressive, and are still used today for summer music concerts and dance shows. ⏱ *25 min. Rue de la Calade.* ☎ *04-90-49-36-25. Admission 3.50€, 2.20€ students 18–25. Nov–Feb 10am–4:30pm; Mar–Apr and Oct 9am–5:30pm (closed 11:30am–2pm); May–Sept 9am–6pm.*

❺ ★ **Musée Réattu.** The former collection of local painter Jacques Réattu includes dozens of works by Picasso, pieces signed by Dufy and Zadkine, and photographs signed by Henri-Cartier Bresson, among others. ⏱ *1 hr. rue Grand Prieuré.*

A bullfight in Arles' Roman arena.

An outdoor cafe near Arles' arena.

☎ 04-90-49-37-58. www.musee
reattu.arles.fr. Admission 7€; 5€
concession. Oct–June Tues–Sun 10am–
12:30pm, 2–6pm; July–Sept 10am–
7pm.

6 **Place du Forum.** On the site of
the original Roman Forum, this coveted square buzzes with cafes and
restaurants that fill up beneath the
erudite gaze of a statue of Frédéric
Mistral.

7 ★★ **Espace van Gogh.**
Vincent van Gogh spent only 15
months in Arles (from 1888), yet
through the filter of his neuroses
and what he called the town's "different light," he painted more than
300 writhingly vivid scenes now
prized by museums and collectors.
The town ironically owns none, but
this library, bookshop, and exhibition space—set in the former hospital where the misunderstood genius
stayed—looks just as it did on his
canvases. ⏲ 30 min. Place du Dr
Félix Rey. ☎ 04-90-49-37-53. Admission free. Daily 7:30am–7pm.

8 ★ **Fondation van Gogh.** This
exhibition space pays homage to
Vincent with tribute works by artists
such as Francis Bacon and Roy Lich-
tenstein. ⏲ 45 min. 24 bis Rond
Point des Arènes. ☎ 04-90-49-94-04.
www.fondationvangogh-arles.org.
Admission 6€; 4€ concession. Apr
to mid-Oct 10am–7pm daily, mid-Oct
to Mar 9:30am–noon, 2–5:30pm.

9 ★★★ **Église St-Trophime.**
Opposite an Egyptian obelisk taken
from the Roman circus across
the Rhône, this church's 12th-
century portal is one of the finest

The gardens of the Espace van Gogh.

achievements of the southern Romanesque style. Frederick Barbarossa was crowned king of Arles here in 1178. Don't miss the spectacular Gothic and Romanesque cloister, noted for its carvings. ⏱ *35 min. Place de la République.* ☎ *04-90-49-33-53. Free admission to church; cloister 3.50€, 2.60€ ages 18–25. Daily 8:30am–6:30pm. Church daily 8:30am–6:30pm. Cloister Nov–Feb daily 10am–4:30pm; Mar–Apr, Oct daily 9am–5pm; May–Sept daily 9am–6pm.*

❿ ★★ **Musée Arlaten.** The poet Frédéric Mistral led a movement to establish modern Provençal as a literary language. He founded this local folklore museum, filled with fascinating costumes and artifacts, using the money from his Nobel Prize for literature in 1904. Closed for renovation until 2013. *29 rue de la République.* ☎ *04-90-93-58-11. www.museonarlaten.fr.*

⓫ ★ **Hôtel de Ville.** While you're on place de la République, enter the city hall and look up at the unusual flat vaulting—a pure 17th-century marvel by Jules Hardouin Mansard, architect of Versailles, south of Paris.

⓬ ★★ **Les Alycamps.** Many tombs were looted, but the main alley of this ancient sacred burial ground is still as atmospheric as when van Gogh painted it. *Avenue des Alycamps. Admission 3.50€, 2.60€ concession. Nov–Feb 10am–4:30pm; Mar–Apr and Oct 9am–5:30pm (closed 11:30am–2pm); May–Sept 9am–6pm.*

Where to **Stay**

★★★ **Galerie Huit** MEDIEVAL CENTER Owner Julia de Bierre, author and creator of period interiors, welcomes guests into her sumptuous and unusual home, a

The bar at the Grand Hôtel Nord-Pinus.

17th-century mansion which doubles as an art gallery and a furniture restoration workshop. *8 rue de la Calade.* ☎ *04-90-97-77-93. www.galeriehuit.com. 5 units. Doubles 100€–150€. MC, V.*

★★ **Grand Hôtel Nord-Pinus** FORUM CENTER Expect glamor, even theater: Rooms are richly upholstered, and representations of bullfights decorate most public areas. *14 pl. du Forum.* ☎ *04-90-93-44-44. www.nord-pinus.com. 26 units. Doubles 170€–310€. AE, MC, V.*

★ kids **Hôtel Calendal** ARENES This place has an unbeatable position overlooking the arena. Rooms are basic, but there are kid's games in the shaded garden, and the restaurant serves simple buffet food. *5 rue Porte de Laure.* ☎ *04-90-96-11-89. www.lecalendal.com. 34 units. 109€–150€ double. MC, V.*

A room at the Grand Hôtel Nord-Pinus.

★★ **Hôtel d'Arlatan** MEDIEVAL CENTER   Roman vestiges lie underfoot in the lobby of this 15th-century residence with a walled courtyard pool. Rooms are furnished with authentic Provençal antiques. *26 rue du Sauvage.* ☎ 04-90-93-56-66. www.hotel-arlatan.fr. 47 units. Doubles 85€–157€. Parking from 13€. AE, MC, V. Closed Jan.

Where to **Dine**

★ **La Charcuterie** MEDIEVAL CENTER *LYONNAIS*   The cheery owner is proud of his Lyonnais origins and the top-class sausages and hams his Lyonnais restaurant cooks so well. Wash everything down with a local Côte du Rhone. *51 rue des Arènes.* ☎ 04-90-96-56-96. www.lacharcuterie.camargue.fr. *Menu 15€; a la carte 25€–30€. MC, V Lunch & Dinner Tues–Sat. Closed Aug 1–15, Dec 23–Jan 6.*

Le Café van Gogh ARENES *CAFE* The famous yellow cafe van Gogh chose for his work *Café de Nuit. 11 pl. du Forum.* ☎ 04-90-96-44 56.

★★★ **Le Cilantro** ARENES *FRENCH FUSION*   Enjoy ultramodern surroundings, inventive cocktails, excellent wine, and chef Jérôme Laurent's successful culinary inventions (think tuna with foie-gras—surprising but delicious). *31 rue Porte-de-Laure.* ☎ 04-90-18-25-05. *Menus 20€–25€ lunch, 35€–99€ dinner. MC, V. Lunch Tues–Sat, dinner Mon–Sat. Closed Mon Sept–June.*

Querida MEDIEVAL CENTER *SPANISH*   This cool restaurant/wine bar serves a heartwarming mix of Spanish tapas, like Pata Negra ham and grilled peppers in salt, larger dishes, and a long list of Spanish and—a rarity in France—New World wines. *37 rue des Arènes.* ☎ 04-90-98-37-81. www.querida.fr. *Fixed-price menu 18€. MC, V. Lunch & dinner Thurs–Mon. Closed 1 week in Nov & mid-Jan to mid-Feb.*

Avignon

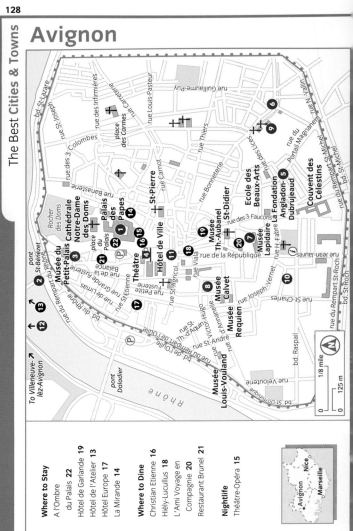

1 Palais des Papes
2 Pont St-Bénézet
   (Pont d'Avignon)
3 Musée du Petit Palais
4 Le Forum
5 Musée Angladon
6 Rue des Teinturiers
7 Musée Lapidaire
8 Musée Calvet
9 Chapelle des
   Pénitents Gris
10 Collection Lambert
11 Place de l'Horloge
12 Villeneuve-lez-Avignon

Where to Stay
A l'Ombre
   du Palais 22
Hôtel de Garlande 19
Hôtel de l'Atelier 13
Hôtel Europe 17
La Mirande 14

Where to Dine
Christian Etienne 16
Hiély-Lucullus 18
L'Ami Voyage en
   Compagnie 20
Restaurant Brunel 21

Nightlife
Théâtre-Opéra 15

+ Church
Ⓟ Parking
ⓘ Tourist Information

Once the center of Christendom, Avignon is still one of Europe's most elegant and captivating medieval cities, bordered by the Rhône River, and encircled by medieval ramparts. The papacy was headquartered here in the 14th century (during what the Romans called the Babylonian Captivity), and the church's legacy prevails, centered on the Palais du Papes (pope's palace). Avignon's city walls encompass architectural treasures, petite bustling squares, and animated café culture. Its festivals, museums, and progressive, contemporary attitude toward film and theater have earned it the distinction of being one of the European Capitals of Culture for the millennium. Accommodations are nearly impossible to find during the summer months and festivals, between July and September, unless you book well ahead. START: **Avignon is 37km (23 miles) northeast of Arles and 45km (28 miles) east of Nîmes. TRIP LENGTH: 2–3 days.**

---

① ★★★ **Palais des Papes.** Dominating Avignon from a hilltop, this 14th-century monument—headquarters of a schismatic group of cardinals who came close to destroying the authority of the popes in Rome—is one of the most notorious palaces in the Christian world. Although stripped of most of its finery, some treasures are still visible. The Chapels of St-Jean and St-Martial contain 14th-century frescoes attributed to the school of Matteo Giovanetti. The pope's bedroom in the Tour des Anges is decorated in tempera foliage on which birds and squirrels perch. In a secular vein, the studium (stag room)—the study of Clement VI—was frescoed in 1343 with hunting scenes. For wine buffs, the monument's very own **bouteillerie** (wine house) offers *dégustations* (tastings) during visiting hours. 🕐 *1 hr. Place du Palais des Papes.* ☎ *04-90-27-50-00. www.palais-des-papes.com. Admission (including audioguide) 11€; 8.50€–7€ reduced mid-Nov to Feb. July 9am–8pm; Aug 9am–9pm; Mar–June & Sept–Oct 9am–7pm; Nov–Feb 9:30am–5:45pm.*

The fortified city of Avignon.

Festival d'Avignon

Created by actor Jean Vilar in 1947 and known throughout the land as merely "the festival," this world-acclaimed jamboree of top-notch theater now encompasses the official Festival d'Avignon as well as a simultaneous fringe festival. This is *the* time to visit (or steer clear), when, for 3 weeks in July, every inch of available floorspace (including sidewalks and parking lots) becomes a stage. **www.festival-avignon.com**.

Money-Saving Tip

Buy a combined ticket for the Pont d'Avignon and Palais des Papes; or get an Avignon Pass (at any attraction) and pay full rate for your first visit then a reduced rate at all other museums in Avignon and Villeneuve-lez-Avignon.

② ★★★ kids **Pont St-Bénézet (Pont d'Avignon).** Spanning the Rhône, much of this 12th-century monument was washed away during floods several hundred years ago. Today it has only four of its original 22 arches. On one pier is the

A mime performing at the Festival d'Avignon.

two-story Chapelle St-Nicolas—one story in Romanesque style, the other in Gothic. If you have children who know the 'sur le pont d'Avignon' song, this is a fine spot for a rendition. There is also a small space recounting the song's history. 🕐 *50 min. Pont St Bénézet.* ☎ *04-32-74-32-74. www.palais-des-papes. com. Admission: 4.50€; 3.50€ concession (reduced to 4€ and 3€, respectively mid-Nov to Feb). July 9am–8pm; Aug 9am–9pm; Mar–June & Sept–Oct 9am–7pm; Nov–Feb 9:30am–5:45pm.*

③ **Musée du Petit Palais.** Overshadowed by its giant neighbor, Le Palais des Papes, this wonderful museum contains an important collection of paintings from the Italian and Avignon schools of the 13th to 16th century. Several galleries also display Roman and Gothic sculptures. 🕐 *45 min. Place du Palais des Papes.* ☎ *04-90-86-44-58. www.petit-palais.org. Admission 6€; 3€ students; under 18 free. Wed–Mon 10am–1pm, 2–6pm. Closed public holidays.*

Take a Break

④ **Le Forum.** Grab a table, a coffee, and a salad, and look out at the glorious Renaissance facade of Avignon's opera house. *20 pl. de l'Horloge.* ☎ *04-90-82-43-17. $.*

The Musée Angladon.

⑤ ★★ Musée Angladon.

Jacques Doucet (1853–1929) was a Belle Epoque dandy, dilettante, and designer of Parisian haute couture. He also collected works of art. He died a pauper, but his former home contains 6th-century Buddhas, Louis XVI chairs, and canvases by Cézanne, Sisley, Degas, Modigliani, Picasso, Max Jacob, and van Gogh. 🕐 *45 min. 5 rue Laboureur.* ☎ *04-90-82-29-03. www.angladon.com. Admission 6€; 4€ concession. Tues–Sun 1–6pm (closed Mon–Tues in winter).*

Love Boat

Avignon is enchanting by night when the monuments are lit. However, a summer dinner cruise along the Rhône is even more enthralling when love is in the air. **GBP Boats** (☎ *04-90-85-62-25; www.mireio.net) leave from Allées de l'Oulle.*

⑥ ★ Rue des Teinturiers.

Named after the textile-working Indians who lived here in the 13th century, this picturesque, cobbled street, shaded by plane trees, is one of the city's most atmospheric spots. Waterwheels still wind alongside the River Sorgue, while locals relax in cafes, secondhand bookstores, and art galleries.

⑦ Musée Lapidaire.

A 17th-century Jesuit church houses this archaeological museum, filled with fascinating Gallo-Roman statues, gargoyles, Etruscan artifacts, mosaics, and glass. 🕐 *45 min. 27 rue de la République.* ☎ *04-90-85-75-38. www.musee-lapidaire.org. Admission 2€; 1€ students. Wed–Mon 10am–6pm.*

⑧ ★ Musée Calvet.

This wonderfully restored fine arts museum has lovely colonnaded rooms that surround a courtyard. Inside Gobelin tapestries adorn the ground floor. French paintings from the

A waterwheel on the Rue des Teinturiers.

Buying Avignon's Wares

The Mouret hat shop.

Les Halles, on Place Pie, is a bustling covered market (7am–1pm) that doubles as a cooking school every Saturday morning (11am–noon), when chefs display their culinary talents before enthusiastic gastronomes. **Place Carmes** holds a morning flower and flea market on weekends. For high-street brands, head to **rue République.** The pedestrian streets around **rue des Marchands** are a maze of boutiques; and several famous designers flock to **rue St Agricol.** Avignon's oldest shop, **Mouret,** is a time-warp hatter, 20 rue des Marchands (☎ 04-90-85-39-38; www.chapelier.com), and **La Tropézienne** sells a rainbow of artisan-crafted sugary delights, 22 rue St Agricol (☎ 04-90-86-24-72; www.latropezienne.net).

18th and 19th century, silverware, clocks, and old locks make up other parts of a surprisingly wide-ranging collection of artifacts, including a good section of Impressionist and modern works. 🕐 *45 min. 65 rue Joseph Vernet.* ☎ *04-90-86-33-84. www.musee-calvet.org. Admission 6€; 3€ concession. Wed–Mon 10am–1pm, 2–6pm.*

⑨ Chapelle des Pénitents Gris. Tucked away on rue des

Teinturiers by a little bridge, the pretty 13th-century **Chapelle des Pénitents Gris** was the scene of a miracle, when, in 1433, flood water reputedly parted like the Red Sea to save it from destruction. *8 rue des Teinturiers. Open Tues & Sat 2–5pm.*

⑩ ★★★ Collection Lambert. Created in 2000 by Parisian art dealer Yvon Lambert, this remarkable gallery presents more than 350 works from his personal collection—a testimony

Yvon Lambert at the Lambert Collection.

The Place d'Horloge.

to his passionate engagement in several art movements—from Minimal, Conceptual, and Land Art from the '60s and '70s, to painting from the '80s, and photography and video from the '90s. ⏱ *50 min. 5 rue Violette.* ☎ *04-90-16-56-20. www. collectionlambert.com. Admission 6€; 4€ concession. July–Aug daily 11am–7pm; Sept–June Tues–Sun 11am–6pm.*

⑪ ★★ Place de l'Horloge. With its cafes, national theater, 19th-century city hall, and adjoining 15th-century clock tower, this vast, shaded square is the hub of Avignon life. During the Festival d'Avignon it becomes the home of a swirling carousel of *artistes.*

⑫ ★★ Villeneuve-lez-Avignon. This sleepy village opposite Avignon, just across the Rhône, contains some architectural gems built by the pope's cardinals. These include France's largest Carthusian monastery, the **Chartreuse du Val-de-Bénédiction,** rue de la République (☎ 04-90-15-24-24); the hauntingly beautiful **Église Notre-Dame,** place Meissonier (☎ 04-90-25-46-24), built in 1333; the **Fort & Abbaye St-André,** Mont Andaon (☎ 04-90-25-45-35), founded in 1360 by Jean-le-Bon to serve as a symbol of might to the pontifical powers across the river; and the region's richest repository of medieval painting and sculpture in the **Musée Pierre de Luxembourg,** rue de la République (☎ 04-90-27-49-66).

Cooking Lessons at La Mirande

kids The region's top chefs descend on **La Mirande's** (p 134) **Marmiton cooking school** each week to teach budding Cordon Bleu's the secret behind Provence's finest cuisine. It's an entertaining way to get a taste of the local way of life. Lessons include morning pastry making (80€), a kids' cooking class (46€), and evening classes (135€), where you share what you prepared with the class.

Where to **Stay**

A l'Ombre du Palais CENTER Nowhere in Avignon will you get better views of the Palais des Papes than in this B&B on the main square. Sabine, the eccentric owner, will cook for you in the evening, if you can't bear to leave (40€). *6 rue de la Vielle Juiverie.* ☎ *06-23-46-50-95. www.alombredupalais.com. 5 units. Doubles 125€–165€. MC, V.*

★ **Hôtel de Garlande** CENTER Down a discreet side street near the Palais des Papes and Place de l'Horloge, you can't ask for anything more central, nor for anything more charming for your money. This old mansion has just 12 rooms, all dressed in warm and cozy tones, and the friendly staff members treat you like a family friend. *20 rue Galante.* ☎ *04-90-80-08-85. www. hoteldegarlande.com. 12 units. Doubles 80€–118€. MC, V.*

★★ **Hôtel de l'Atelier** VILLE-NEUVE-LEZ-AVIGNON Hidden in the heart of Villeneuve-lez-Avignon, 2 minutes from the Pierre de Luxembourg museum, this 16th-century house has great nostalgic style: Soft, pale colored rooms have high beamed ceilings and neatly tiled bathrooms. A rear garden with potted orange and fig trees provides fruit and shade for breakfast. *5 rue de la Foire, Villeneuve-lez-Avignon.* ☎ *04-90-25-01-84. www.hotel delatelier.com. 23 units. Doubles 59€–115€. MC, V.*

★★★ **Hôtel Europe** CRILLON Sleep in this splendid 1580 town house, and you'll follow in the footsteps of Napoléon, Victor Hugo, Tennessee Williams, and Dalí. Rooms are spacious and tastefully clad in antiques, while the shaded courtyard is a fine spot for breakfast or dinner. *12 pl. Crillon.* ☎ *04-90-14-76-76. www.hotel-d-europe.fr. 44 units. Doubles 195€–820€. AE, DC, MC, V.*

★★★ **La Mirande** PALAIS DES PAPES This nest of opulence displays 2 centuries of decorative art, from the 1700s Salon Chinois to the Salon Rouge, with striped walls in Rothschild red. Rooms are huge, the garden is a tranquil haven, and the restaurant is Avignon's finest. Once a month, cooking lessons are organized in the vaulted basement kitchens. Parking 25€. *4 pl. de la Mirande.* ☎ *04-90-85-93-93. www. la-mirande.fr. 21 units. Doubles 310€–690€. AE, MC, V.*

The entrance to La Mirande.

A room at La Mirande.

Where to **Dine**

★★ Christian Etienne PALAIS DES PAPES PROVENÇAL
This 12th-century dining room, still clad in early-16th-century frescoes honoring the marriage of Anne de Bretagne to the French king in 1491, reaches new culinary heights. If you're on a budget, opt for the half-price lunch menu. Or splurge on a dinner specialty such as filet of perch with Châteauneuf-du-Pape. Reservations required. *10 rue Mons.* ☎ *04-90-86-16-50. www.christian-etienne.fr. Fixed-price lunch 31€; fixed-price dinner 65€–125€. AE, MC, V. Lunch & dinner Tues–Sat. Closed early Aug & late Dec–Jan.*

★★★ Hiély-Lucullus HORLOGE CONTEMPORARY FRENCH
Stunning Belle Epoque decor enhances grand, innovative cuisine such as St-Jacques scallops in a coconut crust, and Litchi mousse served with raspberries and sauterne jelly. Wine and service is faultless every time. Reservations required. *5 rue de la République.* ☎ *04-90-86-17-07. www.hiely-lucullus.com. Fixed-price menu 30€–50€. Menu gastronomique including wine 90€. AE, MC, V. Lunch & dinner daily.*

★★★ L'Ami Voyage en Compagnie HORLOGE PROVENÇAL
This is a secret the locals would prefer

The dining room at Hiély-Lucullus.

to keep: a family-run cafe-cum-antiques-bookstore that serves hearty, local cuisine, and decent wine. *5 rue Prévot Place St Didier.* ☎ *04-90-87-41-51. Mains 8€–14€. No credit cards. Lunch Mon–Sat; closed 2 weeks late Aug & 1 week Feb.*

★★ Restaurant Brunel CENTER MEDITERRANEAN
The contemporary red and steely gray interior of Chef Robert Brunel's restaurant is the refreshingly modern setting for delectables such as tarte tatin of tomatoes, duck moussaka, and tasty home-made patisseries. The 15€ lunch menu includes a glass of wine, a main, coffee, and cakes. *46 rue de la balance.* ☎ *04-90-85-24-83. www.restaurantbrunel.fr. Mains from 11€; menus 15€–33€. AE, MC, V. Lunch & dinner Tues–Sat.*

A Night at the Opera

Inside this festoon of 19th-century architecture, Avignon's **Théâtre-Opéra** makes for a perfect evening's entertainment with ongoing opera, ballet, chamber music, comedy, and symphony music concerts year-round. After the show, end your evening with a drink in one of the bars on place de l'Horloge. *Place de l'Horloge.* ☎ *04-90-82-42-42. www.avignon.fr. Box office Mon–Sat 11am–6pm. Tickets 5€–80€.*

Cannes

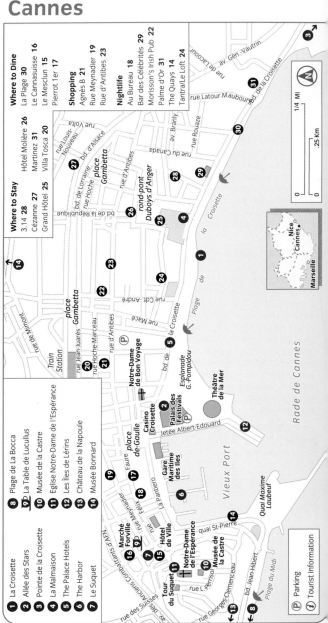

Thanks to its world-acclaimed film festival, this tinsel town on the Riviera is a gloriously excessive place to visit, even when the red carpet is starless. Bronzed beauties, megastars, groupies, and curious first-timers arrive in droves to experience the decadence. Sandwiched between the red rocks of the Esterel and two peaceful off-shore islands (Îles des Lérins), Cannes has attracted high-fashion crowds since 1834, when British Chancellor Lord Brougham stopped here to avoid an outbreak of cholera in Nice. He built a grand home, invited all his friends, and turned Cannes into a winter playground for the English aristocracy. More than a mere resort today, it has become a working port and a busy conference center 365 days a year. START: **Cannes is 37km (23 miles) east of Fréjus and 34km (21 miles) west of Nice. TRIP LENGTH: 1–2 days.**

① ★★ La Croisette. Lined with palm trees, luxury hotels, private beaches, designer shops, and expensive restaurants, this elegant, 3km (2 miles) promenade is where every film star and tourist visiting Cannes ultimately ends up lingering. Just east of the old port, at the top of La Croisette, lies the "bunker"— Cannes' Palais des Festivals—home to miles' worth of that iconic red carpet, a 2,400-seat auditorium, the Debussy Theatre, broadcasting studios, and the tourist office. Guided tours are available 2 days a week. Ask at the tourist office in the Palais des Festivals on La Croisette. ☎ 04-92-99-84-22. www.palaisdes festivals.com.

Tip

Unless you're bent on star-spotting or fond of crushing crowds and exorbitant prices, avoid Cannes during the film festival in May and from July through September.

② kids Allée des Stars. Between the Palais des Festivals and the gardens, kids (and adults) love the trail of more than 200 hand prints of celebrities who have walked Cannes' red carpet during the film festival.

③ ★ Pointe de la Croisette. Stroll eastward along the Croisette to this excellent vantage point, with views over La Napoule bay, Cannes, the Esterel, and Îles de Lérins. In the Middle Ages, a cross (croissette) lay here, facing the islands in defiance of the Saracen invaders. Today, artificial beaches and the **Palm Beach Casino** complex, with traditional games and slot machines, draw in the crowds. *Place Franklin Roosevelt.* ☎ 04-97-06-36-90. www. casinolepalmbeach.com. Daily 11am– 4am (till 5am summer).

La Croisette, Cannes' seaside promenade.

Cannes Film Festival

In 1939, French minister Jean Zay chose Cannes' sunny shores as the venue for an international film festival. WWII broke out, however, and so the first Cannes Film Festival (www.festival-cannes.fr) didn't take place until 1946, in a specially built Palais des Festival on the site of today's Hilton hotel. According to legend, architects forgot to include a projection window and had to chisel out a hole in front of crowds of impatient VIPs. The festival's popularity and renown grew to include star-studded juries presided over by the likes of Jean Cocteau, Marcel Pagnol, and, more recently, David Lynch. For 3 weeks in May each year, in the new Palais des Festivals, celebrities confront frenzied hordes to promote their films and their image, meet directors, and party until sunup.

Whoopi Goldberg's handprint on the Allée des Stars.

❹ ★ **La Malmaison.** This 19th-century pavilion, a former games and tea room, is all that remains of the Grand Hotel, demolished and replaced in 1963. Today, Cannes' Cultural Authority manages the space for two major temporary art exhibitions a year. *47 La Croisette.*

The Hotel Martinez.

☎ *04-97-06-44-90. Admission 4€, 2€ students 18–25. Wed–Mon 10:30am–1pm, 3–6pm. Closed during festivals and between exhibitions.*

❺ ★★★ **The Four Palace Hotels.** Cannes' four iconic palace hotels, dotted along the Croisette, are veritable legends—purpose-built palaces, with private beaches and spas for Cannes' rich and famous clientele. The **Majestic,** built in 1926, No. 10 (☎ 04-92-98-77-00; www.lucienbarriere.com), is part of the Lucien Barrière casino group and has three Venetian-style saloons from the 18th-century, 330 rooms, and two swish bars and restaurants. The oldest is the sumptuous **Carlton InterContinental,** No. 58 (☎ 04-93-06-40-06; www. ichotelsgroup.com), built in 1912 by Charles Dalmas. Its two white *coupoles* were reputedly modelled on the breasts of a Gypsy courtesan called La Belle Otéro. The **Martinez,** No. 73 (see p 142), is a 1927 Art Deco landmark with the largest

The Hotel Martinez dock.

suite in the world. Measuring a phenomenal 1,000 sq. m (1,196 sq. yds.), it costs 35,000€ a night. New kid on the block, the **Palais Stephanie**, No. 50 (☎ 04-92-99-70-00; www.hotel-palais-stephanie-cannes. com), with its panoramic terrace, was built on the site of the original Palais de Festivals in 1992.

6 The Harbor. Lines of fishing boats and luxury yachts bob lazily on the port at the foot of **Le Suquet** (see below), Cannes' old town. The west side is lined with shops and restaurants. Boats for the Lérins islands also embark from here. Near the port, the **Allée de la Liberté** is a shaded square where a daily

flower market (food and antiques Sat–Sun, 10am–6pm) gives way to *pétanque* matches in the afternoon.

7 ★ Le Suquet. Perched on the slopes of Mont Chevalier, a hill overlooking modern Cannes, the old town has one of the best covered markets on the Riviera, rue Forville (produce daily 8am–1pm; Mon antiques). Its streets are mainly pedestrian-only, jam-packed with restaurants. Rue Perrissol leads to place du Castre, with its 12th-century fortified château, church, bell-tower, and **Musée de la Castre** (see p 140).

8 Plage de la Bocca. Most of Cannes' sand is privately owned. Much of the 3km (2 mile)-long plage (beach) de la Bocca, however, west of Le Suquet (see above), is open to the public. The trouble is finding room to pitch your towel.

9 ★★ La Table de Lucullus. Away from the glitz and glamour of La Croisette, join loud shoppers from Forville Market for some cheap and delicious tapas (think fresh sardines, vegetable tarts, and shellfish) in a friendly, unpretentious bistro (a rarity in this town). *4 place du Marché-Forville.* ☎ *04-93-39-32-74. Mains 10€. No credit cards. Tues–Sun noon–2pm. $.*

The Hotel Carlton.

Shopping in Cannes

In Cannes, your budget will dictate the street you shop on. **Rue Meynadier** has the cheapest stores, tempting food and craft displays, and tourist trappings. Try **La Ferme Savoyarde,** No. 22 (☎ 04-93-39-63-68), for the best cheese in Cannes. **Rue d'Antibes, La Croisette,** and the streets that link the two are a paradise for luxury shoppers. Grab inspiration at **Christian Lacroix,** 14 bd. de la Croisette, then spend in **Agnès B,** 3 rue des Frères Casonova, before finding the perfect shoes at **Jacques Loup,** 21 rue d'Antibes. For regional goodies (crockery, oils, and liquors) try **Cannolive,** 16 rue Venizelos (☎ 04-93-39-08-19); and for a novel to read on the beach, browse the wide selection at **Cannes English Bookshop,** 11 rue Bivouac-Napoléon (☎ 04-93-99-40-08).

⑩ ★ **Musée de la Castre.** This 11th- to 12th-century castle was built by the Lérins monks to watch over Cannes' port. It offers breathtaking views from the 12th-century watchtower, and houses a small but fascinating collection of archaeological and ethnological items from five continents, as well as 19th-century paintings by local artists. 🕐 *45 min. Place de la Castre.* ☎ *04-93-38-55-26. Admission 3.40€; 2.20€ youths*

The Carlton's stretch of sand.

under 25. Sept–June Tues–Sun 10am–1pm, 2–5pm (until 6pm Apr–June, Sept); July–Aug daily 10am–7pm (Wed until 9pm June–Sept). Closed public holidays.

⑪ **Église Notre Dame de l'Espérence.** Just behind the Musée du Castre, this 17th-century Gothic church has sheltered the sacred bones of St-Honorat since 1788. *1 pl. du Castre. Open daily.*

⑫ **kids** ★★★ **Les Îles de Lérins.** In contrast to downtown Cannes' effervescence, the offshore islands of St-Honorat and Ste-Marguerite are hauntingly peaceful and teeming with wildlife, just a 15-minute boat ride offshore. **Île St-Honorat** is a striking, pine-studded religious backwater, founded in the 4th century, and now home to Cistercian monks who make and sell their own wines. Laypersons can visit the monastery, but discretion is imperative. **Île Ste Marguerite** is more touristy and ideal for a hike, swim, and a picnic. The star attraction is the **Musée de la Mer,** set inside the **Fort Royal** prison that Alexandre Dumas made famous in his novel *The Man in the Iron Mask.*

Nature trails *(sentiers)* are well indicated all around the island, and the **Plongée Club de Cannes** (☎ 04-93-38-67-57; www.plongee-sylpa.com) takes tourists diving around the island to see the wealth of aquatic flora and fauna. *Musée de la Mer (Marine Museum), Fort Royal.* ☎ *04-93-43-18-17. Admission 3.20€; 2.40€ youths under 25. Oct–Mar Tues–Sun 10:30am–4:45pm; Apr–Sept 10:30am–5:45pm; closed public holidays & lunch Jan–June. Catch Trans Côte d'Azur. Boats to both islands from quai Maubeuf (☎ 04-92-98-71-30; www.trans-cote-azur.com; tickets 12€ adults, 6€ under 10; 1st departure from Cannes 7:30am; last return boat to Cannes 6pm).*

⓭ **Château de la Napoule.** In 1918, after a scandalous love affair, rich Americans Marie and Henry Clews moved to France to shun society and invent their own world. The result is this fairy-tale castle, rebuilt from medieval ruins, entirely decorated with their own artistic creations—a grotesque, sculpted menagerie of gargoyles, monkeys, gnomes, and mythological creatures. *7km (4 miles) west of Cannes in Mandlieu La-Napoule.* ☎ *04-93-49-95-05. www.chateau-lanapoule.com. Mar–Oct daily 10am–6pm; Nov–Feb Mon–Fri 2–6pm, Sat–Sun 10am–5pm. Admission 6€ adult (guided visit 11:30am, 2:30pm, 3:30pm and 4:30pm), 7–17 yrs 4€.*

⓮ **Musée Bonnard.** In the town of Le Cannet, 2km (1¼ miles) north of Cannes, you'll find this new museum dedicated to one of France's most important 20th-century artists, Pierre Bonnard. The painter moved to Le Cannet in 1926, and stayed here until his death in 1939. Here, Bonnard painted what would become some of his most remarkable works—complex compositions of interiors and gardens,

Le Suquet tower.

created with intense colors and textures. *18 bd. de Carnot.* ☎ *04-92-18-24-42. www.lecannet.fr. Ask Le Cannet tourist office for information: place Benidorm, 73 av. du Campon, 06110;* ☎ *04-93-45-34-27; www.lecannet.fr.*

The chic boutiques of Cannes.

Where to **Stay**

The cafe at the Carlton.

★★★ **3.14** CROISETTE This fun, psychedelic hideaway is decorated in bright colors according to feng shui principles. Decor on each floor is inspired by a different continent. Spoil yourself in the rooftop spa, pool, and trendy beach restaurant. *5 rue François Einesy.* ☎ *04-92-99-72-00. www.3-14hotel.com. 96 units. Doubles 155€–700€. AE, MC, V.*

★★ **Cézanne** CENTER NORTH This boutique hotel (with its private beach) mixes bold colors and sleek contemporary design at a pleasant distance from the hurly-burly of the Croisette. *40 bd. d'Alsace.* ☎ *04-92-59-41-00. www.hotel-cezanne.com. 29 units. Doubles 130€–230€. AE, MC, V.*

★★ **Grand Hotel** CROISETTE This neo-1960s luxury hotel is flashy but surprisingly peaceful, thanks to its setting away from the Croisette. Its retro-chic restaurant, le Pré-Carré, serves excellent food. *45 La Croisette.* ☎ *04-93-38-15-45. www.grand-hotel-cannes.com. 76 units. Doubles 240€–410€. AE, MC, V.*

★★ **Hôtel Molière** CENTER This is the preferred haunt for journalists and film critics during the festival. Rooms are old-fashioned, but several have balconies overlooking a pretty garden. *5–7 rue Molière.* ☎ *04-93-38-16-16. www.hotel-moliere.com. 24 units. Doubles 123€–190€ w/breakfast. MC, V.*

★ **Martinez** CROISETTE Art Deco–style razzle-dazzle wows guests in this palatial hotel with wonderful sea views, a private beach, three gourmet restaurants, a cocktail bar, a heated pool, and a sumptuous spa by Givenchy. *73 La Croisette.* ☎ *04-92-98-73-00. www.hotel-martinez.com. 412 units. Doubles 270€–920€. AE, MC, V.*

★★★ **Hôtel la Villa Tosca** CENTER Right in the center of Cannes' shopping district, this small, elegant hotel is refreshingly unpretentious, with comfortable rooms. *11 rue Hoche.* ☎ *04-93-38-34-40. www.villa-tosca.com. 22 units. Doubles 82€–220€. AE, MC, V.*

Where to **Dine**

★★ **La Plage** CROISETTE *MEDITER-RANEAN* The 3.14 hotel's turquoise restaurant, with a surreal plastic ball theme, is very popular with trendy locals looking for good Mediterranean food and a prime location on the Croisette beach. *3.14 plage bd. de la Croisette.* ☎ *04-93-94-25-43. www.3-14hotel. com. Menus 30€–36€. AE, MC, V. Lunch & dinner daily.*

★★★ **Le Cannasuisse** LE SOUQUET *SWISS* Somewhat of an anomaly, this is a rustic spot for cheese lovers. Tuck into large portions of Raclette, fondues, and all sorts of other delights usually found in Alpine ski resorts. *23 rue de Forville.* ☎ *04-93-99-01-27. Menus 26€–27€. MC, V. Dinner Mon–Sat.*

★ **Le Mesclun** LE SOUQUET *FRENCH GOURMET* Warm tones and wooden paneling give this place an intimate feel, while such dishes as fricassee of lobster in wild mushroom sauce, and a heavenly crème-brûlée tantalize taste buds. *16 rue Saint-Antoine.* ☎ *04-93-99-45-19. www.lemesclun-restaurant.com. Menus from 35€. AE, MC, V. Dinner Thurs–Tues.*

★★ **Pierrot 1er** OLD PORT *SEAFOOD* Come here for delicious, well-priced fresh fish dishes served in a chic-rococo dining room overlooking Canne's bustling port. *51 rue Felix Faure.* ☎ *04-93-39-03-95. Mains 12€–30€. MC, V. Lunch & dinner daily.*

Cannes After Dark

Nightlife takes three basic forms in this glitzy town:

- **Star-Studded Tables d'hautes:** Sup or dine while celebrity-spotting at the Carlton's legendary **Bar des Célébrités** and seventh-floor hideaway (see p 138), the **Casino Club** (passport and smart dress required). The Michelin-starred **Palme d'Or** restaurant or ground floor cocktail bar at the Martinez (see p 142) also get constant VIP business.
- **Lounge-Bar Restaurants:** Several chic eateries stay open all night as a bar and disco. Join the mixed clientele at **Au Bureau,** 49 rue Félix Faure (☎ 04-93-68-56-36; www.bars-and-co.fr; daily from 5pm); and at the trendy **Tantra** and upstairs bar **Le Loft,** 13 rue Dr. Gérard Monod (☎ 04-93-39-40-46; www.dalton-group. com; daily evening).
- **Humble Pubs: Morisson's Irish Pub** stages live music 3 nights a week, 10 rue Teisseriere (☎ 04-92-98-16-17; www.cannes-nightlife.com; daily evening); and **The Quays** serves beer to locals and others near the old port, 17 quai St-Pierre (☎ 04-93-39-27-84; www.cannes-nightlife.com; daily evening).

The Best Cities & Towns

Marseille

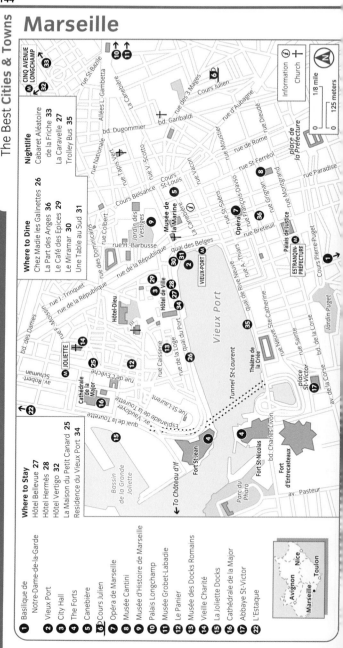

Nightlife
Cabaret Aléatoire
de la Friche **33**
La Caravelle **27**
Trolley Bus **35**

Where to Dine
Chez Madie les Galinettes **26**
La Part des Anges **36**
Le Café des Epices **29**
Le Miramar **30**
Une Table au Sud **31**

Where to Stay
Hôtel Bellevue **27**
Hôtel Hermès **28**
Hôtel Vertigo **32**
La Maison du Petit Canard **25**
Residence du Vieux Port **34**

1 Basilique de
   Notre-Dame-de-la-Garde
2 Vieux Port
3 City Hall
4 The Forts
5 Canebière
6 Cours Julien
7 Opéra de Marseille
8 Musée Cantini
9 Musée d'Histoire de Marseille
10 Palais Longchamp
11 Musée Grobet-Labadie
12 Le Panier
13 Musée des Docks Romains
14 Vieille Charité
15 La Joliette Docks
16 Cathédrale de la Major
17 Abbaye St-Victor
22 L'Estaque

Southern Marseille

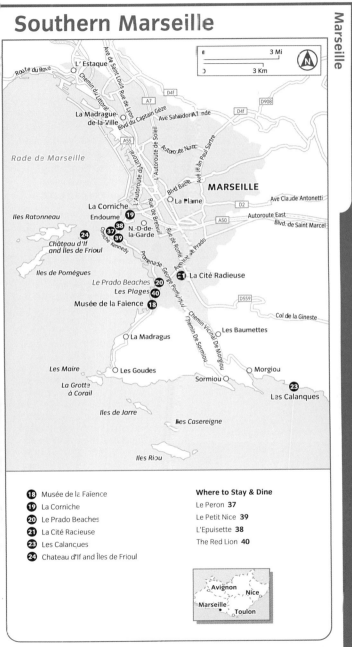

18 Musée de la Faïence
19 La Corniche
20 Le Prado Beaches
21 La Cité Racieuse
23 Les Calanques
24 Chateau d'If and Îles de Frioul

Where to Stay & Dine
Le Peron 37
Le Petit Nice 39
L'Epuisette 38
The Red Lion 40

France's first city, and European Capital of Culture 2013, has been a crossroads of culture, trade, and immigration for more than 2 millennia, since the Phoenicians founded it in 600 B.C. Today Marseille remains a fast-paced, forward-thinking port where Provençal traditions meet exotic influences from North Africa and the Middle East. Flanked by white cliffs, and facing the sea, its stepped streets and tranquil squares contrast with bustling 19th-century thoroughfares, souklike markets, chic shops, and the colorful Vieux Port where fishmongers animate the boat-lined quayside. As Marseille grew, it gobbled up much of the coastline, so stay an extra day or two to visit the outlying urban villages, beaches, and offshore islands that make this city one of the most captivating places on the Mediterranean. **START: Marseille is 32km (20 miles) south of Aix-en-Provence and 30km (19 miles) west of Cassis. TRIP LENGTH: 2–3 days.**

Transportation Tips

Public transport in Marseille is excellent—a cheap and user-friendly subway (Metro) and modern tramway cover most sites. To get your bearings, hop on the tourist bus. It covers more than 18km (11 miles) of the city's key sites. The tour begins at the Vieux Port and lasts for 1½ hours. One-day pass 18€; 2 days 20€. First tour 10am; last tour 4:15pm. Closed Jan.

The golden Madonna atop the Basilique de Notre-Dame-de-la-Garde.

❶ ★★★ **Basilique de Notre-Dame-de-la-Garde.** This Romanesque-Byzantine-style church, crowning a limestone mount, is the symbol of Marseille. Built by Henri Espérandieu in the mid–19th century, and topped by a 9m (30-ft.) gilded statue of the Virgin, it's visible from miles around. From its terrace, admire the sweeping panoramas over the entire city, Marseille's offshore islands, and the sea. Its interior is sumptuously decorated with colored marble and mosaic facings, and an exquisite marble Mater Dolorosa by Carpeaux is in the vaulted crypt. *Rue Fort-du-Sanctuaire.* ⏱ *1 hr.* ☎ *04-91-13-40-80. Free admission. Daily 7am–7pm summer, 7:30am–5:30pm winter. Metro: Vieux Port.*

❷ ★★★ **Vieux Port.** The history of Marseille and the Vieux Port are inseparable. Greek-Phoenicians landed here in 600 B.C., taking over a small Celto-Ligurian settlement. Legend has it that modern "Massalia" (or Marseille) was born of a love affair between Phoenician soldier Protis, and Gyptis, daughter of the Ligurian chieftain, who fell for his good looks. In the 12th century,

Marseille's ancient port.

d'Orves, a giant courtyard lined with restaurants, art galleries, and theaters. *Metro: Vieux Port.*

3 City Hall. The 17th-century City Hall (or Mairie) was the only building to survive WWII Nazi bombing on the Quai du Port. Built upon the site of a 13th-century trading center, it symbolized the city's great political status under Louis XIV. To sail across the port, take the ferry boat in front of City Hall (on Quai du Port, near the cross street rue de la Mairie) to place aux Huiles (free). *Quai du Port. Mairie closed to visitors. Ferry boat daily 7am–7:30pm.* ☎ 04-91-91-45-62. *Metro: Vieux Port.*

ships from Marseille took crusaders to the Holy Land, and in 1666, Louis XIV built two emblematic forts at the harbor entrance. In 1943, most of the Quai du Port was dynamited by the Nazis. Only the 17th-century City Hall remains. The surrounding restaurants and apartments are tasteful post-war constructions, built to plans by Fernand Pouillon. On the north side of the port, take a break in the Cours d'Estienne

Fresh Fish Market

Every morning from 8am to 1pm, head to **quai des Belges** and listen to the velvety drawl of Provençal fishmongers hawking their catches. Metro: Vieux Port.

4 ★ The Forts. The prosperity of Marseille's traders encouraged rebellion against Louis XIV. The Sun King built Fort St-Nicolas (closed to visitors), near today's Pharo gardens, to control both the city's

A fisherman with the day's catch.

Fort St-Jean and the cathedral.

and navigation. It also doubles as a Maritime museum. ◷ *45 min.*
Musée de la Marine et de l'Economie de Marseille. 9 La Canebière.
☎ *04-91-39-33-21. www.ccimp.com. Admission 3€ adult; 1.50€ child. Open daily 10am–6:30pm; closed public holidays. Metro: Vieux Port.*

6 **Cours Julien.** We love this bohemian spot for a coffee break, lunch, or dinner. Try **Le Sud du Haut** for traditional dishes (80 cours Julien; ☎ 04-91-92-66-64; www.lesudduhaut.com; Mon–Sat noon–2pm, Wed–Sat 8–11:30pm), then wander around trendy boutiques where artists design their own clothes and objects.

defenses and contain the rebels. He later gained complete military control by reinforcing the 12th century Fort St-Jean, on the north entrance. Today, Fort St-Jean affords fine views over the harbor and contains the **MUCEM,** a museum on Mediterranean civilizations, whose new wing (set to open in 2012) is one of France's most technically sophisticated architectural structures, built using Befup, an ultrastrong concrete. ◷ *2 hrs. Fort St-Jean, 201 quai du Port.* ☎ *04-96-13-80-90. www.mucem.eu. Open Wed–Mon 1–7pm; closed public holidays. Admission 5€ adult; 3€ concession. Metro: Vieux Port.*

5 **Canebière.** Marseille's illustrious thoroughfare was another of Louis XIV's urban designs. In the 19th century, splendid Haussman-style buildings were added, creating most of what you see today. American soldiers from WWII nicknamed it "Can a' Beer," but the name really stems from *canbe,* the hemp used to make rigging for boats. The best facade belongs to the oldest stock-exchange in France (founded by Henri IV in 1599), with intricate stone carvings that represent trade

7 **Opéra de Marseille.** The originality of the Grand Théâtre opera house stems from its two styles: 18th-century neoclassical and Art Deco. Inaugurated as a temple to music and dance in 1787, it

Marseille's infamous thoroughfare, the Canebière.

burned down in 1919, save for the walls and columns. As you gaze upward, contemplate the text inscribed on the top cornice: "Art receives beauty from Aphrodite, rhythm from Apollo, balance from Pallas, and movement and life from Dionysus." *2 rue Molière.* ☎ *04-91-55-11-10. www.marseille.fr. Tickets 8€–80€. Metro: Vieux Port.*

⑧ ★ Musée Cantini. If you love Fauvism, surrealism, and post-war art, this 17th-century private mansion won't disappoint, with leading works by Francis Bacon, Raoul Dufy, Max Ernst, Fernand Léger, Henri Matisse, Joan Miro, Dennis Hopper, and Pablo Picasso. ⏲ *1 hr. 19 rue Grignan.* ☎ *04-91-54-77-75. Oct–May Tues–Sun 10am–5pm; June–Sept 11am–6pm; closed public holidays. Admission 2€ adult; 1€ concession. Metro: Estrangin/Préfécture.*

⑨ Musée d'Histoire de Marseille. Hidden away behind the Bourse shopping mall, this museum tells the story of Marseille from pre-history to Gallo-Roman times through archaeological finds, models, and documents. Visitors wander through an archaeological garden where 1st-century Greek fortifications have been revealed, and you can see the remains of a 3rd-century Roman merchant shipwreck. ⏲ *1 hr. Centre Bourse, square Belsunce.* ☎ *04-91-90-42-22. Open Mon–Sat noon–7pm; closed public holidays. Admission 2€ adults; 1€ concession. Metro: Vieux Port.*

⑩ ★★ Palais Longchamp. Striking and elaborate, this Second Empire palace is a hymn to the glory of water—something the city lacked until an 85km (53 mile) canal was constructed in 1848 to channel water from the Durance River. A magnificent half-circle colonnade frames a giant fountain symbolizing the Durance, surrounded by

A cafe on cours Julien.

allegories of vine and wheat, on a chariot drawn by bulls from the Camargue. The fountain is flanked by the Fine Arts Museum (closed until 2012), the Natural History Museum, and a pretty park behind. ⏲ *1 hr. Musée d'Histoire Naturelle, Palais Longchamp.* ☎ *04-91-14-59-50. www.museum-marseille.org. Admission 4€ adult; 2€ concession. Open Tues–Sun 10am–5pm; closed public holidays. Metro: Cinq Avenues/Longchamp.*

⑪ ★★★ Musée Grobet-Labadie. Opposite the Palais Longchamp, this sumptuous bourgeois home was bequeathed to the city in 1919, and contains one of the most eclectic art collections in the region. Its original decor has been scrupulously maintained, displaying 10 salons, bedrooms, boudoirs, and libraries laden with treasures: paintings by Fragonard, Constable, and Monticelli; 18th-century furniture; medieval trinkets; Renaissance etchings; and a rare abundance of Aubusson and Gobelin tapestries. ⏲ *1½ hrs. 140 bd. Longchamp.* ☎ *04-91-62-21-82. Oct–May Tues–Sun 10am–5pm; June–Sept 11am–6pm; closed public holidays.*

The Palais Longchamp.

Admission 2€ adult; 1€ concession. Metro: Cinq-Avenues.

⑫ ★★ Le Panier. The hill on the north side of the Vieux Port is Marseille's oldest district, known as Le Panier. It was here that the Phoenicians first settled, and it has subsequently remained a magnet for immigration. Even today, as you wander along its narrow medieval stairwells and passageways, you'll hear a variety of languages, smell exotic cooking, and see laundry drying in windows. *Metro: Vieux Port/ Colbert.*

⑬ Musée des Docks Romains. This maritime museum covers Roman port activity in Marseille from 600 B.C. to A.D. 400 and woos visitors with fascinating objects recovered from local Roman shipwrecks. ⊕ *40 min. Place Vivaux.* ☎ *04-91-91-24-62. Oct–May Tues– Sun 10am–5pm; June–Sept 11am– 6pm; closed public holidays. Admission 2€. Metro: Vieux Port.*

⑭ ★★★ Vieille Charité. This former 17th-century workhouse is one of Marseille's most gorgeous

settings. It almost disappeared entirely until Le Corbusier campaigned to have it classified as a historic monument. Its centerpiece is a baroque chapel, by Pierre Puget, with a fabulous ovoid dome. The surrounding arcaded galleries contain the **Musée d'archéologie méditerranéenne** (Mediterranean Archaeological Museum) and the **Musée des Arts Africains, Océaniens & Amerindiens** (MAAOA or Museum of African, Oceanic, and Native American Art), France's only primitive arts museum outside Paris. ⊕ *2½ hr. 2 rue de la Charité.* ☎ *04-91-14-58-59. www.marseille. fr. Open Oct–May Tues–Sun 10am– 5pm; June–Sept Tues–Sun 11am– 6pm; closed public holidays. Admission 3€ for both museums. Metro: Joliette.*

⑮ La Joliette Docks. After the glorious 19th century, Marseille's wealth and power eroded, leaving widespread poverty and a reputation for crime. Nowhere was this more evident than at La Joliette Docks: Once the pride of Marseille and the largest port in Europe, it became a playground for druggies and petty criminals. This has now changed, thanks to the Euroméditerranée, a European-led rehabilitation program that has transformed the docks into a business district, soon to be adorned with emblematic skyscrapers—the CMA-CGM tower, by Anglo-Iraqi architect Zaha Hadid, already stands at 147m (482 ft.)—restaurants, and a promenade. To see how this area of Marseille will look in the future, head for the Euroméditeranée showroom inside the revamped brick **Compagnie des Docks et Entrepôts** warehouse. ⏲ *30 min. Les Docks, Atrium 10.3, 10 pl. de la Joliette.* ☎ *04-91-14-45-00. www.euromediterranee.fr. Open Mon–Fri 10am–1pm, 2–6pm (till 5pm Fri). Metro: Joliette.*

⑯ ★★ Cathédrale de la Major. In between the Panier and the Joliette Docks, this neo-Byzantine beauty, built between 1852 and 1893, was modelled on Saint Sophia of Constantinople. It houses the tombs of the bishops of Marseille. Its white stone and green stone cladding recall Notre-Dame-de-la-Garde (in the distance on the opposite side of the port), also designed

The Marseille cathedral.

by Espérandieu. Part of the building is a former 12th-century cathedral, sacrificed during the new construction. Regular organ concerts take place here. ⏲ *30 min. Place de la Major.* ☎ *04-91-90-53-57. Open Daily. Metro: Joliette.*

⑰ ★★ Abbaye St-Victor. Founded in A.D. 416, this intriguing example of religious architecture looks more like a medieval fortress

The city's old Panier neighborhood.

Abbaye St-Victor.

than an actual abbey. This is because Abbot Guillaume Grimoard (future Pope Urban V of Avignon) had it fortified in the 14th century, following the barbarian invasions. The crypts form a full-scale underground church and contain the Black Virgin—a painted, walnut statue of Our Lady of Confession. Each year on February 2, she leads a procession around Marseille commemorating the legendary arrival by boat of the three Saintes Maries. To celebrate this event, boat-shaped cookies called *navettes,* flavored with orange zest and orange-flower, are sold throughout the city. ⏱ *30 min. Place St-Victor.* ☎ *04-96-11-22-60. Open daily. Admission for Crypt 2€ (1€ youths under 18).*

Treat Yourself

The best *navettes* come from **Le Four des Navettes,** 136 rue Sainte (☎ 04-91-33-32-12; www.fourdes navettes.com), the oldest bakery in Marseille, dating from 1731.

⑱ ★★ Musée de la Faïence. Sublimely situated between the sea and the hills in Parc Montredon, this ceramics museum is set in the wonderful 19th-century Château Pastré. During WWII it was a sanctuary for the intelligentsia and for threatened Jews. Since 1995, it has showcased more than 1,500 ceramic items representing 7,000 years of history, including some spectacular faience pottery—an art that reached its peak in Marseille in the 18th century. ⏱ *1½ hours. 157 av. de Montre-don.* ☎ *04-91-72-43-47. www. marseille.fr. Admission 2€ adults; 1€ 12–18yrs; free 11 and under. Oct–May daily 10am–5pm, June– Sept Tues–Sun 11am–6pm; closed some public holidays. Bus 19. Get off at Madrague de Montredon. A mini-train transports visitors to the châ-teau via the gardens every 30 min.*

⑲ La Corniche. Beginning at the pretty **Parc du Pharo** peninsula (with its Napoleon III palace and sea views over the islands), the Corniche runs 5km (3 miles) along the south coast. The President

An Insider's View of Marseille

If you're looking for a novel travel experience in Marseille, contact **Marseille Provence Greeters** (www.marseilleprovence greeters.com), a fabulous association of volunteers who are passionately in love with their town, and ready to share their favorites with you—for free. It's a wonderful way to discover Marseille's secrets and explore the city like a local. Walks are tailored to individual tastes and last about 2 hours.

J. F. Kennedy stretch is dominated by late-19th-century villas and a sturdy viaduct that crosses the Auffe Valley. Don't miss the camera candy snugged behind the aqueduct in the **Vallon des Auffes Port**—a jumble of colorful traditional Marseille boats called *pointus*, fisherman's houses, and top-class seaside restaurants (see where to dine), with stunning views of shallow jade-green Mediterranean waters leading to the deeper blue waters off the Côte d'Azur. *Strange fact:* When the Mistral wind is blowing across the Corniche, the Frioul Islands and the Château d'If offshore appear closer to the mainland.

20 ★ **kids** **Le Prado Beaches.** Composed of landfill from metro excavations, the Prado Beaches are where the locals work up a tan. **Roucas Blanc** beach has a bike track, children's play area, volleyball court, and solarium. By day, **Escalé Borely** beach is a fine spot for windsurfing, before it reels in the party crowds at night. The pebbled **Bonneveine** beaches are for water-skiers and sea-scooters, and **Plage de la Vieille Chapelle** has yet more kids' facilities. *Metro: Castellane/Rond Point du Prado, then bus 19.*

21 ★ **La Cité Radieuse.** In the 1950s, Le Corbusier changed the face of modern architecture with his

Cité Radieuse—a revolutionary 18-story village of 337 apartments, schools, shops, sports facilities, a theater, and a hotel. Although it's a private residence, visitors are welcome. Opt for an organized tour with the tourist office or go it alone, but don't miss the roof: Its Daliesque features have earned it the nickname Maison du Fada (crackpot's house), and the sea views are tremendous. ⏱ *1 hr. 280 bd.*

The Vallon des Auffes Port.

The Île de Frioul, off the coast of Marseille.

Michelet. ☎ 04-91-16-78-00. www.
marseille-citeradieuse.org. Metro:
Rond Point du Prado then bus 21(S)
or 22(S) to Le Corbusier.

㉒ ★★ **L'Estaque.** In the northernmost part of Marseille, you'll find
a fishing port forever associated
with Impressionism, Fauvism, and
Cubism. Paul Cézanne, Georges
Braque, Raoul Dufy, August Macke,
André Derain, and August Renoir
flocked here between 1860 and
1920 to paint the eclectic scenery. A
signposted walking tour begins at
the harbor's jetty and presents the
district's colorful history.

Five minutes up the road (by car)
towards Corbières, don't miss the
new **Fondation Monticelli** (☎ 06-
82-87-69-07; www.association

monticelli.com), dedicated to the
Marseilles painter, Adolphe Monticelli, who inpired van Gogh. The
collection is set in a curious 19th-
century lookout building with
breathtaking views across the sea
and onto Marseille. Don't leave
L'Estaque without sampling the
chichis—the town's delicious donut
specialties. *Take bus 35 from the
Vieux Port or drive from place de la
Joliette to boulevard Dunkerque,
then onto the Littoral highway and
follow the Estaque exit.*

㉓ ★★★ **Les Calanques.** Within
15 minutes from the city, you're into
the Calanques massif—a 20km (12
mile) stretch of rocky creeks along
the coastline between Marseille and
Cassis. Their paradisiacal beaches

Marseille After Dark

For a late-night boogie, try the **Trolley Bus,** 24 quai de Rive-Neuve
(☎ 04-91-54-30-45; www.letrolley.com), which plays an eclectic
selection of music. Fight for a spot on the balcony at ★★ **La Caravelle,** 34 quai du Port (☎ 04-91-90-36-64), and enjoy the vintage
surroundings, a breathtaking port view, and free tapas. **The Red
Lion,** 231 av. Mendès-France (☎ 04-91-25-17-17), is a fine English-
style pub at the Prado Beaches, and the ★ **Cabaret Aléatoire de
la Friche,** 41 rue Jobin (☎ 04-95-04-95-04), offers cutting-edge live
concerts and the occasional disco

Marseille Shopping

Marseille has many ways of making you spend, but shopping has to be the most pleasurable. Check out the souk market area on place du Marché des Capucins, then the high street and designer offerings on rue St-Ferréol, rue Sainte, and rue de la Tour, before heading to the quirky boutiques and galleries around cours Julien.

and dramatic white cliffs attract walkers and sunbathers alike. They are home to exceptional protected wildlife, including Peregrine falcons and Bonelli's Eagles. Wear good shoes, take plenty of water, and watch your step—paths are often steep and uneven. For a relaxed approach by boat, excursions begin at the Vieux Port. For detailed maps, guided walks, and information on getting there by public transport, ask at the tourist office. Access is sometimes prohibited from July to mid-Sept. *Croisières Marseille Calanques boat trips, 74 quai du Port.* ☎ *04-91-58-72-23. www. croisieres-marseille-calanques.com.*

Inside the Château d'If.

Open all year. Times vary. Metro: Vieux Port.

㉔ ★★★ **Chateau d'If and Îles de Frioul.** From Marseille's mainland, you can see the mysterious silhouettes of four limestone islands: Pomègues, Ratonneau, If, and Tiboulen. The Île d'If is world famous for its 16th-century fortress, built under François I as a military stronghold, and the setting of Alexandre Dumas's epic tale, *The Count of Monte Cristo.* Although Monte Cristo was a fictional character, many real rebels, villains, and slaves were imprisoned here. In the 17th century, hundreds of Protestants also perished in the château's dank dungeons. The untamed Mediterranean environment of the Frioul islands is captivating. They constitute a refuge for flora and fauna such as sea lavender, the sand lily, and the yellow-legged gull. Summer concerts are held in the Hôpital Caroline on Ratonneau Island—a former hospice for yellow-fever patients. Pomègues houses the world's first official organic fish farm, and Port Frioul accommodates pleasure boats and yachts. *Frioul If Express Boat crossings.* ⏱ *25 min. Quai des Belges.* ☎ *04-91-46-54-65. www.frioul-if-express.com. Open all year; times vary (call for details). Metro: Vieux Port.*

Where to **Stay**

★ **Hôtel Bellevue** VIEUX PORT An Old Port location with views onto Notre-Dame-de-la-Garde, plus Marseille's trendiest tapas bar downstairs (La Caravelle, see p 154). Rooms are small but comfortable. *34 quai du Port.* ☎ *04-96-17-05-40. www.hotel-st-louis.com. 18 units. Doubles 84€–135€ w/breakfast. AE, MC, V. Metro: Vieux Port.*

★ **Hôtel Hermès** VIEUX PORT Recently renovated, with several rooms overlooking the port and Notre-Dame-de-la-Garde, this modern hotel is surprisingly calm despite its central location. *2 rue Bonneterie.* ☎ *04-96-11-63-63. www.hotelmarseille.com. 28 units. Doubles 70€–100€ w/breakfast. AE, MC, V. Metro: Vieux Port.*

★ **Hôtel Vertigo** GARE ST-CHARLES Half hostel and half hotel, the Vertigo offers funky retro design with ecclectic antique furniture. Share a hostel room or book a private double room—either way the atmosphere is cool. There is a communal kitchen if you want to make your own snacks and drinks. *2 rue des Petites Maries.* ☎ *04-91-91-07-11. www.hotel vertigo.fr. 58 beds. Hostel 25€ per person; doubles 60€–70€ w/breakfast. AE, MC, V. Metro: Gare St Charles.*

La Maison du Petit Canard PANIER The "house of the little

duck" bursts with character. Choose between self-contained apartments or a B&B plan. The generous hosts cook hearty meals for just 18€ upon request. *2 Impasse Sainte Françoise.* ☎ *04-91-41-40-31. http://maison. petit.canard.free.fr. 4 independent studios, 1 room. Doubles 60€–80€. No credit cards. Metro: Joliette.*

★★★ **Le Petit Nice** CORNICHE The most chic hotel and restaurant in Marseille opened in 1917. Run by Chef Gérard Passédat, this is France's only fish restaurant with 3 Michelin stars. Set in two mansions, rooms are spacious and brilliantly clad in plush fabrics, all with sea views. *Corniche Président-J.-F.-Kennedy.* ☎ *04-91-59-25-92. www. petitnice-passedat.com. 16 units. Doubles 195€–1,090€ w/breakfast. Main dishes 85€–250€. AE, MC, V. Bus 83b (to Endoume).*

★★ **Residence du Vieux Port** VIEUX PORT Decor in the rooms is based on Le Corbusier's Cité Radieuse (see p 153), so expect lots of 1950s-style furniture and block colors. Order room service and dine on your balcony, taking advantage of the breathtaking views. *18 quai du Port.* ☎ *04-91-91-91-22. www. hotelmarseille.com. 44 units. Doubles 180€–200€ w/breakfast. AE, MC, V. Metro: Vieux Port.*

A room at Le Petit Nice hotel.

Where to **Dine**

Dining Tip

If you plan to try *bouillabaise*, be sure your restaurant prepares it according to traditional methods; otherwise it's not the real deal. Prepared properly, it's going to cost you both time and money, but it's worth it.

★★★ **kids** **Chez Madie les Galinettes** VIEUX PORT *PROVEN-CALE* Dreamy cuisine, including Alibofis (sweet breads), and fish grilled to perfection. *138 quai du Port.* ☎ *04-91-90-40-87. Lunch menu 15€, dinner menu 22€–28€. MC, V. Lunch Mon–Fri, dinner Mon–Sat. Metro: Vieux Port.*

★ **La Part des Anges** ESTIENNE D'ORVRES *WINE BAR* Over 250 types of wine are on the menu (from 2€ up), plus hearty cheese and meat platters. *33 rue Sainte.* ☎ *04-91-33-48-18. www.lapartdes anges.com. Mains 6€–14€; a la Carte 18€–35€. AE, MC, V. Breakfast, lunch & dinner daily. Metro: Vieux Port.*

★ **Le Café des Epices** PANIER *MODERN PROVENCAL* A relaxed bistro with high end, inventive cuisine. Try the chocolate cake with tomato sorbet. *4 rue Lacydon.* ☎ *04-91-91-22-69. Menus 19€–35€ MC, V. Lunch Tues–Fri, dinner Tues–Sat. Metro: Vieux Port.*

★★★ **Le Miramar** VIEUX PORT *BOUILLABAISSE* Bouillabaisse aficionados flock to sample Chef Christian Buffa's version, which may be the culinary highlight of your trip. Reservations required 48 hours in advance. *12 quai du Port.* ☎ *04-9 91-10-40. www.bouillabaisse.com. Main courses 30€–50€;* bouillabaisse from 55€ per person (minimum 2). AE, MC, V. Lunch & dinner Tues–Sat. Metro: Vieux Port.*

★★ **Le Peron** CORNICHE *CONTEMPORARY FRENCH* Come here for gourmet seafood dishes and views to die for over the Île d'If and the sea. *56 pr. de la Corniche.* ☎ *04-91-52-15-22. www.restaurant-peron.com. Menus from 59€. AE, MC, V. Lunch & dinner Tues–Sat. Bus 83.*

L'Epuisette CORNICHE *SEAFOOD* Dine on fine Mediterranean cuisine in a beautiful setting—the dining room juts over the water, visible through glass on the floor, on a pretty port. *Vallon des Auffes.* ☎ *04-91-52-17-82. www.l-epuisette.com. Menu 55€–135€. AE, MC, V. Lunch & dinner Tues–Sat. Bus 83 (get off Vallon des Auffes).*

★★ **Une Table au Sud** VIEUX PORT *MODERN PROVENCAL* See and be seen tucking into creative cuisine such as chestnut and sea urchin soup. Reservations required. *1 quai du Port.* ☎ *04-91-90-63-53. www.unetableausud.com. Lunch 33€–47€, dinner 84€–125€. AE, MC, V. Lunch & dinner Tues–Sat. Closed Aug & Dec 23–27. Metro: Vieux Port.*

Traditional bouillabaise at Miramar.

Monaco

To Grande Corniche ↑
BEAUSOLEIL
av. de Villaini
To Menton ↗
Moulins
bd. des Larvotto
bd. Princesse Grace
MONTE CARLO
av. P. Doumer
FRANCE
bd. Princesse-Charlotte
bd des
14 15 ℹ
av. Princesse Grace
MONEGHETTI
la Costa
pl. du Casino
3
Plage de Larvotto
av. du Jardin-Exotique
av. de
av. d'Ostende
MONACO
⌂
Las Thermes de Monte Carlo
bd. de Belgique
bd. du Jardin-Exotique
Grimaldi
quai des Etats-Unis
Stade Nautique Rainier-III
ℹ Information
✉ Post Office
— Railway
bd. Albert-1er
Rainier-III
13 ✝
Port de Monaco
Parc Princesse Antoinette
12 LA CONDAMINE
Jardin Exotique
7
Station ✉
pl. du Canton
11
Charles-III
pl. de Armes
10 quai Antoine-1er
6
av. de la Porte-Neuve
1
MONACO-VILLE
✉
pl. du Palais
2
Heliport
FONTVIEILLE
8
av. St-Martin
Jardins St-Martin
0   1/5 mile
0   200 meters

Marseille
Monaco
Nice

1 Les Grands Appartements du Palais
2 Musée Océanographique
3 The Casino
4 Café de Paris
5 Avenue Princesse Grace & Beaches
6 Monaco Top Cars Collection
7 Jardin Exotique

Where to Stay
Hôtel Colombus 8
Hôtel de France 12
Hotel Métropole 15

Where to Dine
Avenue 31 16
Mozza 9
Quai des Artistes 10

Shopping
Galeries du
 Métropole 14
Rue Grimaldi 13
Rue Princesse-
 Caroline 11

Glamorous Monaco is a feudal anomaly. Controlled by the Grimaldi family since 1297, it's the only European state (outside of the Vatican) to have an autocratic leader. Taking up some of the most choice coastline on the Côte d'Azur, between Nice and the Italian border, it is exempt of all taxes and gains most of its revenues from gambling and tourism. Its world-famous casino, exclusive boutiques, luxury hotels, and annual Formula 1 Grand Prix make the principality a veritable playground for international jet-setters and the wintering wealthy. Monaco is split into five districts: Monaco-Ville (the old town on the rock *La Rocher*), Fonteveille (west), Moneghetti (northwest), Monte-Carlo (the central hub of luxury around the casino and opera house), and the busy La Condamine port area. To call Monaco from outside the borders add 00-377 at the beginning of the number. **START: Monaco is 21km (13 miles) east of Nice. TRIP LENGTH: 2 days.**

The Musée Océanographique.

❶ ★★★ Les Grands Appartements du Palais. Monaco's royal family resides here, at the Palais du Prince, which dominates the principality from "the Rock." It was built mainly in the 13th century, and then enlarged during the Renaissance. Tour the sumptuous *grands appartements* and get a glimpse of the dazzling red **Throne Room.** To see the 10-minute **Relève de la Garde** (changing of the guard), arrive at 11:55am. In one wing, the **Musée du Palais du Prince** (Souvenirs Napoléoniens et Collection d'Archives) holds a collection of mementos of Napoléon and Monaco. When the royals are in residence, this is the only part of the palace you can visit. ⏱ *1½ hr. Place du Palais.* ☎ *93-25-18-31. www.palais.mc. Palace admission 8€; 3.50€ ages 8–14. Palace Apr 10:30am–6pm, May–Sep 9:30am–6:30pm, Oct 10am–5:30pm, closed Nov–March. Museum admission 4€; 2€ ages 8–14. Museum late Dec–May 10:30am–12:30pm and 2–5pm; June–Sep 9:30am–6:30pm; Oct to mid-Nov 10am–5pm; closed late Nov to mid-Dec.*

❷ ★★★ kids Musée Océanographique. Albert I founded this museum in 1910 to display

The Prince's Palace, home of the Grimaldi family, rulers of Monaco since the 13th century.

The Royals Today

When Prince Rainier III died in 2005, his title went to his son Albert II. Albert and his sisters, Caroline and Stephanie, are the children of American film legend Grace Kelly, who died here in a car crash in 1982. Albert has two illegitimate children on record, and is engaged to former South African Olympic swimmer Charlene Wittstock. This fact, plus Caroline's failed first marriage and Stephanie's less-than-royal choice of suitors (a trapeze artist, an elephant trainer, and her bodyguard), makes them roving targets for the European tabloids.

exotic specimens he collected during 30 years' worth of expeditions. Some species were unknown before he captured them. The underground aquarium is one of Europe's finest. It contains more than 90 tanks of rare and wonderful species and a shark lagoon. The roof restaurant, La Terasse, is good for a light bite. ⏱ *1hr. Avenue St-Martin.* ☎ *93-15-36-00. www. oceano.mc. Admission 13€; 6.50€ ages 4–18; free under 4. Apr–Sept daily 9:30am–7pm (til 7:30pm July–Aug); Oct–Mar daily 10am–6pm. Closed during Grand Prix.*

Monte Carlo's legendary casino.

Travel Tip

The Monaco Tours tourist train operates from 10am to 5pm (from 10:30am in winter). It makes a 30-minute commented trip around Monaco. Jump on in front of the aquarium. ☎ *92-06-64-38. www.monacotours.mc. Closed mid-Nov to Feb.*

❸ ★★★ **The Casino.** Built between 1878 and 1910, this ornate Charles Garnier–designed palace is the draw for wealthy visitors. An

The Café de Paris.

old-fashioned law still prohibits Monégasque citizens and clergymen from entering the gaming rooms. Smart dress (jacket and tie for men) is de rigueur. The minimum bet on roulette tables is 2€. Stakes are higher in the private salons. *Place du Casino.* ☎ *98-06-21-21. www.montecarlocasinos.com. ID required; must be 18 for entry. Admission min. 10€. Daily from 2pm.*

4⃣ Café de Paris. Along with the casino and the sublimely rococo Hôtel de Paris, this turn-of-the-century cafe is a Monégasque institution. The upstairs salon affords fine views over the coastline. Place du Casino. ☎ *98-06-76-23. $$.*

5⃣ Avenue Princesse Grace and Beaches. Most of this seafront stretch is reclaimed land that leads to the **Jardin Japonais** (daily 9am–dusk) and the expensive **Monte-Carlo Beach Club,** 22 av. Princesse Grace (☎ 93-28-66-66). For free sunbathing, head just off avenue Princesse Grace to the **Plage de Larvotto** (☎ 93-30-63-84). At No. 17, a charming villa designed by Charles Garnier (creator of the casino and Paris opera

house) houses the **Musée National** (☎ 98-98-91-26; www.nmnm.mc; admission 6€, 3.50€ youths 18–25; daily 10am–6pm), inside the Villa Sauber, a curious museum of dolls and automata.

6⃣ ★ Monaco Top Cars Collection. The late Prince Rainier's private collection of more than 100 vintage cars contains treasures such as a 1903 De Dion Bouton. ⏱ *45 min. Les Terasses de Fontvieille.* ☎ *92-05-28-56. Admission 6€; 3€ youths 18–25. Daily 10am–6pm; closed Dec 25–Jan 1.*

The Galeries du Metropole.

Partying in Monaco

All VIPs frequent **Jimmy'z**, in the exclusive Le Sporting club seaside complex (av. Princesse Grace; ☎ 98-06-70-68; daily 10:30pm–late). The uber-cool also flock to **Le Maya Bar** for a meal and cocktail (24 av. Princesse Grace; ☎ 97-70-74-67; daily noon–2pm, 8pm–11:30pm) before heading down the road to the nightclub of the moment, **Karé(ment)** (10 av. Princesse Grace, ☎ 99-99-20-20; www.karement.com; Thurs–Sat 11pm–dawn).

The Musée d'Anthropologie Préhistorique.

7 ★★ **kids** **Jardin Exotique.** These gardens, clinging precariously onto cliffs overlooking the principality, are known for their cactus collection. There are also several dolomitic limestone grottoes to explore and the **Musée d'Anthropologie Préhistorique** (☎ 93-15-80-06), with its collection of Stone Age tools and mammoth bones. ⏱ *2 hr. Boulevard du Jardin-Exotique.* ☎ *93-15-29-80. www.jardin-exotique.mc. Admission (includes museum) 7€; 3.70€ children 6–18. Daily 9am–6pm (or sundown). Closed Nov 19, Dec 25.*

Shopping with Billionaires

For glitz, glamor, and designer style, the **Galeries du Metropole** (av. de la Madone, below the hotel; see "Where to Stay") is unrivaled. **Rue Grimaldi** is the principality's most commercial street, near the fruit, flower, and food market, Place des Armes (daily from 7:30am). **Rue Princesse-Caroline** is also loaded with bakeries and flower shops, and it's the closest thing you'll find to funkiness in Monaco.

Where to **Stay**

★★ **Hotel Columbus** FONTVIE-ILLE This contemporary address with big luxurious leather furnishings is a coveted crash pad, so to speak, for Formula 1 drivers and fans. *123 av. des Papalins.* ☎ *92-05-90-00. www.columbushotels.com. 184 units. Doubles 295€–325€. AE, MC, V.*

★ **Hôtel de France** CONDAMINE PORT A small, welcoming hotel, all dressed up in bright yellows and checkered fabrics. *6 rue de la Turbie.* ☎ *93-30-24-64. www.monte-carlo.mc/france. 26 units. Doubles 85€. MC, V.*

★★★ **Hôtel Métropole** MONTE CARLO CASINO Impeccably discreet, yet utterly luxurious, this timeless palace was entirely revamped by designer Jacques Garcia. Joël Robuchon (the world's most Michelin-starred chef, with 25 *macarons* under his belt) runs the two gourmet restaurants. A pool, solarium, and fabulous luxury spa (ESPA) also encourage relaxation. *4 av. de la Madone.* ☎ *93-15-15-15. www. metropole.com. 169 units. Doubles 385€–1,300€. AE, DC, MC, V.*

A waiter at the Café Quai des Artistes.

Where to **Dine**

★ **Avenue 31** LES PLAGES INTER-NATIONAL Located in a prime beach-front spot, this designer eatery, which covers food for all tastes (salads, Brasserie fare, fish dishes, and sushi), offers excellent value. *31 av. Princesse Grace.* ☎ *97-70-31-31. www.avenue31.mc. Lunch from 14€; dinner from 39€. AE, DC, MC, V. Lunch & dinner daily.*

Mozza MONTE CARLO/PLAGES ITALIAN This place offers 15 types of certified Italian Mozzarella cheeses, parma-ham to die for, some of the best pasta in Monaco, and decent wine to wash it down with. What more could you ask for? *11 rue d Portier.* ☎ *97-77-03-04. Mozza Platter 18€; mains 15€–29€. MC, V. Lunch & dinner daily.*

★★★ **Quai des Artistes** CONDA-MINE PORT BRASSERIE Wonderful, traditional French cuisine in a Parisian-style brasserie. On a warm day, tuck into a giant seafood platter under the arcades overlooking the port. *4 quai Antoine 1er.* ☎ *97-97-97-77. www.quaidesartistes.com. Menus: lunch 25€; dinner 53€–65€. AE, MC, V. Lunch & dinner daily.*

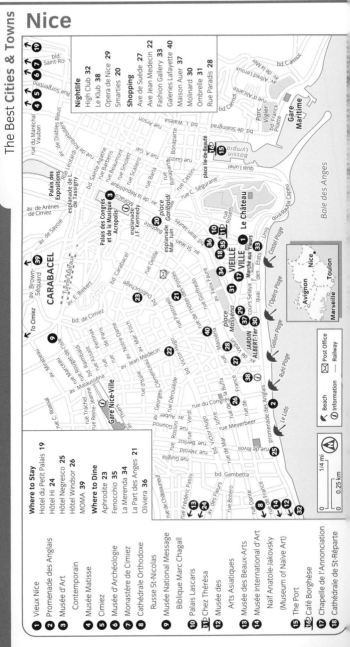

Nice

Nightlife
High Club 32
Le Klub 38
Opera de Nice 29
Smarties 20

Shopping
Ave de Suède 27
Ave Jean Medecin 22
Fashion Gallery 33
Galeries Lafayette 40
Maison Auer 37
Molinard 30
Ombrelle 31
Rue Paradis 28

Where to Stay
Hotel du Petit Palais 19
Hôtel Hi 24
Hôtel Negresco 25
Hôtel Windsor 26
MOMA 39

Where to Dine
Aphrodite 23
Fenocchio 35
La Merenda 34
La Part des Anges 21
Oliviera 36

1 Vieux Nice
2 Promenade des Anglais
3 Musée d'Art Contemporain
4 Musée Matisse
5 Cimiez
6 Musée d'Archéologie
7 Monastère de Cimiez
8 Cathédrale Orthodoxe Russe St-Nicolas
9 Musée National Message Biblique Marc Chagall
10 Palais Lascaris
11 Chez Thérésa
12 Musée des Arts Asiatiques
13 Musée des Beaux-Arts
14 Musée International d'Art Naïf Anatole-Jakovsky (Museum of Naïve Art)
15 The Port
16 Café Borghèse
17 Chapelle de l'Annonciation
18 Cathédrale de St-Réparte

Beach
Information
Post Office
Railway

Tracing the pebbled shores of the Baie des Anges (Angel Bay), and creeping its way up into the surrounding hillside, the capital of the Riviera balances old-world decadence with modern urban energy. Founded by the Greeks in the 4th century B.C., it fell to the Romans, and subsequently the House of Savoy in the Middle Ages, where it remained until Napoleon took it into France in 1860. By the 19th century, the Victorian upper class and tsarist aristocrats were flocking here for the mild winter climate. Nice's spectacular light (averaging 300 days of sunshine a year) also caught the attention of legendary artists such as Marc Chagall and Henri Matisse. Nowadays, Nice throbs with activity. With wonderful markets and an age-old cultural respect for good eating, it has become a paradise for foodies. **START: Nice is 21km (13 miles) west of Monaco and 37km (23 miles) east of Cannes. TRIP LENGTH: 2–3 days.**

Le Grand Tour

The best way to see Nice and get your bearings is to buy a 1- or 2-day pass for the "hop-on, hop-off" Grand Tour bus. It covers 12 sites around the city, and commentary is in seven languages. Buy tickets on board or at the tourist office. ☎ 04-92-29-17-00. www.nice legrandtour.com.

❶ ★★★ **Vieux Nice.** The old town is a maze of narrow streets, teeming with local life and studded with inexpensive restaurants. It begins at the foot of the **Colline du Château**— Nice's former stronghold, which

commands spectacular vistas (daily 3am–dusk; access via an elevator). It stretches to busy **place Masséna,** recognizable by its sienna-tiled roofs and Italianate facades. The fish market takes place every morning but Monday at **Place St-François** (Tues–Sun 6am–1pm). At the same time, the great **Cours Saleya** market is a flamboyant bustle of bright flowers, fresh fruit, and appetizing vegetables (Tues–Sun 6am–1:30pm). Monday it becomes an antiques market, and by evening it's the focal point of Nice's nightlife. The **Chapelle de la Miséricorde** is also here. One of the world's most beautiful baroque churches, it's a requisite stop.

Nice's Old Town.

The Promenade des Anglais.

② ★ **Promenade des Anglais.**
This world-famous promenade owes
its existence to English aristocrats
who, after a bad orange crop in
1822, occupied their idle workers
with the construction of this wide
boulevard fronting the bay. It's split
by islands of palms and flowers.
Stretching for about 7km (4 miles)
between the pebbled beach and the
town, it is lined by rows of grand
cafes, famous hotels, the Musée
Masséna, and villas, some decaying.
Farther east, the promenade
becomes **Quai des Etats-Unis,** the
original boulevard, lined with more
restaurants.

③ ★★★ **Musée d'Art Contemporain.** This modern building—
recognizable by its gargantuan
cube-head statue near the
entrance—is home to exceptional
artworks that trace the avant-garde

movement from the '60s to the
present. U.S. pop artists and European neo-realists are particularly
well represented. The roof affords a
fine panorama over the city and surrounding hills. 🕐 *1 hr. Promenade
des Arts.* ☎ *04-97-13-42-01. www.
mamac-nice.org. Admission free.
Closed public holidays.*

④ ★ **Musée Matisse.** In the
heart of a public olive tree garden,
the 17th-century Italianate villa on
Cimiez Hill is a museum in honor of
the artist who died in Nice in 1954.
The collection contains nude
sketches that will make you ques-
tion how early critics could have
denounced them as renderings of
"the female animal in all her shame
and horror." Other works include
*Nude in an Armchair with a Green
Plant* (1937), *Nymph in the Forest*
(1935–1942), and a chronologically
arranged series of paintings from
1890 to 1919. 🕐 *1hr. 164 av. des
Arènes-de-Cimiez.* ☎ *04-93-81-08-
08. www.musee-matisse-nice.org.
Admission 5€; 2.50€ under 18.
Wed–Mon 10am–6pm; closed Jan 1,
May 1, Easter, and Dec 25.*

⑤ ★★★ **Cimiez.** Five kilometers
(3 miles) north of Nice's *centre-ville*
lies the once-aristocratic hilltop
quarter of Cimiez. Queen Victoria

Nice's Museum of Modern and Contemporary Art (MAMAC).

The Musée Matisse.

used to winter here, in the Hôtel Excelsior, with half the English court in tow. The boulevard de Cimiez still clings to flamboyant remnants of this era. The startling array of magnificent villas ranges in style from Louis XV to Oriental and neo-Gothic. Founded by the Romans, who called it Cemenelum, Cimiez was the capital of the Maritime Alps province. *Drive north, take the Grand Tour, or catch buses 15 or 17 from place Masséna.*

⑥ ★ Musée d'Archéologie. Excavations in Cimiez uncovered the ruins of a Roman town. This museum allows you to wander the dig sites, including old baths and a 5,000-seat amphitheater still used for Nice's **Festival du Jazz** (☎ 04-97-13-36-86; www.nicejazzfestival. fr) for a week in mid-July. Nice's history is also recounted in the small museum through displays of ceramics, sculpture, coins, and tombs. ◔ 1½ hr. 160 av. des Arènes. ☎ 04-93-81-59-57. www.musee-archeologique-nice.org. Admission 3€, 1.50€ youths 18–25, free under 18. Wed–Mon 10am–6pm. Closed some public holidays.

⑦ ★ Monastère de Cimiez. A handful of Franciscan friars still live in this picturesque monastery,

Mardi Gras of the Riviera

More than a million visitors from around the world flock to the Côte d'Azur for the **Nice Carnaval** (www.nicecarnaval.com). Beginning sometime in February (usually 12 days before Shrove Tues), 3 weeks of wild celebration mark the return of spring. Festivities traditionally include spectacularly colorful, bulbous *corsi* (floats), *veglioni* (masked balls), confetti, and glorious battles in which young women toss flowers. The climax is a fireworks display on Shrove Tuesday that lights up the Baie des Anges.

Masked revelers during the Nice Carnaval celebrations.

Nice Shopping

Ave Jean Medecin is the main high-street shopping drag, where you'll find the **Galeries Lafayette** department store. For designer labels, target rue Paradis and avenue de Suède. Vieux Nice is cluttered with food shops, markets, and clothes creators. **Fashion Gallery,** 5 rue St-Suaire (☎ 04-93-80-33-73), brings together several brands in a hip cavelike shop, dressed in chandeliers. **Molinard,** 20 rue St-François de Paule (☎ 04-93-62-90-50; www.molinard.com), sells perfume and offers lessons on scent. **Ombrelle,** 17 rue de la Préfecture (☎ 04-93-80-33-13; http://best agno.exen.fr), has been selling marvelous umbrellas, parasols, and canes since 1850. And **Maison Auer**, 7 rue St-François de Paule (☎ 04-93-85-77-98; www.maison-auer.com) is renowned for its fabulous chocolate and Belle Epoque boutique.

famous for three Louis Bréa altarpieces and the tombs of Henri Matisse and Raoul Dufy, buried in the cemetery. The Musée Franciscain is decorated with 17th-century frescoes. It documents the painful deaths of the Franciscan martyrs. From the magnificent gardens, enjoy the vistas over Nice and the Baie des Anges. ⏱ *1 hr. Place du Monastère.* ☎ *04-93-81-00-04. Free admission. Museum Mon–Sat 10am–noon and 3–6pm. Church daily 9am–6pm.*

⑧ Cathédrale Orthodoxe Russe St-Nicolas. Ordered and built by Tsar Nicholas II, this cathedral is deemed the most beautiful religious edifice of the Orthodoxy outside Russia. It dates from the Belle Epoque era, when the Romanovs, their entourage, and everyone from grand dukes to ballerinas walked Nice's promenades. Richly decorated with icons, it can be seen from afar thanks to its ornate onion-shaped domes. It's closed to visits during church services. ⏱ *30 mins. Avenue Nicolas-II (off bd. du Tzaréwitch).* ☎ *04-93-96-88-02. www.acor-nice.com.*

Admission 2.50€; free under age 12. May–Sept daily 9am–noon & 2:30–6pm; Oct–Apr daily 9:30am–noon & 2:30–5pm.

⑨ ★ Musée National Message Biblique Marc Chagall. This handsome museum, surrounded by pools and a garden, is devoted to Russian-born Marc Chagall's treatment of biblical themes. It is the most important Chagall collection ever assembled, with some 450 of his oils, gouaches, drawings, pastels, lithographs, sculptures, and ceramics. ⏱ *50 min. Avenue du Dr.-Ménard.* ☎ *04-93-53-87-31. www. musee-chagall.fr. Admission 7.50€; 5.50€ youths 18–25; under 18 free. July–Sept Wed–Mon 10am–6pm; Oct–June Wed–Mon 10am–5pm.*

⑩ ★ Palais Lascaris. Imposing yet almost entirely invisible from the street, the baroque Palais Lascaris in the city's historic core is associated with the Lascaris-Vintimille family, whose recorded history predates the year 1261. Built in the 17th century, it contains elaborately detailed ornaments and ceilings frescoed with mythological scenes.

Inside the Palais Lascaris.

Classified as a historic monument, it retains many of its 18th-century panels and plaster embellishments. A pharmacy, built around 1738, complete with many of the original Delftware accessories, is also on the premises. 🕐 *30 min. 15 rue Droite.* ☎ *04-93-62-72-40. Free admission. Wed–Mon 10am–6pm. Closed some public holidays.*

⓫ ★★★ Chez Thérèsa. Locals can't get enough of Thérèsa's *socca*—a thin, crispy pancake made from chickpea flour, garlic, and olive oil. Along with the pizzalike *pissc-ladière* (anchovies and caramelized onions), it's the symbol of Niçoise street food. *28 rue Droite (Théresa also holds a stall on Cours Saleya market).* ☎ *04-93-85-00-04. $.*

⓬ ★ Musée des Arts Asiatiques. In a swanky, minimalist glass and metal construction near Nice's airport, this museum is a tribute to the sculpture and paintings of Cambodia, China, India, Tibet, and Japan. Inside are some rare ceramics and devotional carvings—many brought back by colonials during the 19th and early 20th centuries. Of special interest are the accoutrements associated with Japanese tea ceremonies, in the tea pavilion, shaded by gingko trees. 🕐 *1 hr. 405 pr. des Anglais.* ☎ *04-92-29-37-00. www.arts-asiatiques.com. Admission free. May to mid-Oct Wed–Mon 10am–6pm; mid-Oct to Apr Wed–Mon 10am–5pm.*

⓭ ★★ Musée des Beaux-Arts. This fine collection, devoted to the

Nice Nightlife

For a special evening, opt for a night at the **Opera de Nice** (4 rue St-François de Paule; ☎ 04-92-17-40-40; www.opera-nice. org; tickets from 8€–85€). This sumptuous hall, with red velvet and crystal chandeliers, programs international symphony orchestras, ballets, and operas. **Smarties** (10 rue Défy; ☎ 04-93-62-66-64) is a '70s-themed bar that serves delicious cocktails to a mixed-ages crowd. DJs spin nightly at **High Club** (47 pr. des Anglais ☎ 06-16-95-75-87; www.highclub.fr), and at gay-friendly **Le Klub** (6 rue Halévy; ☎ 06-45-22-07-97; www.leklub.net).

The Musée Asiatique.

masters of the Second Empire and the Belle Epoque, lives in a Genoese-inspired former residence of a Ukrainian prince. The gallery of sculptures includes works by J. B. Carpeaux, François Rude, and Auguste Rodin. Paintings include treasures by the Dutch Vanloo family dynasty (including Carle Vanloo, Louis XV's premier painter), and 19th- and 20th-century artists Felix Ziem, Jean-Francois Raffaelli, Eugène Boudin, Claude Monet, Armand Guillaumin, and Alfred Sisley. ⏲ *45 min. 33 av. des Baumettes.* ☎ *04-92-15-28-28. www.musee-beaux-arts-nice. org. Admission free. Tues–Sun 10am–6pm.*

Nice's harbor.

⓮ Musée International d'Art Naïf Anatole-Jakovsky (Museum of Naïve Art). The setting of this unique museum is the dazzling, pink-faceted Château Ste-Hélène—former home to the perfumier Coty. Anatole Jakovsky, one of the world's leading art critics, once owned the collection—some 600 drawings and canvases, and a rare panorama of naive and primitive art from the 18th century to the present. ⏲ *1hr. Château St-Hélène, avenue de Fabron.* ☎ *04-93-71-78-33. Admission free. Wed–Mon 10am–6pm.*

⓯ The Port. For 2,000 years, ships anchored in a natural bay at the foot of Chateau Hill. It wasn't until the mid–18th century, under the Duke of Savoy, that it became an official port. In the 19th century, it was deepened and extended, and the surrounding houses ornamented with typical Niçoise porticoes. Today ferries, liners, and yachts dwarf the traditional fishing boats. Flea markets are held regularly on the port's Quai Lunel.

⓰ Café Borghèse. Snug behind the port's old church, this is where locals come for cappuccinos, aperitifs, and copious portions of pasta and meat dishes. *9 rue Fodéré.* ☎ *04-92-04-83-83. www.cafe borghese.com. $.*

⑰ Chapelle de l'Annonciation.
St. Rita is the patron saint of the terminally ill and the desperate. This, her chapel, is an atmospheric, gilded baroque gem where hopeful visitors light candles for loved ones *1 rue de la Poissonnerie.* ☎ *04-93-62-13-62. Free admission. Daily 7:30am–noon, 2:30–6:30pm.*

⑱ Cathédrale de St-Réparte.
Set on what is easily Nice's loveliest square, this stucco- and marble-clad cathedral stands out by virtue of its brightly tiled dome. It is named after a young virgin, martyred in the Holy Land, whose body was towed back to Nice by angels (hence the name of Nice's coastline, Baie des Anges, or the Bay of Angels). Frequent classical music concerts take place here—particularly Baroque. *Place Rossetti.* ☎ *04-93-62-34-40. Free admission. Daily 8am–noon, 2–6pm.*

Where to **Stay**

Hotel du Petit Palais CIMIEZ
Sacha Guitry lived in this Belle Epoque building in the 1930s. The decor is plain but pretty, with fine views over Nice and a relaxing garden. *17 av. Emile Bieckiert.* ☎ *04-93-62-19-11. www.petitpalaisnice.com. 25 units. Doubles 100€–180€. AE, MC, V.*

★★ Hi Hotel NEW TOWN The avant-garde Hi offers nine different high-tech room "concepts." They range from hospital white-on-white to birch-wood veneer and acid green. The design is not always practical—some toilets are elevated to a position of theatrical prominence—but it's fun. *3 av. des Fleurs.* ☎ *04-97-07-26-26. www. hi-hotel.net. 38 units. Doubles 200€– 700€. AE, DC, MC, V.*

★ Hôtel Negresco PROMENADE DES ANGLAIS No other palace hotel on the Riviera can boast such a wildly kitschy assemblage of European art treasures (think Louis XIV portraits hanging near psychedelic Niki de St-Phalle statues). The

The Hotel Negresco.

carousel-themed breakfast room is a fun-fair unto itself, and the Michelin-starred restaurant is still one of the best in town. *37 pr. des Anglais. ☎ 04-93-16-64-00. www. hotel-negresco-nice.com. 145 units. Doubles 280€–650€. AE, DC, MC, V. Free parking.*

★★ Hôtel Windsor PROMENADE DES ANGLAIS   One of the most arts-conscious hotels in Provence is in a *maison bourgeoise* built by disciples of Gustave Eiffel in 1895. Each unit is a unique and often wild decorative statement by a different artist. The fifth floor holds the health club, steam room, and sauna. The

garden houses scores of tropical and exotic plants. *11 rue Dalpozzo. ☎ 04-93-88-59-35. www.hotelwind sornice.com. 57 units. Doubles 78€– 175€. MC, V. Parking 10€.*

★★★ MOMA NORTH OF CENTER The Arboireau family renovated their Belle Epoque–era house to create this gorgeous B&B, which doubles as an arts and events space. The jazz room is decorated in cool browns and whites, and the Pop Room incorporates Pop Art touches. Bliss! *5 av. des Mousquetaires. www.moma-nice.com. 2 units. Doubles 90€. No credit cards.*

Where to **Dine**

★★★ Aphrodite NEW TOWN *FRENCH*   This restaurant attracts foodies with the promise of molecular gastronomy—unexpected food associations that create flavor explosions in your mouth. The gourmet dishes include fish with smoked oranges and Irish beef smoked with Alpine pine leaves. The lunch menu

La Part des Anges wine bar.

is particularly good-value. *10 bd. Dubouchage. ☎ 04-93-85-63-53. www.restaurant-aphrodite.com. Lunch menu 25€; 3-courses 70€. AE, MC, V. Lunch & dinner Tues–Sat.*

★ Fenocchio VIEUX NICE *ICE-CREAM*   Hailing back to its former days as an Italian protectorate, Nice and ice cream go hand in hand. This is the best place in town, with around 90 flavors—some rather adventurous (think beer, thyme, tomato, and basil). *2 pl. Rossetti. ☎ 04-93-80-72-52. Scoop 2.50€. MC, V. Afternoon & evening Tues– Sun. Closed Dec–Jan.*

★★ La Merenda VIEUX NICE *TRADITIONAL NICOISE*   Noisy and always bustling, this rustic restaurant wows clients with Niçoise classics such as beef with orange polenta, blette tart (made from a sweet cabbagelike leaf), and *petits farcis* (stuffed tomatoes and peppers). *4 rue Raoul Bosio. No phone. Menus 25€. No credit cards. Lunch & dinner Mon–Fri. Closed Aug 1–15 & public holidays.*

Niçoise Cooking School

Rosa Jackson—a respected restaurant critic, author of several cookbooks, and a self-confessed food fanatic—runs a fabulous cooking school, **Les Petits Farcis**. She takes you on a trail of discovery around the Cours Saleya market before teaching you how to prepare an authentic Niçoise meal. This is the best cooking school in Nice. *7 rue du Jésus.* ☎ *06-81-67-41-22. www.petitsfarcis. com. Prices start at 160€ per person*

Rosa Jackson, who runs Les Petits Farcis.

★ **La Part des Anges** VIEUX NICE *WINE BAR* The aroma will lure you from the street into this intimate wine bistro. The sommelier-owner delights his regulars with fine wines and hearty regional cooking. *17 rue Gubernatis.* ☎ *04-93-85-71-53. Menus 25€. AE, MC, V. Lunch & dinner Mon–Sat.*

Oliviera VIEUX NICE *MEDITERRA-NEAN* Olive oil never has, and ever will, taste better than in this shop/cafe. Passionate owner Nadim serves delicious salads and pastas with oils so good, you can't stop sopping them up. Even the tiramisu gets a drizzle. *8 bis rue du Collet.* ☎ *04-93-13-06-45. www.oliviera. com. Mains 9€–17€; menu 35€. No credit cards. Lunch & dinner Tues–Sat.*

A server pours olive oil at Oliviera.

Nîmes

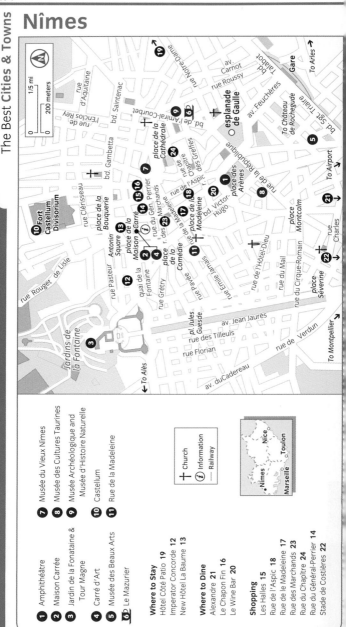

1 Amphithéâtre
2 Maison Carrée
3 Jardin de la Fonataine &
   Tour Magne
4 Carré d'Art
5 Musée des Beaux Arts
6 Le Mazurier
7 Musée du Vieux Nîmes
8 Musée des Cultures Taurines
9 Musée Archéologique and
   Musée d'Histoire Naturelle
10 Castellum
11 Rue de la Madeleine

✝ Church
ⓘ Information
— Railway

Where to Stay
Hôtel Côté Patio 19
Imperator Concorde 12
New Hôtel La Baume 13

Where to Dine
Alexandre 21
Le Chapon Fin 16
Le Wine Bar 20

Shopping
Les Halles 15
Rue de l'Aspic 18
Rue de la Madeleine 17
Rue des Marchands 23
Rue du Chapître 24
Rue du Général-Perrier 14
Stade de Costières 22

On the edge of the Camargue plain, the ancient town of Nemausus (Nîmes) grew to prominence during the reign of Caesar Augustus (27 B.C.–A.D. 14). It possesses some of the world's finest Gallo-Roman relics; its pièce de résistance is one of the world's best-preserved Roman amphitheaters, where bullfights now take place. An honorary part of Provence, due to its Provençal atmosphere and culture, it's technically in the nearby Languedoc. Spain's influence is also palpable—especially when cafes serving paella and sangria spill onto the streets at night, and during the Camargue running of the bulls through the streets. And Nîmes' influence on the U.S. is indisputable: It was a textile known as "serge de nimes," made here in the 18th century that crossed the Atlantic to become the clothing we all call denim (meaning "from Nîmes") today. START: Nîmes is 51km (32 miles) west of Avignon and 31km (19 miles) northwest of Arles. TRIP LENGTH: 2 days.

❶ ★★★ kids Amphithéâtre (Arènes). With its perfect classical proportions, Nîmes' Roman arena is a better-preserved twin of the one in Arles, and it's more complete than Rome's. It has two stories, each with 60 arches, and it was built of huge stones painstakingly fitted together without mortar. Concerts, ballets, and bullfights now take place where the Romans staged gladiatorial combat, wolf or boar hunts, and even mock sea battles during which the ring was filled with water. ⏱ *45 min. Amphithéâtre Romain de Nîmes.* ☎ *04-66-21-82-56. Admission 7.80€, 5.90€ children 7–17 and students; under 7 free.*

June–Aug daily 9am–7pm; Mar, Oct until 6pm; Apr–May, Sept until 6:30pm; Nov–Feb, 9:30am–5pm.

❷ ★★★ Maison Carrée. Built during the reign of Caesar Augustus, this temple is the pride of Nîmes. Consisting of a raised platform with tall, finely fluted Corinthian columns and friezes of acanthus leaves, it's one of Europe's most beautiful, best-preserved Roman temples. It inspired the builders of La Madeleine in Paris as well as Thomas Jefferson. It shows cultural and art exhibits, presented beneath an authentically preserved roof. ⏱ *45 min. Place de la Maison Carrée.* ☎ *04-66-21-82-56.*

Nîmes' Roman ampitheater.

The ancient Maison Carrée.

Roman river god. The grounds encompass the ruined **Temple de Diane,** Roman baths, and the sturdy bulk of the ★ **Tour Magne,** the city's oldest Roman monument. The tower is on a low, rocky hill called **Mont Cavalier,** a 10-minute walk north through the park. Climb 140 steps for views over Les Alpilles mountains. *Admission 2.70€; 2.30€ children 7–17 and students. Gardens Oct–Mar daily 7:30am–6:30pm, Mar–Oct until 10pm.*

Tip

Buy a combined ticket for the Arena, Maison Carrée, and Tour Magne for 9.90€ (7.60€ youths 7–17 and students); children 6 and under free.

Admission 4.50€; 3.70€ children 7–17 and students; under 7 free. June daily 10am–7:30pm; July–Aug until 8pm; Apr–May, Sept until 6:30pm; Mar, Oct until 6pm (closed 1–2pm Oct); Nov–Feb, 10am–1pm, 2–5pm.

❸ ★★★ kids Jardin de la Fontaine and Tour Magne. This oasis of greenery, laid out in the 18th century, surrounds the ruins of a Roman shrine. It's one of France's most beautiful parks, planted with rows of chestnuts and elms, adorned with statues, and intersected by grottoes, canals, and a natural spring that inspired Nimes' ancient name—Nemausus, after the

❹ ★ Carrée d'Art. Opposite the Maison Carrée stands its glass-and-metal modern-day twin. Inside is a research center and exhibition space with a library and newspaper kiosk. The **Musée d'Art Contemporain** displays French art from the 1960s to the present. The terrace affords a panorama of most of Nimes' ancient monuments and medieval churches. 🕐 *45 min. Place de la Maison Carrée.* 📞 *04-66-76-35-70. www.nimes.fr. Admission 5€;*

The Maison Carrée's modern counterpart, the Carré d'Art.

Bridge to the Past

Dating to 19 B.C., the Pont du Gard aqueduct stands strong, spanning the Gard River, 23km (14 miles) northeast of Nîmes. Its huge stones, fitted together without mortar, form three tiers of arches arranged gracefully into symmetrical patterns. One of the region's most vivid Roman achievements, it is now a UNESCO World Heritage site. Frédéric Mistral, national poet of Provence and Languedoc, recorded a legend touting that the devil himself constructed the bridge with the promise that he could claim the soul of the first person to cross it. From Nîmes, take N86 to a point 3km (2 miles) from the village of Remoulins, and follow signs.

The Ponte du Garde.

3.70€ children 7–17 and students. Tues–Sun 10am–6pm.

⑤ ★ Musée des Beaux Arts.

This early-20th-century building exhibits French paintings and sculptures from the 17th to the 20th centuries, as well as Flemish, Dutch, and Italian works from the 15th to the 18th centuries. Seek out the G. B. Moroni masterpiece, *La Calomnie d'Apelle,* and the well-preserved Gallo-Roman mosaic. ⏱ *45 min. Rue de la Cité-Foulc.* ☎ *04-66-67-38-21. www.nimes.fr. Admission 5.20€; 3.80€ children 7–17 and students; under 10 free. Tues–Sun 10am–6pm (until 9pm 2nd Thurs/month and every Thurs July–Aug).*

Take a Break

⑥ **Le Mazurier.** This tasteful Belle Epoque brasserie makes a fine spot for a relaxing coffee, a quick bite on the terrace, or an aperitif at the zinc bar. *9 bd. Am Courbet.* ☎ *04-66-67-27-48. $.*

⑦ Musée du Vieux Nîmes.

Housed in an Episcopal palace from the 1700s, this museum opened in the 1920s to preserve regional antiques, workday objects from the 18th and 19th centuries, and industrial artifacts. Most of the rooms are mock-up interiors illustrating daily life in Nîmes. ⏱ *40 min. Place aux Herbes.* ☎ *04-66-76-73-70. Free admission. Tues–Sun 10am–6pm.*

Musée du Beaux Arts.

Shopping in Nîmes

Most of Nîmes' shops are in the center of town, on rue du Général-Perrier, rue des Marchands, rue du Chapître, and the pedestrian rue de l'Aspic and rue de la Madeleine. A Sunday market runs from 8am until 1pm in the parking lot of the Stade des Costières—site of most of the town's football (soccer) matches, adjacent to the southern edge of the boulevard *périphérique* that encircles Nîmes. The covered market in Les Halles (rue des Halles) is open daily from 7am until 1pm.

⑧ Musée des Cultures Taurines. This small museum, in an annex of the Musée du Vieux Nîmes, is devoted to *tauromachy* (bullfighting) and the role it plays in Nîmes. 🕐 *30 min. 6 rue Alexandre Ducros.* ☎ *04-66-36-83-77. Admission 5.20€; 3.80€ concession. Tues–Sun 10am–6pm.*

⑨ kids Musée Archéologique and Musée d'Histoire Naturelle. Within the former Jesuit college, two museums showcase complimentary collections. The archaeology museum houses Roman statues, coins, pottery mosaics, and statues. The Natural History museum is a taxidermist's dream, with numerous stuffed animals, an interesting anthropological section, and some Iron Age menhirs. 🕐 *1hr. 13 bis bd.*

Amiral Courbet. ☎ *04-66-76-74-80 or 04-66-76-73-45. Free admission. Tues–Sun 10am–6pm.*

⑩ Castellum. In rue Lampèze, to the north of the center, archaeologists recently unearthed these remnants of a Roman water tower, which received water from the Pont du Gard aqueduct. Huge lead pipes, the holes for which are still visible, distributed the water across town.

⑪ ★ Rue de la Madeleine. Locals go about their daily business on this shopping thoroughfare. **Maison Villaret,** No. 13 (☎ 04-66-67-41-79), bakes and sells Nîmes specialty cookies *(croquants),* and the Romanesque facade at No. 1 belongs to the oldest house in Nîmes. Grab a seat at one of the many terrace-cafes on **Place aux Herbes,** just off Madeleine.

Inside the Musée du Vieux Nîmes.

Where to **Stay & Dine**

★★★ Alexandre (Michel Kayser) OUTSKIRTS *TRADITIONAL FRENCH* The most charming restaurant around is 8km (5 miles) south of Nimes in an elegantly rustic setting. Chef Michel Kayser satisfies the palate with dishes such as *ile flottante*—a variation on the French dessert, with truffles and *velouté* of cèpe mushrooms. *Rte. de l Aéroport de Garons.* ☎ *04-66-70-08-99. www. michelkayser.com. Reservations recommended. Mains 28€–54€; menus 64€–134€. AE, DC, MC, V. Lunch & dinner Tues–Sat. From town center, take rue de la République southwest to av Jean-Jaurès; then head south and follow signs to the airport (toward Garons).*

Hôtel Côté Patio CENTER A 10-minute walk from the Arènes, this brightly-colored friendly hotel offers excellent value. Rooms are small, but they're modern, airy, and well-decorated. Most rooms open out onto a large patio—a fine spot for breakfast. *31 rue de Beaucaire.* ☎ *04-66-67-60-17 www.hotel-cote-patio.com. 17 units. Doubles 63€–77€. MC, V. Parking 9€.*

★★ Imperator Concorde CENTER NORTH This hotel, the largest and finest in town, is adjacent to Les Jardins de la Fontaine. The cozy but ample rooms have traditional or French furniture, in one or another of the Louis styles. *L'Enclos de la Fontaine. Quai de la Fontaine.* ☎ *04-66-21-90-30. www.hotel-imperator.com. 62 units. Doubles 130€–250€. AE, DC, MC, V. Parking 13€.*

★★ Le Chapon Fin CENTER *TRADITIONAL NÎMES* This tavern-restaurant is an institution in Nimes. Specialties include foie gras with truffles, casserole of roasted lamb and eggplant, sauerkraut, and brandade of codfish. *3 rue du Château-Fadaise.* ☎ *04-66-67-34-73. www.chaponfin-restaurant-nimes. com. Reservations required. Mains 16€; menus 22€–30€. MC, V. Lunch Mon–Fri; dinner Mon–Sat.*

★ New Hotel La Baume CENTER NORTH One of my favorite nests in Nimes bears the name of the Marquis de la Baume, whose family built this 17th-century mansion. A magnificent staircase ornaments the interior courtyard and lends the place a sense of grandeur. In contrast to the stately exterior, the guest rooms are hyper-contemporary. *21 rue Nationale.* ☎ *04-66-76-28-42. www.new-hotel.com. 34 units. Doubles 140€–260€. AE, DC, MC, V.*

★ Wine Bar "Le Cheval Blanc" ARENA *TRADITIONAL FRENCH* Michel Hermet makes his own wine at vineyards that have been associated with his family for many generations. More than 300 varieties of wine are in stock. Typical dishes are magret of duckling, top-notch beefsteaks, and fresh fish. *1 pl. des Arènes.* ☎ *04-66-76-19-59. www. winebar-lechevalblanc.com. Main courses 11€–25€; menus 12€–21€ lunch; 18€–30€ dinner. AE, MC, V. Lunch Tues–Fri, dinner Mon–Sat.*

The Café Mazurier (see p 177).

St-Rémy

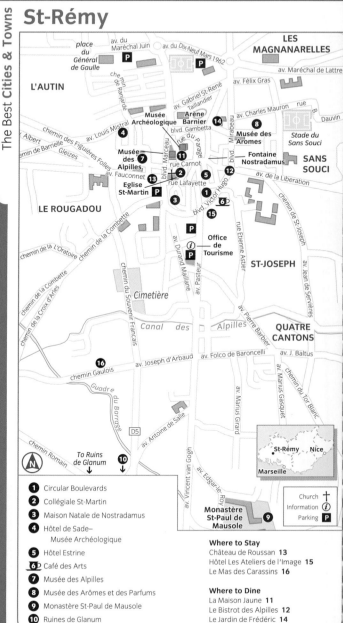

1 Circular Boulevards

2 Collégiale St-Martin

3 Maison Natale de Nostradamus

4 Hôtel de Sade–
   Musée Archéologique

5 Hôtel Estrine

6 Café des Arts

7 Musée des Alpilles

8 Musée des Arômes et des Parfums

9 Monastère St-Paul de Mausole

10 Ruines de Glanum

Where to Stay

Château de Roussan 13
Hôtel Les Ateliers de l'Image 15
Le Mas des Carassins 16

Where to Dine

La Maison Jaune 11
Le Bistrot des Alpilles 12
Le Jardin de Frédéric 14

Church †
Information (i)
Parking P

At the foot of the mysterious Alpilles hills, elegant St-Rémy is the archetypal Provençal town, with tree-lined boulevards, bubbling fountains, lively squares, atmospheric alleys, and chic residents who have made an art form of posing in cafes. Nostradamus, the physician and astrologer, was born here in 1503. Now it is more closely associated with Dutchman Vincent van Gogh, who committed himself to an asylum just outside town in 1889. Just south of the center, don't miss the ancient ruins of the city of Glanum, which date to the 1st century. START: St-Rémy is 21km (13 miles) south of Avignon and 75km (47 mile) northwest of Aix-en-Provence. TRIP LENGTH: 1–2 days.

❶ ★★ Circular Boulevards.
The most vibrant parts of town are the boulevards **Victor Hugo, Mirabeau, Gambetta,** and **Marceau,** which follow St-Rémy's old ramparts and positively burst with cafes, restaurants, and boutiques. **Place de la République** seals the loop with yet more activity and bustling cafe terraces. On Wednesday morning on the streets of the old town, vendors spread out their wares, including spices, olives, fabrics, and crafts. On Saturday morning, a small vegetable market is held near the Église St-Martin on boulevard Marceau.

❷ ★ Collégiale St-Martin. The 14th-century vestiges of this collegiate church line rue Hoche. The rest—aside from the bell tower, which also dates from the 14th century—had to be rebuilt around 1820, when the building caved in. The 5,000-pipe organ, renowned throughout France, is used for summer concerts. 🕐 30 min. Boulevard Marceau. 📞 04-90-92-10-51. Admission free. Daily 9–11am, 3–5pm, but check with tourist office.

❸ Maison Natale de Nostradamus. On December 14, 1503, Nostradamus was born to a wealthy family of merchants in this 15th-century house (no visits—seen from the street only). A doctor adept in astrology, astronomy, and clairvoyance, he wrote a collection of prophecies (Les Propheties, 1555)

A shop in St-Rémy.

construed to have predicted some of history's most pivotal events: the Great Fire of London (1666), the French Revolution (1789), Hitler's birth and rise to power, the assassination of John F. Kennedy, and even the destruction of the space shuttle Challenger. This abode, where he resided for 20 years before studying medicine in Avignon and Montpellier, would have been much larger than what remains today. The surrounding squares, narrow passages, and Renaissance mansions still convey a sense of St-Rémy's famously wealthy past. Rue Hoche.

The asylum in the monastery of St-Paul de Mausole, where van Gogh convalesced.

④ ★★ Hôtel de Sade–Musée Archéologique.

This stunning Renaissance mansion belonged to the family of the Marquis de Sade (1740–1814), France's infamous Libertine writer, imprisoned on several occasions for sexual debaucheries. Built on the site of Roman baths, it shows fragments found at Glanum, an impressive array of pre-Roman sculpture, and a stone lintel with grooves once used to display the severed heads of enemies. *Closed until further notice for renovations. Rue du Parage.* ☎ *04-90-92-64-04. Check with tourist office for new opening times and admission prices.*

⑤ Hôtel Estrine.

Joseph de Pistoye, judge to the Prince of Monaco, built this handsome mansion in 1748. It takes its name from Louis Estrine, a master rope maker from Marseille who resided here. Built from ashlar masonry, this three-story building pays homage to 20th-century artists such as Pierre Alechinsky, Edouard Pignon, Léon Zack, and Ossip Zadkine. Two rooms are devoted to the cubist artist Albert Gleizes, who lived in St-Rémy from 1939 to 1953. *Rue Estrine.*

☎ *04-90-92-34-72. Admission 3.20€; 2.30€ youths 18–25. Thurs–Sun, Tues 10am–12:30pm, 2–6pm. Wed 10:30am–6pm.*

⑥ Café des Arts.

The terrace of this cafe has been a center for people-watching since the 1950s. Soak up the hustle and bustle over a cool pastis or a glass of wine (no food is served). *30 bd. Victor Hugo.* ☎ *04-90-92-08-50. $.*

⑦ ★ Musée des Alpilles.

The former Mistral de Montdragon family mansion is devoted to the arts and traditions of the Alpilles area, with permanent collections on the landscape, flora and fauna, and *tauromachy*. The 16th-century galleried courtyard, embellished with a turreted staircase and a 20th-century

A statue of van Gogh at St-Paul de Mausole.

A fountain in St-Rémy.

bust of van Gogh by Ossip Zadkine, is a masterpiece unto itself. ⏱ *45 min. 1 pl. Flavier.* ☎ *04-90-92-68-24. Admission 3€; 2€ youths 18–25. Nov–Feb Tues–Sat & 1st Sun each month 2–5pm, Mar–June 2–5pm, Sept–Oct 10am–noon, 2–6pm. (July–Aug until 7pm).*

❽ Musée des Arômes et des Parfums. For thousands of years, Provence has been a center for fragrance and aromatherapy. This unexpected museum recounts that history with a vast collection of perfume bottles and stills, and some heady essential oils. ⏱ *40 min. 34 bd. Mirabeau.* ☎ *04-90-92-48-70. Free admission. Daily 10:30am–12:30pm, 2:30–7pm (closed Sun Sept–Easter).*

❾ ★★★ Monastère St-Paul de Mausole. Van Gogh rendered this asylum's 12th-century cloisters famous when he admitted himself as a patient in 1889, commencing a period of creative fury. Between treatments and moods of despair, he produced some 150 paintings in 1 year here, including *Starry Night*, *Olive Trees*, and *Cypresses*. The complex is a former Augustinian and Franciscan monastery that became a convalescence hospital in the 18th century. A self-guided walking tour leads visitors through van Gogh's daily paces, through the cloisters and surrounding gardens, indicating various spots that are still recognizable in his paintings. ⏱ *1 hr. Avenue Van Gogh.* ☎ *04-90-92-77-00. www.cloitresaintpaul-valetudo.com. Admission 5€; 3.50€ youths 13–18; under 12 free. Apr–Oct daily 9:30am–7pm; Nov–Mar daily 10:30am–4:45pm.*

❿ ★★★ Ruines de Glanum. In a bucolic spot, with rolling panoramas across the Durance Valley to Mont Ventoux, lie the mishmash vestiges of a Gallo-Roman settlement. Ruins include a triumphal arch from the time of Julius Caesar; the oldest cenotaph in Provence, called the Mausolée des Jules (a mausoleum raised to honor the grandsons of Augustus); and some impressive remains from a Gallo-Greek town of the 2nd century B.C. ⏱ *1½ hr. Av. van Gogh/rte. des Baux. From St-Rémy, take D5 1.5km (1 mile) south, following signs to les antiques.* ☎ *04-90-92-23-79. www.glanum. monuments-nationaux.fr. Admission 7€; 4.50€ youths 18–25. Apr–Sept daily 10am–6:30pm; Oct–Mar Tues–Sun 10:30am–5pm. Times subject to change.*

Where to **Stay**

★★ Château de Roussan

You'll be pressed to find more breathtakingly romantic lodgings than this château, Nostradamus's ancestral home, just outside St-Rémy. It's set in 15 acres of park-land, where swans swim in the lake and streams gurgle over rounded pebbles. Furnished with antiques, rooms are plush and romantic. *Route de Tarascon.* ☎ *04-90-90-79-00. www.chateauderoussan.com. 22 units. Doubles 180€–380€. MC, V.*

★★★ L'Hôtel Les Ateliers de L'Image

This radical photography-themed hotel, in a cinema converted by Roland Paillat, is an absolute treat. Rooms strike an ideal balance between comfort and concept—the tree-house suite, for instance, has its own private tree-house. The gardens are beautifully landscaped, with pools and even a

The Hôtel Les Ateliers de l'Image.

Inside the Hôtel Les Ateliers.

sushi bar. *36 bd. Victor Hugo.* ☎ *04-90-92-51-50. www.hotelphoto. com. 32 units. Doubles 165€–305€. AE, MC, V.*

★★★ Le Mas des Carassins

CENTER/GLANUM This converted 19th-century farmhouse is an oasis of calm, with views onto the Alpilles; a magnificent, lavender-filled garden, shaded by century-old olive trees; a pool; an excellent restaurant; and individually decorated, rustic rooms that leave you feeling pampered. *1 chemin Gaulois.* ☎ *04-90-92-15-48. www.masdes carassins.com. 14 units. Doubles 99€–216€ w/breakfast. AE, MC, V.*

Where to **Dine**

★★ **La Maison Jaune** CENTER
PROVENCAL This local haunt
charms, with its yellow facade and
two-story shaded terrace. Food is
fresh, flavorful, and inventive, with
dishes such as sardines roasted
with fennel, or roast pigeon on a
bed of red cabbage, drizzled with
hazelnut oil. *15 rue Carnot.*
☎ *04-90-92-56-14. www.lamaison
jaune.info. Menus 36€–66€. MC, V.
Lunch Wed–Sat, dinner Tues–Sat.
Closed some evenings in winter and
entirely Jan–Mar.*

The chef at La Maison Jaune.

★ **Le Bistrot des Alpilles** CEN-
TER *FRENCH* This bustling brasserie serves decadent cuisine, fresh
from the market. Try the specialty
lamb *gigot* cooked in the restaurant's open fire. Wine buffs will
appreciate the long wine list. *15 bd.
Mirabeau.* ☎ *04-90-92-09-17. Menus
25€; a la Carte 40€. Lunch and dinner daily. MC,V.*

Le Jardin de Frédéric CENTER
FRENCH Diners tuck into inventive
delights such as lamb in garlic sauce
and saffron flavored cod soufflé
here at this pretty green-painted
villa. *8 bd. Gambetta.* ☎ *04-90-92-
27-76. A la Carte 25€–30€. MC, V.
Lunch Fri–Wed; dinner daily.*

Outdoor seating at La Maison Jaune.

St-Tropez

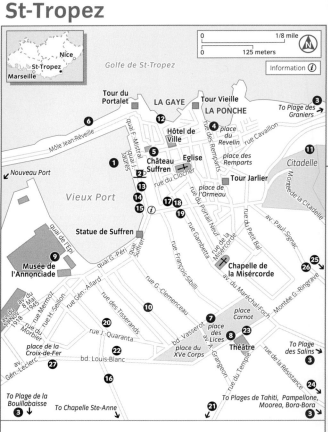

1 The Port

2 Café Sénéquier

3 The Beaches

4 La Ponche Quarter

5 Château Suffran

6 Môle Jean-Réveille

7 La Tarte Tropézienne

8 Place des Lices

9 Musée de l'Annonciade

10 Maison des Papillons

11 Citadelle

Where to Stay

Bastide de St-Tropez **24**

Hôtel La Ponche **12**

Hôtel Lou Cagnard **16**

Where to Dine

Le Café **23**

Le Girelier **13**

Spoon Byblos **25**

Shopping

Atelier Ivan Hor **19**

Bach'Stage **20**

Duf 100-Design **27**

Le Dépôt **22**

Lion de Sable **21**

Nightlife

Café de Paris **14**

Le Bar du Port **15**

Le Papagayo **18**

Le VIP Room **17**

Les Caves du Roy **26**

At its most **Bacchanalian**, between May and September, St-Tropez is as steamy and sun-kissed as ever. The Brigitte Bardot vehicle, *And God Created Woman,* may have put St-Tropez on the tourist map, but Colette also lived here, and Anaïs Nin famously posed for a little cheesecake on the beach in 1939 in a Dorothy Lamour–style bathing suit. In summer, artists, composers, novelists, and the film colony still drop anchor here in extortionately expensive yachts. The rest of the year, however, St-Tropez goes back to doing what it knows best: being a simple port, for simple (if not monied) folk, with a darling old historic center. **START: St-Tropez is 37km (23 miles) southwest of Fréjus and 50km (31 miles) east of Hyères. TRIP LENGTH: 1 day.**

---

1 **★★★ The Port.** Fishing boats, commercial vessels, and luxury yachts moor in this harbor while their owners disappear into St-Tropez's narrow streets lined with pink and yellow houses. Every year the port fills with more than 800 boats and 10,000 crew members for the annual Mediterranean regatta. Behind the tourist office, the **Porte de la Poissonnerie**—with its tiny fish market dressed in colorful mosaics and marble slabs—is the entrance to the old town and the Place aux Herbes miniature fruit, vegetable, and flower market.

St-Tropez's lively harbor.

2 **Café Sénéquier.** This legendary cafe is historic, venerable, snobbish, and, at its worst, dauntingly stylish. But no trip to St-Tropez is complete without a stop here. *Quai Jean-Jaurès.* ☎ *04-94-97-00-90. $.*

3 **★★ kids The Beaches.** St-Tropez has the hottest Riviera beaches. The best for families are closest to the center, including the **Plage de la Bouillabaisse** and **Plage des Graniers.** More daring are the 9.5km (6 miles) crescents at

The beach in St-Tropez.

Plage des Salins and at **Plage de Pampelonne,** with its riotous cash-only club **La Voile Rouge** (☎ 04-94-79-84-34)—the most outrageous, sexiest, and exhibitionist of the beaches (leave the kids at home). **Plage des Jumeaux** (☎ 04-94-55-21-80) is another active beach, drawing in families with its playground equipment. Notoriously decadent **Plage de Tahiti,** a strip of golden sand long favored by exhibitionists, occupies the north end of the 5.5km-long (3 miles) Pampelonne. Gay men tend to gravitate to **Coco Beach** in Ramatuelle, about 6.5km (4 miles) from the center of St-Tropez.

A sunbather.

❹ ★★★ **La Ponche Quarter.** *Ponche*—or *pouncho* in Provençal—means point or extremity. Tucked between the port and the citadel, this district is the oldest and prettiest part of town, once inhabited by fishermen and artists.

❺ **Château Suffran.** On place de l'Hôtel de Ville (City Hall), the massive 16th-century tower is all that remains of the Château Suffran, home to the seigneurs of St-Tropez. It houses occasional art and photography exhibitions.

❻ ★ **Môle Jean-Réveille.** For sweeping vistas along the coastline, head to this stone jetty. It was destroyed during the Allied landings in 1944, rebuilt in 1950, and extended in 1966. The beacon at the end is an exact replica of the original, dating from 1837.

❼ ★★ **La Tarte Tropézienne.** St-Tropez's famous eponymous cake was invented here by Polish baker Alexandre Micka. It is a spongelike cake, flavored with orange-blossom, filled with cream-custard, and sprinkled with icing sugar. Delightful! *Place des Lices.* ☎ 04-94-97-04-69. www.tarte-tropezienne-traiteur.com. Daily 6:30am–9pm.

❽ ★★ **Place des Lices.** After the port, this is St-Tropez's second

Lively Place des Lices.

hub—a favorite local meeting place, lined with restaurants, plane trees, and sandy patches for playing *boules*. A market is held here every Tuesday and Saturday morning.

⑨ ★★★ Musée de l'Annonciade. Near the harbor, this museum occupies the former chapel of the Annonciade. It houses one of the Riviera's finest collections of post-Impressionist masters, many of whom depicted the port of St-Tropez. The collection includes works such as Van Dongen's *Women of the Balustrade,* as well as paintings and sculptures by Pierre Bonnard, Henri Matisse, Georges Braque, Raoul Dufy, Maurice Utrillo, Georges Seurat, André Derain, and

Where to Drop Euros in St-Trop

Most shops in St-Tropez are tucked in out-of-the-way corners of the old town. Big names include Hermès, Sonia Rykiel, and Dior. For discounts, **Le Dépot** (bd. Louis-Blanc; ☎ 04-94-97-80-10) sells secondhand designer clothes, some still with original tags. **Bach'Stage** (3 rue Joseph Quaranta; ☎ 04-94-97-00-60) is the town's first concept store, selling everything from prêt-à-porter to accessories and furniture. Chic **Lion de Sable** (av. Paul Roussel; ☎ 04-94-97-21-05) offers interesting objects to decorate your home. For intriguing modern art, head to **Atelier Ivon Hor** (40 rue Gambetta & 20 rue des Ramparts; ☎ 04-94-97-73-82), where artist Ivon Hor sells eccentric 3D paintings, which often feature origami paper boats. Try **Dufloo-Design** (34 bd. Louis Blanc; ☎ 06-98-43-62-57) for quirky indoor and outdoor ornaments.

The Bravade of St-Tropez

Every year from May 16th to 18th, St-Tropez becomes a sea of red and white—the colors of the Corsairs—as locals celebrate the bravery *(bravade)* of their patron Saint Tropez. St. Paul converted the Roman citizen Tropes to Christianity. Refusing to renounce his faith before the Romans, he was decapitated, and his body set to sea. It washed up on the shores of St-Tropez, where the residents worshiped him as a martyr. Twenty-one shots of gunpowder mark the beginning of the celebrations, including a religious parade, conducted in traditional dress, with much merrymaking.

Aristide Maillol. ⏱ *45 min. Place Grammont.* ☎ *04-94-17-84-10. Admission 6€; 4€ age 12–18; under 12 free. Wed–Mon 10am–noon, 3–7pm (2–6pm Oct–May). Closed Nov & public holidays.*

⑩ ★ Maison des Papillons. Hidden down a narrow alley, this Provençal house is filled with mounted butterflies. Entomologist Dany Lartigue (son of the photographer J. H. Lartigue) has collected more than 25,000 specimens from all four corners of the earth—all displayed in an informative and artistic manner. ⏱ *30 min. 9 rue*

Etienne-Berny. ☎ *04-94-97-63-45. http://maisondespapillons.ifrance. com. Admission 3€ (free under 10). Wed–Mon 10am–noon, 3–7pm.*

⑪ kids Citadelle. At the top of a steep, touristy street, the citadel is a fine example of 16th- and 17th-century military architecture. Today it houses a somewhat forlorn marine museum, but it's worth a visit for the spectacular views from the ramparts over the Bay of St-Tropez, Ste-Maxime, and the Maure hills. ⏱ *30 min. La Citadelle.* ☎ *04-94-97-59-43. Museum admission 4€; free under 8. Wed–Sun 10am–12:30pm, 1:30–6:30pm.*

Mounted butterfly specimens at the Maison des Papillons.

Where to **Stay**

★★★ La Bastide de Saint-Tropez NORTH   This pink *mas* (country house) is an elegant, friendly oasis for those who can afford to splurge here, north of Place des Lices, in an exotic garden that overlooks a swimming pool. Rooms are smothered in plush fabrics, many have a private terrace, and the restaurant (dine by the pool or in the beautiful glass veranda) serves fine Provençal cuisine. *Route des Carles.* ☎ *04-94-55-82-55. www.bastide-saint-tropez.com. 26 units. Double 260€–710€. AE, MC, V.*

★ Hôtel La Ponche PORT   This family-run hotel is the most discreet and charming establishment in town, with the least celebrity ostentatiousness. Filled with the original airy paintings of Jacques Cordier, who died in 1978, the redecorated rooms are well equipped and open onto sea views. Sun-colored walls with subtle lighting lend a homey feel. *Port des Pêcheurs.* ☎ *04-94-97-02-53. www.laponche.com. 18 units. Doubles 240€–555€. AE, MC, V. Parking 21€. Closed Nov to mid-Feb.*

The pool at the Bastide de St-Tropez.

★★ Hôtel Lou Cagnard CENTER   This charming centrally-located Provençal *bastide* (house) offers bright and airy rooms and a sumptuous garden for an excellent value. *18 av. Paul Roussel.* ☎ *04-94-97-04-24. www.hotel-lou-cagnard.com. 19 units. Doubles 56€–140€. AE, MC, V.*

Where to **Party**

On the lobby level of the Hôtel Byblos, **Les Caves du Roy,** avenue Paul-Signac (☎ 04-94-97-16-02; www.byblos.com), is the most self-consciously chic nightclub in St-Tropez. Entrance is free, but drink prices begin at a whopping 18€. **Le Papagayo,** in the Résidence du Nouveau-Port, rue Gambetta (☎ 04-94-97-76-70), is one of the largest nightclubs in town with psychedelic 1960s-inspired decor. Adjacent is the all steeled, chromed, and mirrored **Le VIP Room** (☎ 04-94-97-78-92). On the port, the **Café de Paris's** long zinc bar (☎ 04-94-97-00-56) is frequently propped up by joyous locals; and **Le Bar du Port,** adjacent to the Café de Paris (☎ 04-94-97-00-54), is breezy, airy, and almost obsessively hip and self-consciously trendy.

Where to **Dine**

★★ **Le Café** LICES *FRENCH* The terrace of this trendy restaurant, with its famous zinc bar, doubles as a sports ground for watching the endless matches of *boules* played on the sand in front. The blackboard menu is the best value, with plenty of well-cooked fish. The desserts never fail here either. *5 pl. des Lices.* ☎ *04-94-97-44-69. www.lecafe.fr. Lunch menu 18€; dinner menu 30€. AE, MC, V. Lunch & dinner daily.*

★ **Le Girelier** PORT *PROVENÇAL* The blue-and-white color scheme has become the trademark of this coveted restaurant. They serve many versions of grilled fish, as well as bouillabaisse (for two). Also on the menu are brochette of monk-fish, a kettle of spicy mussels, and *pipérade* (a Basque omelette with pimientos, garlic, and tomatoes). *Quai Jean-Jaurès.* ☎ *04-94-97-03-87. www.legirelier.fr. Mains 28€–90€;* menu 42€. AE, DC, MC, V. Lunch & dinner daily.

★★★ **Spoon Byblos** PORT *FRENCH/INTERNATIONAL* This is one of many entrepreneurial statements by Alain Ducasse, widely considered the world's greatest chef—or at least the most acclaimed. Originally launched in Paris, Spoon draws special inspiration from the food of Catalonia, Andalusia, and Morocco, and offers more than 300 wines. Dig into shrimp and squid consommé with a hint of jasmine and orange, then try delectable lamb couscous or spit-roasted John Dory. The chef's favorite cheesecake is to die for. *Hôtel Byblos, avenue Paul-Signac.* ☎ *04-94-56-68-20. www.byblos. com. Reservations required. Mains 30€–50€. AE, DC, MC, V. Dinner Thurs–Tues. Closed mid-Oct to mid-Apr.* ●

Le Café waiter.

The
Savvy Traveler

Before You Go

Government Tourist Offices

Aigues-Mortes Place St-Louis 30220; ☎ 04-66-53-73-00; www. ot-aiguesmortes.fr

Aix-en-Provence 2 pl. Gén de Gaulle 13100; ☎ 04-42-16-11-61; www.aixenprovencetourism.com

Antibes 11 pl. Gén de Gaulle 06600; ☎ 04-97-23-11-11; www. antibesjuanlespins.com

Apt 20 av. Philippe de Girard 84400; ☎ 04-90-74-03-18; www. ot-apt.fr

Arles Boulevard des Lices 13200; ☎ 04-90-18-41-20; www.tourisme. ville-arles.fr

Avignon 41 cours Jean Jaures 84000; ☎ 04-32-74-32-74; www. ot-avignon.fr

Bandol Allée Alfred Vivien 83150; ☎ 04-94-29-41-35; http:// tourisme.bandol.fr

Les Baux de Provence Rue Porte Mage 13520; ☎ 04-90-54-34-39; www.lesbauxdeprovence.com

Biot 46 rue St-Sébastien 06410; ☎ 04-93-65-78-00; www.biot.fr

Bormes-les-Mimosas 1 pl. Gambetta 83230; ☎ 04-94-01-38-38; www.bormeslesmimosas.com

Brignoles Carrefour Europe 83170; ☎ 04-94-72-04-21; www. la-provence-verte.net

Cagnes 6 bd. Maréchal Juin 06800; ☎ 04-93-20-61-64; www. cagnes-tourisme.com

Cannes Bureau Palais des Festivals La Croisette; ☎ 04-92-99-84-22; www.cannes.travel

Carpentras 97 pl. du 25 Août 1944 84200; ☎ 04-90-63-00-78; www.carpentras-ventoux.com

Cassis Quai des Moulins 13260; ☎ 08-92-25-98-92; www.ot-cassis. com

La Castellet Hôtel de Ville 83330; ☎ 04-94-98-57-90; www. tourisme83.com

Le Cannet Place Benidorm, 73 av. du Campon 06110; ☎ 04-93-45-34-27; www.lecannet.fr

Cavaillon 79 pl. François Tourel 84300; ☎ 04-90-71-32-01; www. cavaillon-luberon.fr

Chateauneuf-du-Pape Place Portail 84230; ☎ 04-90-83-71-08; www.ccpro.fr

Draguignan Avenue Lazare Carnot 83300; ☎ 04-98-10-51-05; www.dracenie.com

Eze Place Gén de Gaulle 06360; ☎ 04-93-41-26-00; www.eze-riviera.com

Fontaine de Vaucluse Chemin Fontaine 84800; ☎ 04-90-20-32-22; www.oti-delasorgue.fr

Fréjus 325 rue Jean Jaurès 83600; ☎ 04-94-51-83-83; www. frejus.fr

Gordes Place Château 84220; ☎ 04-90-72-02-75; www.gordes-village.com

Grasse 22 cours Honoré Cresp 06130; ☎ 04-93-36-66-66; www. grasse.fr

Hyères Avenue Ambroise Thomas 83400; ☎ 04-94-01-84-50; www.hyeres-tourisme.com

L'Isle-sur-la-Sorgues Place Liberté 84800; ☎ 04-90-38-04-78; www.oti-delasorgue.fr

Lorgues Place Trussy 83510; ☎ 04-94-73-92-37; www.lorgues-tourisme.fr

Previous page: Idling outside the Monte Carlo Casino.

Malaucène   Place de la Mairie 84340; 📞 04-90-65-22-59; http://villagemalaucene.free.fr

Manosque   6 pl. du Docteur Joubert 04100; 📞 04-92-72-16-00; www.manosque-tourisme.com

Marseille   4 La Canebière 13001; 📞 04-91-13-89-00; www.marseille-tourisme.com

Menton   8 av. Boyer 06500; 📞 04-92-41-76-76; www.menton.fr

Monaco   2 a bd. Moulins 98000; 📞 92-16-61-16; www.visit monaco.com

Mougins   18 bd. Courteline 06250; 📞 04-93-75-87-67; www.mougins.fr

Moustiers-Sainte-Marie   Place de l'Église 04630; 📞 04-92-74-67-84; www.moustiers.fr

Nice   5 pr. des Anglais 06302; 📞 08-92-70-74-07; www.nice tourisme.com

Nîmes   6 rue Auguste 30000; 📞 04-66-58-38-00; www.ot-nimes.fr

La Rayol   Place Michel Goy 83820; 📞 04-94-05-65-69; www.tourismevar.com

Roussillon   Place Poste 84220; 📞 04-90-05-60-25; www.roussillon-provence.com

St-Jean-Cap-Ferrat   Avenue Denis Semeria 06230; 📞 04-93-73-08-90; www.saintjeancapferrat.fr

Stes-Maries-de-la-Mer   5 av. van Gogh 13460; 📞 04-90-97-82-55; www.saintesmaries.com

St-Paul de Vence   2 rue Grande 06570; 📞 04-93-32-86-95; www.saint-pauldevence.com

Salon de Provence   56 cours Gimon 13300; 📞 04-90-56-27-60; www.visitsalondeprovence.com

St-Raphaël   Quai Albert 1er 83702; 📞 04-94-19-52-52; www.saint-raphael.com

St-Rémy   Place Jean Jaurès 13210; 📞 04-90-92-38-52; www.saintremy-de-provence.com

St-Tropez   Quai Jean Jaurès 83990; 📞 08-92-68-48-28; www.ot-saint-tropez.com

Saut-en-Provence   Avenue Promenade 84390; 📞 04-90-64-01-21; www.saultenprovence.com

Taradeau   1 av. St-Joseph 83460; 📞 04-94-73-01-07; www.ville-taradeau.com

Toulon   334 av. de la République 83000; 📞 04-94-18-53-00; www.toulontourisme.com

La Turbie   Place Detras; 📞 04-93-41-21-15; www.ville-la-turbie.fr

Vaison-la-Romaine   Place du Chanoine Sautel 84110; 📞 04-90-36-02-11; www.vaison-la-romaine.com

Vallauris   Square du 8 Mai 1945 06220; 📞 04-93-63-82-58; www.vallauris-golfe-juan.com

Venasque   Grande Rue 84210; 📞 04-90-66-11-66; www.tourisme-venasque.com

Vence   8 pl. Grand Jardin 06140; 📞 04-93-58-06-38; www.vence.fr

When to Go

In terms of weather, the most idyllic months for visiting the south of France are May and June. Though the sun is intense, it's not uncomfortable. Coastal waters have warmed up by then, so swimming is possible. The resorts have come alive after a winter slumber but aren't yet overrun. The flowers and herbs in the countryside are at their peak, and driving conditions are ideal. In June, it remains light until around 10:30pm.

The hottest, most overcrowded times are July and August, when seemingly half of Paris shows up in the briefest of bikinis. Reservations

AVERAGE TEMPERATURE & RAINFALL IN PROVENCE & THE RIVIERA

MARSEILLE	JAN	FEB	MAR	APR	MAY	JUNE
Temp. (°F)	44	46	50	55	62	70
Temp. (°C)	6.7	7.8	10	13	17	21
Rainfall (in.)	1.9	1.6	1.8	1.8	1.8	1.0
Rainfall (cm)	4.8	4.1	4.6	4.6	4.6	2.5

	JULY	AUG	SEPT	OCT	NOV	DEC
Temp. (°F)	75	74	69	60	51	46
Temp. (°C)	24	23	21	16	11	7.8
Rainfall (in.)	0.6	1.0	2.5	3.7	3.0	2.3
Rainfall (cm)	1.5	2.5	6.4	9.4	7.6	5.8

NICE	JAN	FEB	MAR	APR	MAY	JUNE
Temp. (°F)	48	49	52	55	62	68
Temp. (°C)	8.9	9.4	11	13	17	20
Rainfall (in.)	3.0	2.9	2.9	2.5	1.9	1.5
Rainfall (cm)	7.6	7.4	7.4	6.4	4.8	3.8

	JULY	AUG	SEPT	OCT	NOV	DEC
Temp. (°F)	74	74	70	62	54	50
Temp. (°C)	23	23	21	17	12	10
Rainfall (in.)	0.7	1.2	2.6	4.4	4.6	3.5
Rainfall (cm)	1.8	3	6.6	11.2	11.7	8.9

are difficult to get, discos are blasting, and space is tight on the popular beaches. The worst traffic jams on the coast occur all the way from St-Tropez to Menton.

Aside from May and June, our favorite time is September and even early October, when the sun is still hot and the great hordes have headed back north.

In November, the weather is often pleasant, though some of the restaurants and inns you'll want to visit might take a sudden vacation: It's the month when many chefs and hoteliers elect to go on their own vacations after a summer of hard work.

Winter hasn't been the fashionable season since the 1930s. In the early days of tourism, when Queen Victoria came to visit, all the fashionable people showed up in winter,

deserting the Côte by April. Today it's the reverse. However, winter on the Riviera is being rediscovered, and many visitors elect to visit then. If you don't mind the absence of sunbathing and beach life, this could be a good time to show up—especially if you're into mimosa flowers, which blossom on the hillsides between Bormes-les-Mimosas and Grasse between January and March. However, some resorts, such as St-Tropez, become ghost towns when the cold weather comes, though Cannes, Nice, Monaco, and Menton remain active year-round.

The Mediterranean coast has the driest climate in France. Most rain falls in spring and autumn. Summers are comfortably dry—beneficial to humans but deadly to vegetation, which (unless it's irrigated) often dries and burns up in the parched months.

Provence dreads *le mistral* (a cold, violent wind from the French and Swiss Alps that roars south down the Rhône Valley). It most often blows in winter, sometimes for a few days, but sometimes for up to 2 weeks.

Festivals, Special Events & Public Holidays

In France, holidays are known as *jours feriés*. Shops and many businesses (banks and some museums and restaurants) close on holidays, but hotels and emergency services remain open.

The main holidays—a mix of secular and religious—include New Year's Day (Jan 1), Easter Sunday and Monday (early Apr), Labor Day (May 1), V-E Day in Europe (May 8), Whit Monday (mid-May), Ascension Thursday (40 days after Easter), Bastille Day (July 14), Assumption of the Blessed Virgin (Aug 15), All Saints' Day (Nov 1), Armistice Day (Nov 11), and Christmas (Dec 25).

For more information on the following, call the local tourist office, listed above.

JAN. Monte Carlo Motor Rally. The world's most venerable car race.

Cannes' Shopping Festival. The glitziest town on the coast celebrates its designer shops with a 4-day festival of fashion shows, galas, and private sales. www.cannesshoppingfestival.com.

FEB. Fête de la Chandeleur (Candlemas), Basilique St-Victor, Marseille. A celebration in honor of the arrival in Marseille of the three Marys.

Carnival of Nice. Float processions, parades, confetti battles, boat races, street music and food, masked balls, and fireworks are part of this ancient celebration. The climax

follows a 114-year-old tradition in which King Carnival is burned in effigy, an event preceded by Les Batailes des Fleurs (Battles of the Flowers), during which members of opposing teams pelt one another with flowers. Come armed with a hotel reservation. Mid-February to early March.

Fête de Citron. Menton's fun and famous lemon festival.

Fête du Mimosa. See the pretty yellow flowers adorn floats and people alike in Bormes-les-Mimosas and Mandelieu-la-Napoule.

MAR. Féria Pascale (Easter Bullfighting Festival), Arles. This is a major bullfighting event that includes not only appearances by the greatest matadors, but also *chrivados* and *bodegas* (wine stalls).

APR. La Fête des Gardians (Camargue Cowboys' Festival), Arles. This event features a procession of Camargue cowboys through the streets of town. Activities feature various games involving bulls, including Courses Camarguaises, in which competitors have to snatch a rosette from between the horns of a bull. On the last Sunday in April and in May.

Festival des Musiques d'Aujourd'hui, Marseille. This festival presents the works of young French and European composers in music and dance. For more information, call **Experimental Music Groups of Marseille** at ☎ 04-96-20-60-10; www.gmem.org. End April to early May.

MAY. Cannes Film Festival. Movie madness transforms this city into the kingdom of the media deal, but you probably won't want to stay for more than a day. It is nearly impossible to find accommodation during this time, let alone see a film (unless you have industry accreditation). For information, see the website, www.festival-cannes.fr. Mid-May.

Monaco Grand Prix de Formula 1. Hundreds of cars race through the narrow streets and winding roads in a surreal blend of high-tech machinery and medieval architecture. For more information, call ☎ 377-93-15-26-00; www.acm.mc. Late May.

JUNE. **Festival Aix en Musique,** Aix-en-Provence. Concerts of classical music and choral singing are held in historic buildings, such as the Théâtre de l'Archevêché and the Hôtel Maynier d'Oppède. For more information, call ☎ 08-20-92-29-23; www.festival-aix.com. Late June to late July.

Luberon Jazz Festival. Over a dozen towns between Cavaillon and Apt come alive with jazz music over this 5-day festival. Musicians often play in little churches, bars, and in outside squares. For more information, call ☎ 04-90-74-55-98; www.luberonjazz.net.

Festival de Marseille Méditerranée. This festival features concerts and recitals of music from the entire Mediterranean region. Theater and dance are also presented. For more information, call ☎ 04-96-11-04-60; www.festivaldemarseille.com. Late June to late July.

JULY. **Bastille Day.** Celebrating the birth of modern-day France, the festivities in the south reach their peak in Nice with street fairs, pageants, fireworks, and feasts. The day begins with a parade down the promenade des Anglais and ends with fireworks in the Vieille Ville. No matter where you are, by the end of the day you'll hear Piaf warbling "La Foule" (The Crowd), the song that celebrated her passion for the stranger she met and later lost in a crowd on Bastille Day. Similar celebrations also take place in Cannes, Arles, Aix, Marseille, and Avignon. July 14.

Les Rencontres d'Arles (photography festival), Arles. This vast international photography festival draws professionals and amateurs alike for three month of cutting-edge exhibitions and projections. For more information, call ☎ 04-90-96-76-06; www.rencontres-arles.com. Early July to Sept.

Nuit Taurine (Nocturnal Bull Festival), St-Rémy. At this festival, the focus is on the age-old allure of bulls and their primeval appeal to roaring crowds. *Abrivados* involve bulls in the town square as "chaperoned" by trained herders on horseback; *encierros* highlight a Pamplona-style stampeding of bulls through the streets. For more information, call ☎ 04-90-92-05-22. Mid-July.

Nice Jazz Festival. This is the biggest, flashiest, and most prestigious jazz festival in Europe, with world-class entertainers. Concerts begin in early afternoon and go on until late at night on the Roman Arènes de Cimiez, a picturesque hill above the city. Reserve hotel rooms way in advance. For information, call ☎ 08-92-70-74-07; www.nicejazzfestival.fr. Mid-July.

Festival d'Avignon. One of France's most prestigious theater events, this world-class festival has a reputation for exposing new talent to critical acclaim. The focus is usually on avant-garde works in theater, dance, and music by groups from around the world. Make hotel reservations very early on; or just come in for the day. For information, call ☎ 04-90-14-14-60; www.festival-avignon.com. Last 3 weeks of July.

AUG. **Féria de St-Rémy,** St-Rémy. This event features a 3-day celebration of bulls with *abrivado* and *encierro* (see the Nuit Taurine entry, above), branding, and Portuguese bull fighting (matadors on horseback). For more information, call ☎ 04-90-92-38-52. Mid-August.

SEPT. **Féria des Prémices du Riz** (Rice Harvest Festival), Arles. Non-bloody bullfights are held in the amphitheater with leading matadors. There are also a procession of floats and traditional events with cowboys and women in regional costume. For more information, call ☎ 04-90-18-41-20. Early September.

OCT. **Foire Internationale de Marseille.** Join the throngs who flock to see this annual fair—a jamboree of music, crafts, sport, and entertainment from all over the world. For more information, call ☎ 04-91-76-16-00; www. foiredemarseille.com. Late September to early October.

Fête de la Châtaigne. (Chestnut festival), Gonfaron and Collobrières. Several villages in the Massif des Maures (mountains) come alive with chestnut markets selling honey, chestnut cream, chestnut breads, and anything else made with chestnuts. Mid-October to mid-November.

NOV. **Fête du Prince,** Monaco. Fabulous fireworks over the harbor mark the end of Monaco's National day on November 19.

DEC. **Fête du Millesime du Vin de Bandol** (wine festival), Bandol. Discover the notes and flavors of the latest Bandol wine vintages, fruits of the *Mourvèdre* grape-variety. For more information, call ☎ 04-94-29-41-35. First or second Sunday of December.

Noël Provençal, Église St-Vincent, Les Baux. The procession of shepherds is followed by a traditional midnight Mass, including the *pastrage* ceremony, traditional songs, and performance of a nativity play. For more information, call ☎ 04-90-54-34-39. December 24.

Fête de St-Sylvestre (New Year's Eve), nationwide. Along the Riviera, it's most boisterously celebrated in Nice's Vieille Ville around place Garibaldi. At midnight, the city explodes. Strangers kiss strangers, and place Masséna and the promenade des Anglais become virtual pedestrian malls. December 31.

Getting **There**

By Plane
From North America

From Paris, if you're heading for the French Riviera, your connecting flight will probably land in Nice's international airport, **Aéroport Nice–Côte d'Azur.** There are also small airports in Avignon, Marseille, Montpellier, Nîmes, and Toulon-Hyères.

Once you fly into Paris's **Orly** or **Charles de Gaulle** airports, you must take **Air France** (☎ 800/237-2747; www.airfrance.com) to reach your destination in Provence or the Riviera. From Orly and Charles de Gaulle, there are several flights per day to Marseille, Nice, and Avignon.

American Airlines ☎ 800/433-7300; www.aa.com) offers daily flights to Paris from Dallas–Fort Worth, Chicago, Miami, Boston, and New York. **Delta Airlines** (☎ 800/241-4141; www.delta.com) flies nonstop to Paris from Atlanta, Cincinnati, and New York. Note that Delta also offers nonstop service from New York to Nice.

United Airlines ☎ 800/538-2929; www.united.com) flies nonstop to Paris from Newark, Chicago, Houston, and Washington, D.C.

several times a week. **US Airways** (☎ 800/428-4322; www.usairways. com) offers daily service from Philadelphia to Paris.

Air France (☎ 800/237-2747; www.airfrance.com) offers a daily nonstop flight between New York and Nice and also offers regular flights between Paris and various North American cities.

Canadians usually choose the **Air Canada** (☎ 888/247-2262 in the U.S. and Canada; www.air canada.com) flights to Paris from Toronto and Montréal. Two of Air Canada's flights from Toronto are shared with Air France and feature Air France aircraft.

From the U.K.
Nice Côte d'Azur Airport is served by several companies: **BMI Baby** (☎ 0905-828-2828; www. bmibaby.com), **British Airways** (☎ 0844-493-0787; www.british airways.com), **Jet2** (☎ 0871-226-1737; www.jet2.com), **Ryan Air** (☎ 0871-246-0000; www.ryanair. com), and **Flybe** (☎ 0871-700-2000; www.flybe.com), which flies from Edinburgh, Glasgow, Inverness, Leeds-Bradford, Manchester, Newcastle, and Southampton. **Marseille Provence Airport** is covered by **EasyJet** (www.easyjet.com) from Bristol and London Gatwick, **British Airways, Ryan Air,** and **Aerlingus** (☎ 0818-365000; www.aerlingus. com) from Dublin.

By Train
The world's fastest trains link some 50 French cities, allowing you to get from Paris to just about anywhere else in the country in hours. With 39,000km (24,233 miles) of track and about 3,000 stations, **SNCF** (French National Railroads; www. voyages-sncf.com) is fabled for its on-time performance. You can travel in first or second class by day and in couchette by night. Most trains have dining facilities.

Information
If you plan to travel a lot on European railroads, get the latest copy of the ***Thomas Cook Timetable of European Passenger Railroads.*** This 500-plus-page book documents all of Europe's main passenger rail services with detail and accuracy. It's available online at www.thomas cookpublishing.com.

In the United States: For more information and to purchase rail passes before you leave, contact **Rail Europe** (☎ 800/622-8600; www.raileurope.com).

In Canada: Contact Rail Europe at ☎ 800/361-RAIL (7245) or www. raileurope.ca.

In the United Kingdom: Call ☎ 08448-484-064 for general enquiries or ☎ 08448-484-051 if you need to travel within seven days. Visit www.raileurope.co.uk for more information

In Paris: For information or reservations, visit www.voyages-sncf. com or call ☎ 36-35. A simpler way to buy tickets is to use the *billetterie* (ticket machine) in every train station, which accept most credit cards (with a PIN).

France Rail Passes
Working cooperatively with SNCF, Air Inter Europe, and Avis, Rail Europe offers three flexible rail passes that can reduce travel costs considerably.

The **France Railpass** provides unlimited rail transport in France for a choice of 3 to 9 days within a 1-month period. Prices start at $248 for one adult in second class, or $291 in first. Children 4 to 11 travel for half price and tickets for travelers 25 and under start at $182 for second class.

The **France Rail 'n' Drive Pass,** available only in North America, combines good value on both rail travel and Avis car rentals, and is best used by arriving at a major rail depot and then striking out to

Have a Seat

Remember that with Eurail and France Rail passes a train ticket does not guarantee you a seat; it merely gets you from one place to another. On crowded trains during peak times, you'll have to make a **seat reservation** (and pay for the privilege) if you want to guarantee a seat somewhere other than atop your luggage. Seat reservations can cost 10€ per person.

explore the countryside by car. It includes the France Railpass (see above) and use of a rental car. You have 1 month to complete your travel on this pass that grants 2 days of unlimited train travel and 2 days of car rental with unlimited mileage in France. Prices for an economy car begin at $319.

The best deal if you're traveling in France with a friend—or even 3 or 4 friends—is the **France Saverpass,** granting 3 to 9 days of unlimited travel in a 1-month period. The ticket prices starts at $249 per person first class or $214 second class for 3 days. For travelers age 60 and over there is the **France Senior Pass,** which allows 3 to 9 days of unlimited first-class travel within 1 month from $266. There's also a **France Youthpass** for travelers 25

or under, granting 3 to 9 days of unlimited train travel within a month. The cost starts at $215 in first class or $182 in second class.

Eurailpass
The Eurailpass permits unlimited first-class rail travel in any country in western Europe except the British Isles (good in Ireland). Passes are available for purchase online (www.eurail.com) and at various offices/agents around the world. Travel agents and railway agents in such cities as New York, Montreal, and Los Angeles sell Eurailpasses. It is strongly recommended that you purchase passes before you leave home as not all passes are available in Europe; also, passes purchased in Europe will cost about 20% more. See the website for details and options.

Getting **Around**

The most charming Provençal villages and best country hotels always seem to lie away from the main cities and train stations. Renting a car is usually the best way to travel once you reach the south of France, especially if you plan to explore in depth.

However, the south of France also has one of the most reliable bus and rail transportation systems

in Europe. Trains connect all the major cities and towns, such as Nice and Avignon. Where the train leaves off, you can most often rely on local bus service.

By Car
Driving time in Europe is largely a matter of conjecture, urgency, and how much sightseeing you do along the way. The driving time from

Driving in Provence

- **On the road, routes are designated by destinations,** even though they're numbered on most maps. If you're planning to take the D22 to St-Rémy, for instance, don't look for signs for the D22; you won't find them. Follow signs for St-Rémy instead.
- **Directionals appear then disappear for long distances.** But rest assured: Once you've followed a signpost toward your destination, you can follow that road until further notice—even if it means covering several kilometers and islands without seeing another directional. It's easy to feel like you've taken a wrong turn, but your destination will reappear—provided you were on the right track to start with!
- **Be prepared for many turnabouts,** or rotaries, on the roads. You'll get used to driving them after a few turns, but the first time can be harrowing as you're looking for directionals and oncoming traffic at once.

Marseille to Paris is a matter of national pride, and tall tales abound about how rapidly the French can do it. With the accelerator pressed to the floor, you might conceivably make it in 7 hours, but we always make a 2-day journey of it.

Car Rentals

To rent a car, you'll need to present a passport, a driver's license, and a credit card. You'll also have to meet the minimum-age requirement of the company. (For the least expensive cars, this age is 21 at Hertz, 23 at Avis, and 25 at Budget. More expensive cars might require that you be at least 25.) It usually isn't obligatory within France, but certain companies have at times asked for the presentation of an International Driver's License, even though this is becoming increasingly superfluous in western Europe.

For rentals of more than 7 days, in most cases cars can be picked up in one French city and dropped off in another, but there are additional charges. **Budget** (www.budget. com) has an office in **Nice** at the

airport (☎ 04-93-21-36-50) and in **Cannes'** center (69 La Croisette; ☎ 08-20-61-16-35). **Hertz** (www. hertz.com) is also well represented, with offices in **Avignon** at the airport (☎ 04-90-84-19-50) and at the train station (☎ 04-32-74-62-80); in **Marseille** at the airport (☎ 08-25-09-13-13) and at the Gare St-Charles station (☎ 04-91-05-51-20); and in **Nice** at the airport (☎ 08-25-34-23-43) and the rail station (☎ 04-97-03-01-20).

Avis (www.avis.com) has offices in **Avignon** at the airport (☎ 04-90-87-17-75) and at the railway station (☎ 04-90-27-96-10); in **Marseille** at the airport (☎ 04-42-14-21-67) and at 267 bd. National (☎ 04-91-50-70-11); in **Nice** at the airport (☎ 04-93-21-36-33) and at Place Massena, 2 av. des Phocéens (☎ 04-93-80-63-52); and in **Cannes** on La Croisette (☎ 04-93-94-15-86) and at the train station (☎ 04-93-39-26-38).

Europcar (www.europcar.com) has locations in **Avignon** at the airport (☎ 04-90-84-05-74) and train station (☎ 08-25-08-89-45);

in **Marseille** at the airport (☎ 08-25-00-30-80) and at the St-Charles train station, 96 bd. Rabatau (☎ 08-25-82-56-80); and in **Nice** at the airport (☎ 08-25-81-00-81). You can rent a car on the spot at any of these offices, but lower rates are often available by making advance reservations from your country of residence.

Two United States–based agencies that don't have France offices but act as booking agents for France-based agencies are **Kemwel Drive Group** (☎ 877/820-0668 or 207/842-2285; www.kemwel.com) and **Auto Europe** (☎ 888/223-5555; www.autoeurope.com). These can make bookings in the United States only, so call before your trip.

Driving Rules
Everyone in the car, in both the front and the back seats, must wear seat belts. Children under 12 must ride in the back seat. Drivers are supposed to yield to the car on their right, except where signs indicate otherwise, as at traffic circles.

If you violate the speed limit, expect a big fine. Those limits are about 110kmph (70 mph) on expressways, about 90kmph (55 mph) on major national highways, and country roads. In towns, don't exceed 50kmph (30 mph).

Maps
For France as a whole, most motorists opt for Michelin map 989. For regions, Michelin publishes a series of yellow maps that are quite good. Big travel-book stores in North America carry these maps, and they're commonly available in France (at lower prices). In this age of congested traffic, one useful feature of the Michelin map is its designations of alternative *routes de dégagement*, which let you skirt big cities and avoid traffic-clogged highways. They also highlight routes in green, which are recommended for tourists.

Another recommended option is *Frommer's Road Atlas Europe*.

Breakdowns/Assistance
A breakdown is called *une panne* in France. Call the police at ☎ 17 anywhere in France to be put in touch with the nearest garage. If the breakdown occurs on an expressway, find the nearest roadside emergency phone box, pick up the phone, and put a call through. You'll be connected to the nearest breakdown service facility.

By Train
Rail services around Provence, particularly the coastline, are excellent. If you don't have a car, you can tour nearly all the major hot spots by train. Service is fast and frequent.

The ancient city of Nîmes, one of the most visited in the area, is a major rail terminus, a stop on the rail link between Bordeaux and Marseille. Marseille, the largest city in the south of France, has rail connections with all major towns on the Riviera as well as with the rest of France. Seventeen high-speed TGVs arrive from Paris daily (trip time: 3 hr. 15 min.). The major rail transportation hub along the French Riviera is Nice, although Cannes also enjoys good train connections. Nice and Monaco are linked by frequent service, and in summer about eight trains per day connect Nice with the rapid TGV train from Paris to Marseille. In winter, the schedule is curtailed depending on demand. The most visited Riviera destination in the east, Monaco also has excellent rail links along the Riviera.

The website for the national rail service is www.voyages-sncf.com. Otherwise, call ☎ 36-35, or ☎ 08-92-35-35-35 when outside France.

Hiring a Gîte

While this book covers hotels and B&Bs, another fabulous way to discover the region is by renting a *gîte* (pronounced *jheet*)—a house—as a base for your sightseeing. Renowned for their charm, *gîtes* are often cheaper in the long run. To find a *gîte*, try these reputable companies: **Gîte de France** (www.gites-de-france.com), France's oldest *gîte*-listing institution; **La Clé Verte** (www.laclefverte.org), which suggests eco-friendly *gîtes*; and British-based **Alastair Sawdays** (www.sawdays.co.uk), which lists some of France's châteaux and unusual buildings.

By Bus

While the trains are faster and more efficient if you are traveling between major cities, both the towns and villages of Provence, including the French Riviera, are linked by frequent bus service. You can use the network of buses that link the villages and hamlets with each other and the major cities to get off the beaten path.

Plan to take advantage of the bus services from Monday to Saturday when they run frequently; very few buses run on Sunday.

Sodetrav (☎ 04-94-54-78-91; www.sodetrav.fr) has some of the best bus routes, and is especially strong in the western Riviera, taking in stopovers at such destinations as St-Raphaël, St-Tropez, Arles, Grasse, Avignon, Marseille, Nimes, and Hyéres. One of its most popular routes is the run between Toulon and St-Tropez.

Fast **Facts**

AUTO CLUB An organization designed to help motorists navigate their way through breakdowns and motoring problems is **Club Automobile de Provence**, 149 bd. Rabatau, 13010 Marseille (☎ 04-91-78-83-00; www.automobileclub provence.com).

BUSINESS HOURS Business hours here are erratic. Most banks are open Monday to Friday from 9:30am to 4:30pm. Many, particularly in smaller towns or villages, take a lunch break at varying times. Hours are usually posted on the door. Most museums close 1 day a week (often Tues), and they're generally closed on national holidays. Usual

hours are from 9:30am to 5pm. Some museums, particularly the smaller ones, close for lunch from noon to 2pm. Again, refer to the individual museum listings.

Generally, shops are open Monday to Friday from 9am to 5pm, but always call first. In larger cities, stores are open from 9 or 9:30am (often 10am) to 6 or 7pm without a break for lunch. Some shops, particularly those operated by foreigners, open at 8am and close at 8 or 9pm. In some small stores, the lunch break can last 2 hours, beginning at 1pm.

CELLPHONES If your phone has GSM (Global System for Mobiles) capability, and you have a world-compatible phone, you should be able to make and receive calls from Provence and the Riviera. Check with your service operator first to see if your phone has this capability. Call charges can be high. Alternatively, you can rent a phone through Cellhire (www.cellhire.com, www.cellhire.co.uk, and www.cellhire.com.au). After a simple online registration, they will ship a phone (usually with a U.K. number) to your home or office. Usage charges can be astronomical, so read the fine print. U.K. mobiles work in France; call your service provider before departing your home country to ensure that the international call bar has been switched off and to check call charges, which can be extremely high. Also remember that you are charged for calls you receive on a U.K. mobile used abroad.

CUSTOMS Customs restrictions for visitors entering France differ for citizens of the European Union and for citizens of non-E.U. countries.

For U.S. Citizens For specifics on what you can bring back, download the invaluable free pamphlet *Know Before You Go* online at www.cbp.gov, or contact the **U.S. Customs Border Protection (CBP),** 1300 Pennsylvania Ave. NW, Washington DC 20229 (☎ 877/CBP-5511 [227-5511] or ☎ 703/526-4200 from abroad).

For Canadian Citizens For a clear summary of **Canadian** rules, call for the booklet *I Declare,* issued by the **Canada Customs and Revenue Agency** (☎ 800/461-9999 in Canada, or 204/983-3500 from outside Canada; www.cbsa-asfc.gc.ca).

For U.K. Citizens For more information, contact **HM Revenue & Customs** at ☎ 0845/010-9000 (from outside the United Kingdom, 02920/501-261), or consult the website www.hmrc.gov.uk.

For Australian Citizens A helpful brochure available from Australian consulates or Customs offices is

Know Before You Go. For more information, call the **Australian Customs Service** at ☎ 1300/363-263, or log on to www.customs.gov.au.

For New Zealand Citizens Request the free pamphlet *New Zealand Customs Guide for Travellers, Notice no. 4* from **New Zealand Customs Service,** The Customhouse, 17–21 Whitmore St., Box 2218, Wellington (☎ 0800/428-786; www.customs.govt.nz).

DRUGSTORES In France they are called *pharmacie.* Pharmacies take turns staying open at night and on Sunday; the local Commissariat de Police will tell you the location of the nearest one.

ELECTRICITY In general, expect 200 volts, 50 cycles. Adapters are needed to fit sockets.

EMBASSIES & CONSULATES All embassies are in Paris. The Embassy and Consulate of the **United States** are at 2 av. Gabriel (☎ 01-43-12-22-22; Metro: Concorde). The United States also maintains a consulate in Marseille at Place Varian Fry, 13286 Marseille (☎ 04-91-54-92-00). The Embassy of **Canada** is at 35 av. Montaigne (☎ 01-44-43-29-00; Metro: Franklin-D-Roosevelt). The Embassy of the **United Kingdom** is at 35 rue du Faubourg St-Honoré (☎ 01-44-51-31-00; Metro: Concorde), open Monday through Friday from 9:30am to 1pm and 2:30 to 5pm; the U.K. consulate, 18 bis rue d'Anjou (☎ 01-44-51-31-02; Metro: Concorde), is open Monday through Friday from 9am to noon and 2 to 5pm.

EMERGENCIES In an emergency while at a hotel, contact the front desk to summon an ambulance or do whatever is necessary. But for something like a stolen wallet, go to the police station in person. Otherwise, you can get help anywhere in France by calling ☎ 17 for the **police,** ☎ 18 for the **fire department** *(pompiers)*

The Savvy Traveler

who also double as paramedics, *and* ☎ 15 for an ambulance. For roadside emergencies, see "Getting Around," earlier in this chapter.

LEGAL AID The French government advises foreigners to consult their embassy or consulate (see above) in case of an arrest or similar problem. The staff can generally offer advice on how you can obtain help locally and can furnish you with a list of local attorneys. If you are arrested for illegal possession of drugs, the U.S. embassy and consular officials cannot interfere with the French judicial system. A consulate can advise you only of your rights.

LOST & FOUND To speed the process of replacing your personal documents if they're lost or stolen, make a photocopy of the first few pages of your passport and write down your credit card numbers (and the serial numbers of your traveler's checks, if you're using them). Leave this information with someone at home—to be faxed to you in an emergency—and swap it with your traveling companion. Be sure to tell all of your credit card companies the minute you discover your wallet has been lost or stolen, and file a report at the nearest police station. Your credit card company or insurer may require a police report number or record of the loss.

Use the following numbers in France to report your lost or stolen credit card: **American Express** (call collect), ☎ 336/393-1111, www.americanexpress.com; MasterCard, ☎ 08-00-90-13-87, www.mastercard.com; **Visa,** ☎ 08-00-90-11-79, www.visaeurope.com. Your credit card company may be able to wire you a cash advance immediately or deliver an emergency card in a day or two.

MAIL Most post offices in France are open Monday through Friday from 8am to 7pm, and Saturday from 8am to noon. Allow 5 to 8 days to send or receive mail from your home. Airmail letters to North America cost .90€ for 20 grams. Letters to the U.K. cost .56€ for up to 20 grams. An airmail postcard to North America or Europe (outside France) costs .90€.

You can exchange money at most post offices. Many hotels sell stamps, as do local post offices and cafes displaying a red TABAC sign outside.

POLICE Call ☎ 17 anywhere in France.

RESTROOMS If you're in dire need, duck into a cafe or brasserie. It's customary to make some small purchase if you do so. France still has many "hole-in-the-ground" toilets, so be forewarned.

TAXES As a member of the European Union, France imposes a value-added tax (VAT) on many goods and services. The standard VAT on merchandise is 19.6%. Refunds are made for the tax on certain goods, but not on services. The minimum purchase is 175€ for nationals or residents of countries outside the E.U.

TELEPHONE The French use a **télécarte,** a phone debit card, which you can purchase at rail stations, post offices, and other places. Sold in two versions, it allows you to use either 50 or 120 charge units by inserting the card into the slot of most public phones. Alternatively most phone boxes nowadays accept credit cards. If possible, avoid making calls from your hotel; some French establishments double or triple the charges.

TIME The French equivalent of daylight saving time lasts from around April to September, which puts it 1 hour ahead of French winter time. Depending on the time of year, France is 6 or 7 hours ahead of U.S. Eastern Standard Time.

TIPPING All bills, as required by law, are supposed to say *service compris*, which means that the tip has been included. Here are some general guidelines: You are rarely expected to tip hotel staff, unless you feel you have had outstanding service. In cafes, **waiter** service is usually included, but .50€ to 1€ is an acceptable amount to leave if you feel you have had excellent service. For **porters,** there's no real need to tip extra after their bill is presented, unless they've performed some special service. For **taxi drivers** round up the fare to the nearest euro. In theaters give **cloakroom attendants** at least 1€. Give **restroom attendants** about .30€ in nightclubs and such places. Give **cinema and theater ushers** about .50€. Tip the **hairdresser** about 10%, and don't forget to tip the person who gives you a shampoo or manicure 2€. For **guides** of group visits to sights, 1€ to 1.50€ per person is reasonable.

Survival **French**

Basic French Vocabulary & Phrases

ENGLISH	FRENCH	PRONUNCIATION
Yes/No	**Oui/Non**	wee/nohn
Okay	**D'accord**	*dah*-core
Please	**S'il vous plaît**	seel voo play
Thank you	**Merci**	*mair*-see
You're welcome	**De rien**	duh ree-*ehn*
Hello (during daylight)	**Bonjour**	bohn-*jhoor*
Good evening	**Bonsoir**	bohn-*swahr*
Goodbye	**Au revoir**	o ruh-*vwahr*
What's your name?	**Comment vous appellez-vous?**	ko-*mahn*-voo-z a- pell-ay-*voo*?
My name is	**Je m'appelle**	*jhuh* ma-pell
How are you?	**Comment allez-vous?**	kuh-mahn-tahl-ay-*voo*?
So-so	**Comme ci, comme ça**	kum-see, kum-*sah*
I'm sorry/excuse me	**Pardon**	pahr-*dohn*

Getting Around/Street Smarts

ENGLISH	FRENCH	PRONUNCIATION
Do you speak English?	**Parlez-vous anglais?**	par-lay-voo-ahn-*glay*?
I don't speak French	**Je ne parle pas français**	jhuh ne parl pah frahn-*say*
I don't understand	**Je ne comprends pas**	jhuh ne kohm-*prahn* pas
Could you speak more loudly/ more slowly?	**Pouvez-vous parler plus fort/ plus lentement?**	Poo-*vay* voo par-lay ploo for/ ploo lan-te-*ment*?
What is it?	**Qu'est-ce que c'est?**	kess-kuh-*say*?
What time is it?	**Quel heure est-il?**	kel uhr eh-*teel*?
What?	**Quoi?**	kwah?
How? or What did you say?	**Comment?**	ko-*mahn*?

ENGLISH	FRENCH	PRONUNCIATION
When?	Quand?	kahn?
Where is?	Où est?	oo eh?
Who?	Qui?	kee?
Why?	Pourquoi?	poor-kwah?
here/there	ici/là	ee-see/lah
left/right	à gauche/à droite	a goash/a drwaht
straight ahead	tout droit	too-drwah
Fill the tank (of a car), please	Le plein, s'il vous plaît	luh plan, seel-voo-play
I want to get off at	Je voudrais descendre à	jhe voo-dray day-son drah-ah
airport	l'aéroport	lair-o-por
bank	la banque	lah bahnk
bridge	le pont	luh pohn
bus station	la gare routière	lah gar roo-tee-air
bus stop	l'arrêt de bus	lah-ray duh boohss
by means of a car	en voiture	ahn vwa-toor
cashier	la caisse	lah kess
cathedral	le cathédral	luh ka-tay-dral
church	l'église	lay-gleez
driver's license	le permis de conduire	luh per-mee duh con-dweer
elevator	l'ascenseur	lah sahn seuhr
entrance (to a building or a city)	une porte	ewn port
exit (from a building or a freeway)	une sortie	ewn sor-tee
gasoline	du pétrol/de l'essence	duh pay-trol/de lay-sahns
hospital	l'hôpital	low-pee-tahl
luggage storage	la consigne	lah kohn-seen-yuh
museum	le musée	luh mew-zay
no smoking	défense de fumer	day-fahns de fu-may
one-day pass	le ticket journalier	luh tee-kay jhoor-nall-ee-ay
one-way ticket	l'aller simple	lah-lay sam-pluh
police	la police	lah po-lees
round-trip ticket	l'aller-retour	lah-lay re-toor
second floor	le premier étage	luh prem-ee-ehr ay-taj
slow down	ralentir	rah-lahn-teer
store	le magasin	luh ma-ga-zehn
street	la rue	lah roo
subway/under-ground/Tube	le Métro	le may-tro
telephone	le téléphone	luh tay-lay-phone
ticket	un billet	uh bee-yay
toilets	les toilettes/les WC	lay twa-lets/les vay-say

Necessities

ENGLISH	FRENCH	PRONUNCIATION
I'd like	**Je voudrais**	jhe voo-*dray*
a room	**une chambre**	ewn *shahm*-bruh
the key	**la clé (la clef)**	la clay
How much does it cost?	**C'est combien?/ Ça coûte combien?**	say comb-bee-*ehn?*/ sah coot comb-bee-*ehn?*
That's expensive	**C'est cher/chère**	say share
Do you take credit cards?	**Est-ce que vous acceptez les cartes de credit?**	es-kuh voo zaksep-*tay* lay kart duh creh-*dee?*
I'd like to buy	**Je voudrais acheter**	jhe voo-dray ahsh-tay
aspirin	**des aspirines/ des aspros**	deyz ahs-peer-*een*/ deyz ahs-*proh*
gift	**un cadeau**	uh kah-*doe*
map of the city	**un plan de ville**	uh plahn de *veel*
newspaper	**un journal**	uh zhoor-*nahl*
phone card	**une carte téléphonique**	uh cart tay-lay-fone-*eek*
postcard	**une carte postale**	ewn cart pos-*tahl*
road map	**une carte routière**	ewn cart roo-tee-*air*
stamp	**un timbre**	uh *tam*-bruh

Numbers & Ordinals

ENGLISH	FRENCH	PRONUNCIATION
zero	**zéro**	*zare*-oh
one	**un**	oon
two	**deux**	duh
three	**trois**	twah
four	**quatre**	*kaht*-ruh
five	**cinq**	sank
six	**six**	seess
seven	**sept**	set
eight	**huit**	wheat
nine	**neuf**	noof
twenty	**vingt**	vehn
forty	**quarante**	ka-*rahnt*
fifty	**cinquante**	sang-*kahnt*
one hundred	**cent**	sahn
one thousand	**mille**	meel

The Calendar

ENGLISH	FRENCH	PRONUNCIATION
Sunday	**dimanche**	dee-*mahnsh*
Monday	**lundi**	luhn-*dee*
Tuesday	**mardi**	mahr-*dee*
Wednesday	**mercredi**	mair-kruh-*dee*
Thursday	**jeudi**	jheu-*dee*
Friday	**vendredi**	vawn-druh-*dee*
Saturday	**samedi**	sahm-*dee*

Food & Menu

ENGLISH	FRENCH	PRONUNCIATION
I would like	**Je voudrais**	jhe voo-*dray*
to eat	**manger**	mahn-*jhay*
Please give me	**Donnez-moi,**	doe-nay-*mwah*,
	s'il vous plaît	seel-voo-*play*
a bottle of	**une bouteille de**	ewn boo-*tay* duh
a cup of	**une tasse de**	ewn tass duh
a glass of	**un verre de**	uh vair duh
a plate of breakfast	**une assiette de**	ewn ass-ee-*et* duh
	le petit-déjeuner	luh puh-*tee*
		day-zhuh-*nay*
a cocktail	**un apéritif**	uh ah-pay-ree-*teef*
the check/bill	**l'addition/la note**	la-dee-see-*ohn*/
		la noat
dinner	**le dîner**	luh dee-*nay*
a knife	**un couteau**	uh koo-*toe*
a napkin	**une serviette**	ewn sair-vee-*et*
a spoon	**une cuillère**	ewn kwee-*air*
a fork	**une fourchette**	ewn four-shet
Cheers!	**A votre santé!**	ah vo-truh sahn-*tay*!
fixed-price menu	**un menu**	uh may-*new*
Is the tip/	**Est-ce que le service**	es-kuh luh ser-*vees*
service included?	**est compris?**	eh com-*pree*?
Waiter!/	**Monsieur!/**	muh-*syuh*/
Waitress!	**Mademoiselle!**	mad-mwa-*zel*
wine list	**une carte des vins**	ewn cart day *van*
appetizer	**une entrée**	ewn en-*tray*
main course	**un plat principal**	uh plah pran-see-*pahl*
tip included	**service compris**	sehr-*vees* cohm-pree
wide-ranging	**menu dégustation**	may-*new*
sampling of the		day-gus-ta-see-*on*
chef's best efforts		

Photo **Credits**